A HISTORY OF THE
GLOBAL STOCK MARKET

ALSO BY B. MARK SMITH

Toward Rational Exuberance:
The Evolution of the Modern Stock Market

A HISTORY OF THE
GLOBAL
STOCK MARKET

FROM ANCIENT ROME
TO SILICON VALLEY

B. MARK SMITH

the university of chicago press

The University of Chicago Press, Chicago 60637
Copyright © 2003 by B. Mark Smith
All rights reserved.
Published by arrangement with Farrar, Straus and Giroux, LLC.
First published by Farrar, Straus and Giroux in 2003
University of Chicago Press edition 2004

Printed in the United States of America
13 12 11 10 09 08 07 06 05 04   1 2 3 4 5

ISBN: 0-226-76404-4

Library of Congress Cataloging-in-Publication Data

Smith, B. Mark, 1953–
    [Equity culture]
    A history of the global stock market : from ancient Rome to Silicon Valley / B. Mark
Smith. — University of Chicago Press ed.
        p. cm.
    Originally published: The equity culture. New York : Farrar, Straus, and Giroux, 2003.
    Includes bibliographical references and index.
    ISBN 0-226-76404-4 (pbk. : alk. paper)
    1. Stock exchanges. 2. Stocks. 3. Securities. I. Smith, B. Mark, 1953– Equity culture. II.
Title.
    HG4551.S568 2004
    332.63'2—dc22

                                                                        2004049777

Contents

A HISTORY OF THE
GLOBAL STOCK MARKET

Introduction

IN MAY 2000, shortly after what would prove to be the top of the great bull market of the 1990s, a conversation between Federal Reserve Board chairman Alan Greenspan and an aide was reported in the *Wall Street Journal*. The subject was Greenspan's seeming preoccupation with the stock market and the impact the market had on Federal Reserve policy decisions. "I could readily stop talking about the stock market," Greenspan admitted to his aide. "But if I do, I will not be explaining how the process is working . . . There is no way to understand what is going on in this economy without reference to [stock] prices."[1]

Greenspan was not alone. Business and political leaders around the world at the turn of the twenty-first century struggled to come to grips with a radically changed economic environment, in which unpredictable, and often volatile, equity* markets could wreak havoc on entire economies. Only a generation earlier, stock markets (if they existed at all) had typically been regarded as economic backwaters to

---

*The word "equity" actually derives from the Latin *aequitas*, which in turn derives from *aequus*, meaning even, or fair. In a financial sense, "equity" refers to the residual value of a business after its liabilities are subtracted, and is a synonym for "stock." As used in this book, the term refers to the publicly traded ownership interest of private companies.

be ignored or treated with disdain. Now, suddenly, they had burgeoned into powerful institutions that played decisive roles in national economies.

To millions of new investors who had for the first time acquired significant amounts of stock (either directly or indirectly through mutual funds and retirement plans), the market held out the prospect of financial security and a comfortable retirement. To entrepreneurs seeking financing, the market offered a cornucopia of options that had not existed a few years earlier, and promised great riches to those shrewd enough to exploit them. To developing countries, equity markets provided a source of permanent investment capital, making it possible to avoid the dangerous dependency on debt that had led to so many crises before.

But the newly potent global stock market could also take on a very different form. Often it seemed like a wild and dangerous beast that threatened to wipe out the retirement savings of inexperienced investors, undermine traditional practices and ways of doing business, and rip asunder social compacts that had governed societies for decades.

Countless books and articles have been written about the "globalization" of equity markets at the turn of the twenty-first century. Many focus (correctly) on the dramatic impact the process is having on countries and populations around the world. But most fail to provide a much-needed sense of perspective. The global stock market of today is in fact not new; in the late nineteenth and early twentieth centuries, another era of "globalization" linked active stock markets together across national borders. Surprisingly, the total capitalization of all the world's stock markets, as a percentage of the world's gross national product, was greater in 1913 than it would be seventy years later.

Pronounced cultural and legal differences among nations, which have been the source of much friction as financial market forces transcend national boundaries, also have roots firmly embedded in the past. It is not possible to understand the Japanese stock market, for example, without understanding Japan's peculiar form of "administered" capitalism and how it evolved from the breakneck nineteenth-century effort by the Japanese government to forcibly modernize Japanese society. Likewise, it is not possible to understand why the development of equity markets in Germany has been so stunted (until recently) without understanding how and why the German system of "universal banking" evolved as a substitute for a vigorous stock market. Perhaps most important, it is not possible to understand the visceral antipathy toward modern "stock market capitalism" felt by many people around the world without recognizing that vigorous equity markets historically have been almost exclusively an Anglo-American phenomenon, with all the related political and cultural baggage that implies.

Even in nations with a significant history of organized stock markets, the perception of those markets has been tainted by suspicions that can be traced back for generations. Denunciations of speculative excess by St. Augustine and St. Thomas Aquinas still reverberate in modern times. During the 1930s a prominent United States senator voiced a widely held opinion when he declared that the stock market was "evil," and that the New York Stock Exchange should be "shut down and padlocked." Successive British Labour Party governments saw stockbrokers and dealers as "parasites," and the market itself as a "plaything for wealthy speculators." In the late 1990s the prime minister of Malaysia accused foreign fund managers of "stock manipulation" that "sabotaged" the Malaysian economy. And as recently as 2002, the Japanese minister of finance described his country's stock market as little more than a "gambling den."

This jaundiced view of stock markets has proven to be profoundly influential. In the nineteenth century, new industries, based on new technologies, created pressing demands for equity capital and for more robust equity markets. But these nascent stock markets were inevitably tainted by the abuses associated with them. In some countries (such as Germany and France), critics succeeded in enacting legislation that set back the development of stock markets, with long-lasting consequences for the economies of those nations. Even in Victorian Britain, where laissez-faire economic liberalism was nearly sacrosanct, spirited debates erupted over the proper role of the stock market in the economy and the proper role of government in the stock market.

In the twentieth century much of the early securities regulation was specifically created to contain the "excesses" of unfettered equity markets. One of the central concepts underpinning the Bretton Woods accords of 1944, which established the rules for the international economy in the post–World War II era, was the assumption that uncontrolled international capital markets were inherently unstable and hence dangerous. It is safe to say that by the middle of the twentieth century, equity markets were largely discredited in the eyes of both the public and governmental authorities.

In the decades following the war, stock markets for the first time became a respectable subject of academic inquiry. A new theory of stock market behavior—broadly identified as the *efficient market hypothesis*—gained gradual acceptance. Meanwhile, glaring failures of welfare state capitalism presaged a revival of intellectual support for laissez-faire economic policies. These two strands of thought combined neatly in support of the notion that stock markets, free of heavy-handed government intervention, were the best mechanisms for allocating capital in a modern economy.

But the story does not end there. Since 1980, a new body of thought—loosely termed "behavioralism"—has challenged the notion that modern stock markets are "efficient," and provided crucial ammunition for those who argue that unrestrained markets can do more damage than good. In a very significant way, behavioralism provides an intellectual basis for long-standing suspicions of speculative market excess. The behavioralist view has gained wide popular acceptance; a steady stream of books and articles about "speculative bubbles" (a behavioralist concept) has found a ready audience. The belief that stock markets are often subject to irrational gyrations coexists uneasily with the "free market" ideology that is now the foundation for much government economic policy.

All these intellectual, economic, political, and cultural influences have combined to create what can best be termed an *equity culture*. This culture is pervasive. It is now commonplace for citizens in many countries to invest a substantial portion of their savings, including retirement monies, in equities; fifty years ago, this was unheard of, and would have been deemed grossly imprudent. Medium-sized businesses in Europe and Asia that a mere ten years ago would never have dreamed of selling stock in a public market now suddenly not only have the opportunity to do so, but frequently find themselves with no choice but to consider equity offerings as other, more traditional, modes of financing disappear. Countries as diverse as Malaysia and France have been forced by the new market realities to reconsider their entire structure of corporate governance and economic regulatory legislation, which in turn requires them to reconsider some of the fundamental underpinnings of their social compacts.

This book is the story of how and why this equity culture has come into being. Of necessity, it focuses on the development of ideas, showing how the concept of a market for stocks has evolved over time. It is the story of a phenomenon—the global equity market—that is both very new and very old. It is a story that must be understood to truly comprehend the complex workings of the international economy in the twenty-first century.

A FINANCIAL REVOLUTION

TO MAKE MONEY from money is a sin. Or so it was widely believed for centuries. In ancient Greece, Aristotle developed the notion of a "fair price" for anything that could be bought or sold. In his view, "fair" prices should govern economic transactions between men in much the same way that the immutable laws of physics governed the universe. It was not for man (or a marketplace created by man) to interfere with the work of nature or the gods. Any attempt to make a profit solely from fluctuations in prices was by definition unjust.

In the thirteenth century, St. Thomas Aquinas expanded upon the concept, declaring it improper to "sell dearer or to buy cheaper than a thing is worth."[1] Loaning money out at interest, or usury, was condemned. The very pursuit of profit for its own sake was immoral. In this St. Thomas followed St. Augustine, for whom the unlimited lust for gain—*appetitus divitarum infinitus*—was one of the three principal sins, along with a craving for power and sexual lasciviousness.[2] Such strictures were prominent in Islamic doctrine as well.

But what is a stock market, or any market for that matter, if not an organized forum in which the participants attempt to "sell dearer or to buy cheaper"? For generations a profound moral ambiguity plagued the development of financial markets. Practical considerations dictated the need for such markets, to provide the capital necessary for business. But the nascent markets for securities were never able to fully escape the suspicion that market participants engaged in activities akin to vice. Those suspicions persist even to this day.

The earliest example of an organized market for equities can be found in the Roman republic of the second century B.C., not yet subject to the theological restraints later imposed by monotheistic religions. Three essential prerequisites for a viable equity market had come to exist in Rome: freely transferable *capital*, readily available *credit*, and a willingness to take *risk*. Flourishing commerce throughout the republic caused wealth to accumulate in Rome, where it became available as capital for investment under a comprehensive system of laws and property rights that made capital easily transferable. In addition, the concept of credit* in a commercial sense had developed and become widely accepted, as evidenced by the ready availability of money lent out at interest, and by the general acceptance of bank drafts as a means of financing trade. And finally, a class of investors willing to invest capital at risk to earn a return, rather than simply stockpiling or hoarding it, provided the entrepreneurial spark to ignite a market. Much as would later occur in financial capitals such as Amsterdam, London, and New York, ancient Rome provided the crucible in which capital, credit, and risk taking came together. It was through this process that the first stock market was born.

The Roman republican government contracted out many of its functions, from temple-building to tax collection, to groups of investors known as *publicani*. Like modern corporations, the *publicani* were legal entities whose ownership was divided into *partes*, or shares. The *publicani* were often run by executive managements, producing public accounts (*tabulae*) and holding regular meetings for shareholders. Some were substantial concerns, employing tens of thousands of slaves and operating across different regions.

The ownership shares in *publicani* concerns were of two types: large executive shareholdings of the great capitalists, known as *soccii*, and smaller shares, called *particulae*, which were much more widely held. Purchases and sales of *particulae* seemed to occur frequently

---

*The English word "credit" derives from the Latin *credere*, to entrust, and *creditum*, loan.

from the second century B.C. onward. The place where trading occurred in Rome was the Forum, near the Temple of Castor. As described by the classical historian Mikhail Rostovtzeff, "crowds of men bought and sold shares and bonds of tax farming companies, various goods for cash and on credit, farms and estates in Italy and the provinces, houses and shops in Rome and elsewhere, ships and storehouses, slaves and cattle." Another historian wrote that "the Forum, with its immense basilicae, may be regarded as an immense stock exchange where money speculation of every kind was going on."[3] Shares fluctuated in value, with uncertain results; Cicero stated that buying shares in public companies was seen as a gamble that conservative men avoided.[4]

The Roman republic was "international" in nature, having conquered or otherwise acquired previously foreign lands, and the Forum market was likewise internationalized. Noncitizens were permitted to own shares of most *publicani*, and many did so. Because the importance of timely information was widely recognized, a network of couriers extending to the far reaches of Rome's possessions was maintained to systematically gather useful financial intelligence. Dealings in foreign currency (foreign exchange) were commonplace, making transactions with outsiders relatively easy to execute.

The Roman stock market declined and eventually disappeared when Rome itself fell from prominence. The Christian feudal system that followed in medieval Europe, and the Islamic order that came to dominate large parts of Asia and Africa, were innately hostile to financial markets. Primitive economies existed by a system of barter, and injunctions against profiteering, speculation, and hoarding were commonplace. The very idea of a financial market of any sort was completely inimical to the fundamental organizing principles upon which these societies were based.

The modern world of markets could not have come into existence in this stultifying environment. But grudgingly, at first only in a few small city-states on the Italian peninsula, glimmers of change began to appear. Merchants from states like Venice and Genoa expanded their dealings across greater distances. This inevitably involved greater risks: to be successful, merchants had to learn to accept and manage these risks. Ultimately, it is the need to manage risks that creates the need for financial markets. It was probably inevitable that securities—paper representations of assets—would eventually come to be traded among merchants who had acclimated themselves to the systematic taking of risk.

The first securities traded were actually government debt obligations, issued by Italian city administrations to raise funds. Government borrowing was certainly not unique; what made these loans different was that they were *negotiable*, meaning that they could be freely transferred (bought and sold) by individuals. In Venice, government bonds were traded at the Rialto, and by the mid-fourteenth century these transactions were apparently significant enough to warrant what would now be called government regulation. A law was passed in 1351 banning the circulation of false rumors intended to depress the prices at which government bonds traded; subsequently, in 1390, 1404, and 1410, there were attempts to restrain speculation in government notes by prohibiting transactions with deferred settlements (which allowed the buyer to own a security he had not yet paid for). Efforts were made by the Ducal Council to forbid what would now be called insider trading (using nonpublic information to profit from trading securities).[5] Despite these regulatory restraints, trading in government bonds flourished in Venice, and became commonplace in other cities as well. By the fifteenth century markets in government securities had appeared in Florence, Genoa, Pisa, and Verona.

Fernand Braudel writes in *The Wheels of Commerce* that "all the evidence points to the Mediterranean as the cradle for the stock market."[6] Most Italian city-states farmed out tax collection to organizations called *monti*, similar to the ancient Roman *publicani*. Capital for the *monti* was divided into shares, called *luoghi*. Once markets for government bonds developed, it was natural that other securities would also come to be traded. In the fifteenth century, transactions in *luoghi* occurred alongside trades in government bonds. This was arguably the first true stock market of the post-Roman era.

Outside of the Italian peninsula, early financial markets developed as adjuncts to the large trade fairs that had been held throughout Western Europe since the eleventh century. Big fairs drew merchants and traders from great distances; the attraction was not only that the fairs provided a central gathering place to do business, but also that they were generally granted special exemptions from the heavy duties and taxes imposed on most commercial transactions. As Fernand Braudel describes them, the fairs can best be seen as pyramids. Markets in many local goods, usually cheap and often perishable, formed the broad bottom of the pyramid. Higher up in the pyramid were smaller numbers of more expensive luxury goods, often transported from far away. And finally, at the very top, was an active money market controlled by a few major dealers.

At the Leipzig fairs, shares of German mines changed hands in the fifteenth century. At the St.-Germain fairs, near Paris, municipal bonds, IOUs, and lottery tickets* were traded. Antwerp, with its two lengthy annual fairs in the spring and autumn and its yearlong tax exemption, was described as a "continuous fair."[7] To establish important international connections, foreign merchants often relocated permanently to cities like Antwerp where fairs were held frequently.

By the sixteenth century, rudimentary mechanisms for the trading of financial assets like stocks and bonds existed in several locales. This primitive financial system was then hit by an external shock—a sudden influx of gold and silver from Portuguese possessions in Africa and Spanish territories in the New World. The history of modern financial capitalism arguably begins at this point, with a "price revolution." Because coins made from gold or silver were the accepted medium of exchange, anything that dramatically increased the supply of specie also increased the amount of money in the economy. Such an increase in the money supply, unaccompanied by a corresponding increase in the supply of goods and services available to be purchased, produced inflation. Earl Hamilton, in a classic work published in 1934, demonstrated that price levels in Europe more than doubled in the early 1500s and remained at high levels through the next century. Hamilton found that money wages lagged behind rising prices, creating profit increases that made capital accumulation (and thus modern capitalism) possible.[8]

---

*"Lottery" tickets in the Middle Ages were a form of government bonds that included a chance to win a large prize in addition to normal interest and principal payments.

While some historians have disputed parts of this thesis, there is substantial evidence that significant changes were occurring in the European economy in the sixteenth century. Prices actually rose faster than supplies of specie, indicating that specie was used more efficiently (or, in other words, the velocity at which money was employed in the economy increased). Interest rates also appear to have fallen, even though inflation should have caused rates to rise.[9] Together, these observations support the notion that innovative new techniques to use and invest money—the precursors of modern financial markets—were evolving during this time of turbulence.

The value of various European currencies (measured in terms of the goods and services they would buy) seems to have declined over this period even more rapidly than did the value of specie, implying that governments were debasing their coinage by reducing the amount of specie in coins in order to finance ever more grandiose military ventures. As conflicts became more international in nature (across the Continent and across entire oceans), merchants struggling to supply the voracious war machines were forced to invest more money for longer periods, across greater distances, and in transactions involving more counterparties. Fixed capital, such as ships and the inventories in their holds, gradually came to be represented by transferable claims on those assets. *Bills of exchange*, which were essentially negotiable IOUs issued between merchants, became acceptable as payments in many transactions, eliminating the need to transfer large, bulky quantities of precious metals. The first, primitive form of paper money had been created.

The pressing need of European governments to finance war inevitably led to new techniques for raising money, in the form of both taxes and borrowing. Rulers borrowed from whomever they could, and under whatever terms were available. But large loans from a few wealthy individuals were not sufficient; some new devices were necessary to broaden the base from which money could be extracted. The Hapsburg regime of Charles V created a new instrument in the mid-sixteenth century, the *annuity*, which proved to have lasting popularity. In the most widely used form, the government would sell an annuity contract to a purchaser, committing the state to make fixed interest payments to any person designated by the purchaser for the life of that designee. Other annuities were perpetual and could be passed on to heirs of the annuitant, although the government usually reserved the right to repay the principal amount at any time, and thus cancel the annuity, if it so decided and could afford to do so. Both types of annuities were transferable, meaning that a market for annuity contracts could develop.

Meanwhile, fairs had begun to decline in importance as centers of market activity, as "enlightened" rulers reduced the burden of taxes and duties imposed on commerce, thereby reducing the attraction of the tax-exempt fairs. Incipient financial markets now tended to operate year round, in fixed locations, and were becoming more active and sophisticated. As more securities issued by diverse foreign jurisdictions came to be traded in a given location, the market began to differentiate systematically between the creditworthiness of different issuers, so that prices fluctuated in response to changing perceptions of credit quality. But more active markets also had a downside; overt efforts at market manipulation occurred. In one early incident in sixteenth-century Lyons, a syndicate organized by the Florentine Gaspar Ducci deliberately attempted to suppress the prices of government securities.[10]

By the mid-sixteenth century, Antwerp, with its "continuous fair," emerged as the leading financial center in the West. It became home to the first permanent stock exchange, or bourse, so named after the Hôtel des Bourses in nearby Bruges, built by a nobleman from the the ancient aristocratic family Van der Bourse, who inscribed over the door his coat of arms—three purses (bourses)—which can still be seen today.[11] The name Bourse caught on; in the seventeenth century, the writer Samuel Ricard, author of *The New Businessman*, specifically defined the term "bourse" as a "[stock] exchange" that was the "meeting-place of bankers, merchants and businessmen, exchange currency dealers and banker's agents, brokers and other persons."

The incessant warfare of the sixteenth century, which created the stresses on economies that forced financial innovation, sometimes had a devastating effect on the very marketplaces it spawned. Most notably, the sack of Antwerp by Spanish troops in 1585 led to the permanent decline of the city's bourse. Amsterdam benefited as Jewish and Protestant refugees fled Antwerp to escape the Spanish-imposed Inquisition, setting a pattern that would recur in future times of crisis. Jews and Protestants were not bound by tight religious strictures against moneylending and moneymaking, so they came to dominate professions in finance and banking. They took with them to Amsterdam the innovative financing techniques they had already developed. The ingredients for the Dutch "economic miracle" of the early seventeenth century were now in place.

Amsterdam soon replaced Antwerp as the financial capital of Western Europe. In 1609 the Amsterdam Wisselbank was founded; merchants could now transfer payments to one another, denominated in bank money (called *banco*) issued by the Wisselbank. The bank was operated on the basis of very conservative principles, and did not seek to expand the supply of money and credit in the economy beyond the quantity of specie it held in its vaults. But by providing a commonly accepted medium of exchange (the *banco*), the bank facilitated a prodigious expansion of Dutch trade.

The year 1609 also saw the creation of the Dutch East India Company, one of the defining events in the evolution of the modern stock market. The new entity was organized as a *joint-stock company*, which differed from the standard partnership form of organization normally employed by merchants. Adam Smith wrote that the joint-stock company was developed because of problems of "distant trade" that tied up large amounts of capital for long periods, more capital than a single merchant or small group of merchants could (or would) put up. Investors, rather than being partners in the firm, held shares in the new company, making the firm itself an entity independent of its owners. This meant that the firm would not have to be dissolved upon the death or departure of one of its partners, and made it much easier to attract capital from a larger number of investors, many of whom would take only passive roles.

The concept behind the joint-stock company originated in medieval trading partnerships called *societas maris* and *commenda*. These were partnerships used to finance shipping and to spread the risks inherent in such ventures. Partners were divided into investors, who stayed on land, and voyagers, who went with the ships. In the *commenda*, the voyagers risked no capital (only their lives), and received one-fourth of the profits. In the *societas*, the voyagers put up one-third of the money and received half of the profits.

The first joint-stock companies had actually been created in England in the sixteenth century. These early joint-stock firms, however, possessed only temporary charters from the government, in some cases for one voyage only. (One example was the Muscovy Company, chartered in England in 1533 for trade with Russia; another, chartered the same year, was a company with the intriguing title Guinea Adventurers.) The Dutch East India Company was the first joint-stock company to have a permanent charter.

Significantly, the joint-stock form of organization did not gain acceptance in the Islamic world, even though Arabic shipping fleets had dominated Mediterranean trading routes since the eighth century. These Arab traders faced the same problems associated with financing long, risky voyages that European traders confronted, but Islamic inheritance laws effectively prevented the development of joint-stock companies. It may well be that rigid Islamic rules, rooted in the Koran, contributed to the gradual decline of the Arab merchant fleets, whose owners were unable to develop new, more efficient means for financing their trade.[12]

The Dutch East India Company was the forerunner of the modern corporation, which, like the ancient Roman *publicani*, is a separate entity distinct from the investors who own it. This meant that partners could not demand that their capital be returned after a successful voyage; if they wished to cash in their holdings, they could do so only by selling to a third party. Thus the need for a market in shares was created.

Capital from across Europe flowed into Holland to be invested in Dutch East India stock. The company was consistently profitable; an envious French author in 1664 wrote, "there are few years wherein [the company's investors] got less than 30 per cent."[13] To accommodate the increased volume of trading, a "New Exchange" was opened in Amsterdam in 1610. Braudel describes the different assets that were traded: "Commodities, current exchange, shareholdings, maritime insurance . . . a money market, a finance market, a stock market."[14] Futures contracts (called actions) on shares of the East India Company were available, as was financing for the purchase of shares (what would now be called "margin" loans). Over the course of the seventeenth century, the practices developed in Amsterdam would come to be known as "Dutch finance," and would have a profound impact on developing markets elsewhere in Europe.

The first treatise on stock market speculation was published in 1688 in Amsterdam. Entitled (perhaps appropriately) "Confusion de Confusiones," it was printed in Spanish, and directed to an audience primarily composed of Jews of Portuguese descent who had come to be prominent players in the trading of Dutch East India shares. The author, Joseph de la Vega, admitted to having gone broke five times playing the market, and described in a folksy yet practical manner the functioning of an active, organized stock exchange in Amsterdam. He attributed the rapid growth of the Amsterdam stock market primarily to the success of the Dutch East India Company.

"Dutch" techniques of finance spread to England after the "Glorious Revolution" of 1688 brought the Protestant William of Orange to the throne. This transition of power occurred at a time of unprecedented prosperity, when traditional ideas of the proper place of money and finance in society were gradually yielding to those of market capitalism. A new generation of "moneyed men," who spurned the old theological critiques of profit and interest, came to prominence in London. The new liberal ideology replaced traditional feudal beliefs, making what had formerly been seen as vices (such as profit, moneylending, and consumption) into attributes. Anticipating Adam Smith's writings of nearly a century later, the new creed held that the active pursuit of personal profit actually benefited, not harmed, society. William of Orange was not a proponent of market capitalism. But the need to bring some semblance of order to chaotic state finances so as to fund the periodic wars of the era made him and his government dependent on the new capitalists.

Prior to the 1690s there had been no real distinction between short-term and long-term government borrowing. The government debt was a hodgepodge of different arrangements, often negotiated separately with individual lenders. Creditors demanding repayment were often given land in lieu of cash. Lenders invariably wanted debts repaid as quickly as possible, since there was no marketplace in which they could sell the debt instruments in order to raise cash.

In the years following 1688, laws were enacted that created what has been termed by historians the Financial Revolution in England, parallel to the Industrial Revolution. A parliamentary guarantee of the government debt was established, making that debt no longer simply a personal obligation of the monarch. A Promissory Notes Act passed, making all debts negotiable and hence transferable. And perhaps most important, a privately owned central bank—the Bank of England—was established in 1694 to provide a stable mechanism for creating and allocating credit. Like the Amsterdam Wisselbank, the Bank of England issued banknotes that became widely accepted as a convenient and trustworthy medium of exchange.

Religious convulsions on the Continent in the late seventeenth century created a flow of refugees to England that provided the human raw material necessary to build a new financial economy. Jews expelled from Spain, and driven by persecution from other parts of Europe, as well as Protestant Huguenots forced out of France, sought refuge in England, bringing with them both the capital and the skills needed for the new financial culture. (One estimate is that the refugees transferred to England roughly £3 million of capital.)[15] Dutch Jews in particular became quite prominent in the City of London, the crowded section of the capital that became the financial center of Britain.

These foreign influences were not seen as an unmixed blessing by all Englishmen. Daniel Defoe is credited with authoring the following doggerel lamenting the important role of foreign advisers to William III:

> We blame the King that he relies too much
> On Strangers, Germans, Huguenots, and Dutch
> And seldom does his just affairs of State
> To English Councillors communicate.[16]

One idea imported from Holland was the sale of annuities to finance wars. The first government-backed annuities in England were sold in 1693 and 1694. These were life annuities, payable to the holder as long as he lived. The contracts proved popular, and the use of this device proliferated quickly to meet the government's burgeoning revenue requirements. Inexorably, in the scramble by the Crown to raise money for seemingly never-ending military expenditures, an oppressive financial burden was accumulated. The wartime interest rates paid on the annuities ran as high as 7 percent, far higher than peacetime rates would likely be. But since the contracts were not redeemable, the government would not be able to refinance them at lower interest rates when peace finally arrived. The annuity contracts were also unwieldy, with all sorts of different lengths, based on the unpredictable life expectancies of the various holders. These limitations would later create serious problems for the British government, and prove to have profound consequences.

A lively stock market (in joint-stock company shares) sprang up in London in the 1690s. It should be noted that the term "stock," as used at the time, also included government bonds and annuities, which were often called government "stock." (The word derives from the wooden tallies, or stocks, that were commonly used to represent government debt, with notches being cut in the tallies as each interest payment was made.) Words like "stockjobber," "director," "subscription," underwriting, "puts," "refusals" (calls), which had a few years earlier been unknown, were now commonplace in financial circles. The term "broker,"* which had previously meant a pimp or procurer, now took on an entirely different (although some would say only slightly more respectable) connotation.

Transactions took place informally in coffeehouses clustered among the twisted warren of narrow streets called Exchange Alley. Shares in the British East India Company, which had formerly been auctioned off along with the company's wares, were now actively traded, as were shares in the newly created Bank of England and other chartered firms such as the Hudson's Bay Company and the Royal African Company. Heightened interest in the market created a demand for more information, causing a financial press of sorts to come into existence. *The Merchants Rememberancer* had carried very

---

*A broker was a man who acted as an agent for others, negotiating purchases or sales of stock, for which he received a commission.

limited market quotations since 1681; by the mid-1690s it had been joined by several other publications. The most comprehensive market information was included in a biweekly paper somewhat incongruously called *A Collection for the Improvement of Husbandry and Trade*, published by an apothecary and coffee trader named John Houghton. A fellow of the Royal Society, Houghton wanted to bridge the gap between pure science and applied technology in all fields; in addition to tackling questions about planting wheat and raising cattle, he took on the subject of the stock market. Houghton wrote the first known descriptions of options and futures contracts, which were then referred to as "actions" and "time bargains." In short order, the number of stocks quoted by Houghton's publication increased from ten to fifty-seven, as many new joint-stock companies were created.[17]

Most of the new joint-stock companies were small, and not formally chartered by the government, unlike large chartered entities such as the East India Company and the Bank of England. The new firms operated in a legal limbo between corporate and partnership forms of organization. Some were businesses dealing in entirely new product lines, often brought in by Huguenots, such as white paper and lustrings. Other firms dealt in more traditional businesses such as saltpeter, sword blades, guns, mines, salvage, fishing, waterworks, and ironworking. The historian W. R. Scott estimates that £4.25 million of capital was raised by new stock issues in the mid-1690s, with the number of joint-stock companies in existence rising from a mere handful at the beginning of the decade to over 150 by 1695.

Houghton explained to his readers how and why the new stock market had come into being, and defined the term "stockjobbing" in the following paragraph:

> A great many Stocks have arisen since this War with France; for Trade being obstructed at Sea, few that had Money were willing it should be idle, and a great many that wanted Employments studied how to dispose of their Money, that they might be able to command it whenever they had occasion, which they found they could more easily do in Joint-Stock, than in laying out the same in Lands, Houses or Commodities, these [shares] being more easily shifted

from Hand to Hand. This put them upon Contrivances, whereby some were encouraged to Buy, others to Sell, and this is . . . called Stock-Jobbing.[18]

Houghton correctly identified a crucial advantage of joint-stock companies: shares that could be easily bought and sold. A ready market for these shares meant that joint-stock company investors were not locked into long-term, illiquid investments, like real estate or unwidely forms of government debt. This was extremely important, because it made investors much more willing to buy joint-stock company shares, and pay higher prices for those shares. This in turn meant that entrepreneurs could now raise significant quantities of new capital at attractive terms through joint-stock ventures, making modern capitalism feasible.

The London stock market was international; there was steady communication with investors in European cities bordering on the North Sea. (Such was the state of roads in England at the time that messages could often be delivered to London from coastal Europe faster than from inland English towns.) By the mid-1690s international flotations of new stock issues were being attempted. The most prominent was that of a Scottish firm called the Darien Company, created for the purpose of settling the isthmus of Panama and using it as a base for trade. The company raised £300,000 from investors in Scotland itself, while additional funds came from parallel offerings in London, Amsterdam, and Hamburg.[19]

The new English stock market suffered its first "crash" in 1696. The immediate causes seem to have been worry over wartime reverses suffered by government forces and concern over the government's plans to retire old coins and replace them with new ones, which created fears that the currency might be debased. Of 140 public English and Scottish companies operating in 1693, only 40 survived until 1697, a failure rate of over 70 percent.[20]

Predictably, many observers were outraged. Grotesque speculative excess in the market was presumed to have led to the catastrophe; it was an accusation that would be repeated time and time again in the future. Complaints about the allegedly manipulative, self-serving activities of brokers at a moment of national crisis led to enactment in

1697 of legislation to "refrain the number and ill-practices of brokers and stock-jobbers."[21] The number of licensed brokers was henceforth to be limited to one hundred, and those brokers were forbidden to deal in government securities without the specific consent of the Treasury. They were not to trade securities for their own accounts, and were prohibited from charging commissions of more than one-eighth of 1 percent. (This act was widely evaded; by one estimate, no more than one-third of all brokers were ever formally "sworn" as required by the law.)[22]

Despite the initial shock and recriminations resulting from the Crash of 1696, the British stock market recovered substantially by 1698. Additional legislation was introduced to restrain the new financial contrivances employed in 'Change Alley, but failed to pass. Most of the new instruments that had made the stock market possible survived. The Financial Revolution in England had created the essential ingredients necessary for a modern market economy.

BUBBLES

> We are now to enter upon the year 1720; a year remarkable beyond any other which can be pitched upon by historians for extraordinary romantic projects, proposals and undertakings . . . and which . . . ought to be held in perpetual remembrance . . . never to leave it in the power of any, hereafter, to hoodwink mankind into so shameful and baneful an imposition on the credulity of the people, thereby diverted from their lawful industry.

SO SAID ADAM ANDERSON, who wrote from personal experience. Anderson was a clerk for the South Sea Company, and published his recollection of the times in a cumbersome work entitled *An Historical and Chronological Deduction of the Origin of Commerce, from the earliest accounts.*[1] The events Anderson decried—later to be known as the South Sea Bubble—made it clear that the new market for stock could be badly abused, and was now of sufficient importance to do damage to the British economy.

The story of the South Sea Bubble has taken on elements of a parable in which foolish speculators become victims of their own greed, first pushing share prices to astronomical levels, then losing everything in the inevitable collapse that follows. The theme of this parable, rooted in traditional religious objections to speculation, has been picked up and repeated over the centuries by writers such as

Charles MacKay, Charles Kindleberger, and Edward Chancellor, who claim that such irrational behavior recurs periodically in the history of markets.

Kindleberger, in *Manias, Panics and Crashes*, defines a speculative bubble as a situation in which the relationship between the market value of an asset and its intrinsic value breaks down due to overzealous trading and unrealistic appraisals. First, something new occurs (such as the development of new technology, a dramatic change in the political climate, etc.) that seems to create great potential for profit. Savvy market participants step in and buy affected securities, causing them to rise. For a bubble to develop, however, this "smart" investment must at some point be supplemented with buying from other, less informed sources; easy credit and low interest rates, which make it possible to borrow money cheaply to invest in the new speculative vehicles, is also usually a prerequisite. According to Kindleberger, if these conditions are met, a boom may ensue, with speculation spreading to segments of the population that normally don't play the market. The new entrants have little experience and thus are prone to react emotionally, exacerbating the severity of price swings. As prices rise, still more investors are attracted by the apparent easy gains. The bubble continues to inflate until finally the supply of buyers is exhausted.

The reality of the South Sea episode, however, appears somewhat less clear-cut. Certainly the ability of inexperienced investors to delude themselves, and lose their money in ways that would subsequently appear to be quite foolish, is self-evident. But the evidence suggests that there was more reason, and less folly, behind the events of 1720 than conventional interpretations allow.

The calamitous occurrences of 1720 did not first manifest themselves in London or in Amsterdam, the two financial centers of eighteenth-century Europe. The financial earthquake first hit in Paris, then radiated out along fault lines to shake the rest of Western Europe. Unlike Holland and England, which had traditions of legal and parliamentary restraints on the monarch, in France royal authority was absolute. Virtually all aspects of the economy were controlled by the central government; any new markets could only come into being through the direct action of the state.

The person who would revolutionize French (and eventually European) finance was a physically imposing man named John Law. Born in Edinburgh in 1671, Law was trained as a goldsmith at a time when many such craftsmen were active participants in the newly liberalized money markets. Standing over six feet tall in an era when few men attained such height, Law was a strikingly attractive man who took great pains to dress and carry himself in a manner that commanded attention. In his youth he was a notorious womanizer and gambler, although early reverses at the gaming tables soon caused him to call upon his impressive mathematical prowess to develop gaming strategies calculated to ensure better results in the future. In this he was remarkably successful; at many points during his life he was able to support himself from gambling winnings. But Law's inquisitive mind soon turned beyond gaming to larger issues of international finance.

Unfortunately, Law was unable to participate in the English Financial Revolution of the 1690s because he had been clapped in jail for killing a young man from a prominent family in a sword duel. After complex behind-the-scenes legal machinations, he was allowed to "escape," and forced to flee England. During a stay in Amsterdam, Law observed how the Dutch central bank helped facilitate the expansion of trade by issuing paper notes guaranteed by the government that were ubiquitously accepted as legal tender. Law realized that if state-sponsored banks could be created that would issue copious new supplies of banknotes as a substitute for specie, constraints on trade that resulted from a limited supply of money could be eliminated. This idea was generations ahead of its time, anticipating the modern system of bank credit and paper money that are today's money supply. But how could Law, technically an escaped felon, hope to sell the concept to Europe's rulers?

He first attempted to persuade the English Queen Anne, who not only declined to consider his arguments but also refused to grant him the royal pardon required if he was to return to England. Undaunted, Law turned his attention to France, and was able to insinuate himself into the confidence of the Duc d'Orleans, who as regent for the underage French king was the de facto ruler of France. Law's first action was to set up a new bank—the Banque Générale—which was supported by a large personal deposit from the regent himself. The bank, soon to be taken over directly by the French government (at great profit to Law), was to provide the credit necessary to stimulate the sagging French economy. Law's favorite dictum was: "Wealth depends on commerce, and commerce depends on circulation."[2] No longer would economic activity in France be stifled by a lack of circulating specie.

Law then in 1717 created the instrument with which his name will always be associated: the Company of the West, known popularly ever since as the Mississippi Company. The concept was breathtaking, in that it offered potentially large benefits for two groups whose interests were theoretically in conflict: the nearly bankrupt French government and its creditors. The Company of the West received from the French government the exclusive right to trade with the French colony of Louisiana, a vast area in North America extending from the mouth of the Mississippi up to the river's distant headwaters. Shares would be sold to private investors, but these shares could be purchased in part with government bonds (at face value) in lieu of cash. Since the market value of the bonds (called billets) was greatly depressed because of the extremely poor state of the government's finances, the ability to exchange the bonds at face value for shares in the new enterprise was seen as an appealing inducement for bondholders to invest in the new company.

As part of the arrangement, the Mississippi Company allowed the French Treasury to pay a lower interest rate on the government bonds the company took in from investors who exchanged the bonds for Mississippi Company shares. Everyone seemed to benefit. The government would be able to slash the burdensome interest it was paying on its debt, bondholders would be able to recognize full value for their badly depreciated investments, and the Mississippi Company would gain the exclusive (and presumably lucrative) right to trade with French Louisiana.

Law became managing director of the new company, which possessed its own army and navy, and at least in theory ruled half of North America. But even with the favorable terms offered, few government bondholders chose to exchange their bonds for Mississippi Company stock. Law was a foreigner, and joint-stock companies were not as well known in France as in Holland or England. The company's shares languished below par.*

Undaunted, Law pushed to expand the scope of the company's activities. He acquired from the government exclusive rights to raise tobacco (which was rapidly becoming popular in France) as well as the right to trade in slaves and other products from the French colony of Senegal. He had the company buy out the old French East India and China trading companies in an effort to secure a worldwide monopoly on all French foreign trade. Law paid for these purchases by issuing new Mississippi Company (now formally called the Company of the Indies) shares.

In order to sell the new stock, Law aggressively hyped the company's prospects in a promotional blitz that resembled a modern public relations campaign. He arranged for the state bank to provide easy credit; it is estimated that over 1.2 billion livres were loaned to purchasers of shares in 1719 alone. At a crucial moment immediately before a share offering, he announced that he and a few friends stood ready to buy all the new shares. The strategy was successful; investors assumed that Law had favorable inside information about the company. The new share offerings sold out, and the stock traded to a substantial premium.

Law was not finished. The company next bought the rights to the royal mint for 50 million livres, put forward a controversial plan to purchase tax-farming rights for another 52 million livres, and finally proposed to take over the entire national debt of 1.2 billion livres in return for further trade concessions. By October 1719, Mississippi Company shares that had struggled at 490 livres five months earlier hit 6,500.

It soon became clear that Law was orchestrating the rise in the price of Mississippi Company shares. In fact he explicitly stated that his objective was to fix the share price at 10,000 livres. This was not to be done to reward investors; instead, it was part of Law's grand "System," in which plentiful credit and low interest rates would provide the basis for a permanent boom in the French economy.

---

*The term "par" refers to the face value of a security, usually the price at which it is issued, and the price at which the security is carried on the issuing entity's books.

Given the rate the government paid the Mississippi Company on the state debt the company had assumed, a share price of 10,000 livres would imply an interest rate on capital invested of 2 percent, the rate that Law believed was appropriate and desirable for the overall economy. Law intended to use the Mississippi share price as a means of fixing French interest rates at low levels.

Shares were traded out of the Mississippi Company's new offices on the rue Quincampoix, a long, narrow street (not much wider than an alley) located in the ancient commercial center of Paris. The rue Quincampoix had long been a meeting place for moneylenders, entrepreneurs seeking to raise capital, and traders of government billets. As activity increased, trading spilled out of the company offices onto the street; the rue Quincampoix and surrounding lanes became clogged with crowds. In an effort to control the chaos, gates were erected at either end and guards were posted to prevent trading at night, which was said to disturb residents of the area. One gate was reserved for "speculators of quality," while the other was to be used by everyone else.[3]

A bell was sounded each morning, at which time the gates opened and trading commenced. Daniel Defoe described the scene:

> Nothing can be more diverting than to see the hurry and clatter of the stock-jobbers in Quincampoix street; a place so scandalously dirty, as if it had not been the sink of the city only, but of the whole kingdom . . . The inconvenience of the darkest and nastiest street in Paris does not prevent the crowds of people of all qualities . . . coming to buy and sell their stocks in the open place, where, without distinction, they go up to their ankles in dirt every step they take.[4]

Speculation in Mississippi Company stock had startling side effects, one of which was the undermining of the existing class structure. Many people from lower social orders prospered spectacularly (at least temporarily) from the boom. Thanks in large part to Law's easy credit policies, people from all walks of life could purchase stock by putting as little as 10 percent down. Law's own coachman is said to have made profits sufficient to retire from his position. In one of the most bizarre legends of the time, a hunchback was said to have earned significant sums by leaning against a mulberry tree and renting out his hump, on which contracts to purchase shares were written out and signed.[5]

The Mississippi Company boom provided the first example of a stock market–induced "wealth effect," defined by economists as a change in personal consumption patterns arising from dramatic moves in stock prices. The demand for luxury goods soared; goldsmiths, tapestry weavers, carpet factories, and porcelain makers were deluged with orders. A foreign diplomat exclaimed: "It is certain that the number of people here increases every day and that all manner of luxury does too; the Hollanders have drawn several millions from hence for jewels, lace and linen; I was told yesterday that one shop had sold in less than three weeks lace and linen for 800 thousand livres and this chiefly to people who never wore any lace before."[6]

The regent's mother took note of the frenzy. She observed: "It is inconceivable what immense wealth there is in France right now. Everybody speaks in millions. I don't understand it at all, but I clearly see that the god Mammon reigns as an absolute monarch in Paris."[7]

By December 1719, Mississippi Company shares hit 10,000 livres, the price Law desired. A new word—"millionaire"—entered the common lexicon to describe stock market winners. Law proceeded apace to build and outfit ships to carry on trade with Louisiana, and vowed publicly that his "System" would firmly establish France as the premier power in the world.

The British government watched the apparent success of Law's "System" in France with apprehension. It was feared that the French economic revival would enable France to renew its quest for military conquest, directly threatening Britain. There was also concern that the French stock market boom was sucking money out England, jeopardizing the economy. Numerous anecdotal accounts confirm the active involvement of English investors in Paris. In one instance, the agent for Lord Strafford, who had invested substantial sums in the Mississippi Company, complained in a letter that he was forced to be in attendance in the damp in the rue Quincampoix from dawn to dusk, "so faint without eating that I have been ready to drop."[8]

Money flowing out of England to Paris was money that would not be available to finance commerce in Britain.

Lord John Dalrymple, the Earl of Stair, who was serving as British ambassador in Paris, sent increasingly apprehensive letters to London describing events in France. Openly hostile to Law, Lord Stair charged that Law "pretends he will set France much higher than she ever was before and put her in a condition to give the law to all of Europe; that he can ruin the trade and credit of England and Holland whenever he pleases; that he can break our bank whenever he has a mind, and our East India Company."[9]

Law's own remarks gave credence to Lord Stair's fears. An English acquaintance of Law's noted that Law "said publicly the other day . . . at his own table that there was but one great kingdom in Europe . . . [and] that he would bring down our East India stock."[10] To show his contempt for Britain's economy and stock market, Law entered into a well-publicized transaction to sell short* £100,000 worth of East India shares, thus betting that the price would decline.

In late 1719, a new edition of Law's treatise, entitled *Money and Trade Considered*, circulated in London. Brilliant in its simplicity, it is seen by modern scholars as one of the first truly insightful works in economics. The two central ideas that lay behind the "System" Law had implemented in France are described in detail. The first is that credit, if circulated, acts as money just as if it were conventional currency. The second is that there is a direct relationship between the circulating medium (or money supply) and the volume of commercial activity. The implication—quickly seized upon in Britain by those hoping to emulate Law's success in France—was that a greatly expanded supply of credit, and of paper representations of value (such as banknotes, shares, etc.), would stimulate economic activity and lead to the creation of more wealth.

The vehicle by which the new economic theories would be sprung on Britain was an obscure entity called the South Sea Company. The firm had been chartered in 1711 using an approach that actually an-

---

*A short sale occurs when a speculator sells a security that he does not own, with the expectation that he will be able to buy it back later at a lower price, thus profiting from a decline in the value of the security.

ticipated the structure of Law's Mississippi Company. The South Sea Company was to "take over" British government debt in exchange for the exclusive right to engage in trade with Spanish America. As would be the case with the Mississippi Company, government bond-holders could use their depreciated bonds at face value to acquire South Sea shares. The company agreed to accept reduced interest payments on the government bonds it received in exchange for its newly issued shares. As in the case of the Mississippi Company, in theory everyone benefited; the government was able to reduce the interest payments required on the public debt, bondholders would receive full value for their bonds, and the new company itself would presumably be able to reap large profits from future trade with the Americas.

Enthusiastic projections appeared in the press. A typical article claimed that a strong demand existed in the Spanish New World possessions for such items as "silk handkerchiefs, worsted hose, sealing wax, spices, clocks and watches, Cheshire cheese, pickles and scales and weights for gold and silver."[11] Frequent references were made to large deposits of precious minerals in South America. Prospective investors could look to the large profits the East India Company had been able to make from exploiting trade opportunities with Portuguese colonies in the Far East. Was it not reasonable to assume the South Sea Company could achieve similar results trading with Spanish colonies in the New World?

Some observers were skeptical, noting that at the time the South Sea Company was formed, the Spanish government forbade foreign nationals from trading with its colonies, a policy that seemed unlikely to change. Daniel Defoe commented, "Unless the Spaniards are to be divested of common sense, . . . abandoning their own commerce, throwing away the only valuable stake they have left in the world, and in short, bent on their own ruin, we cannot suggest that they will ever . . . part with so valuable, indeed so inestimable a jewel, as the exclusive power to trade to their own plantations."[12]

Initially, the only concession the Spanish seemed willing to allow to foreigners was the right to engage in the slave trade. As a result, South Sea stock drifted lower in the company's early years; it was not until May 1715 that it recovered to par for the first time. The rebound occurred in part because of a new deal the company made with the government, allowing it to increase its capital. In effect this was a paper transaction of little significance, but it did result in renewed publicity for the company. After the restructuring, the total paper capital of the South Sea Company exceeded that of all other British joint-stock companies combined, and was considerably more than the entire amount of joint-stock capital that had existed in England as recently as 1703. All the same, prospects for profitable trade with South America continued to prove elusive; by 1718, when Spain once again went to war with Britain, they seemed to vanish altogether.

But in late 1719, just as John Law's economic theories—and the spectacular boom in Mississippi Company shares in Paris—were the talk of the London market, King Philip V of Spain announced his intention to make peace with Britain. Immediately it was assumed that trade with Spanish America would soon be permitted. South Sea stock shot up. Just as Law had done in France, to ensure favorable treatment from the government, South Sea officers secretly dispensed shares, on very favorable terms, to highly placed officials. In this way the South Sea Company engaged in what would today be called "crony capitalism." The inevitable, and intended, result was that persons in important positions of authority now had a vested interest in a continuing stock price rise.

The year 1720 would prove to be one of the most chaotic years in the history of financial markets. But the two investment vehicles whose fates would define the times—the Mississippi and South Sea Companies—traveled very different trajectories. Just as the market in South Sea shares was gathering steam in Britain in early 1720, John Law was struggling in France with severe economic dislocations that had resulted from his "System." Most dangerous was the rampant inflation created by the rapid expansion of the (paper) money supply. A sharp dip in Mississippi Company stock had occurred in December 1719 (from 10,000 livres to 7,500), when Law attempted to restrain the growth of credit that fed inflation and speculation in the stock market. He quickly backed off, allowing the stock to recover to 9,400, but the episode starkly illustrated the choices he faced. Law wished to fix share prices, and effectively fix interest rates, at levels that would make cheap money readily available. But he did not want to create a runaway inflation. As would be discovered many times in the future, puncturing an inflationary boom without precipitating a disastrous economic collapse was a very difficult task.

In January 1720, Law was given virtually absolute power over the French economy when the regent appointed him controller general of finance. In the following months Law issued draconian edicts designed to tighten controls on the stock market and the economy. As foreign and domestic investors sought to sell shares and exchange banknotes for specie in order to transfer wealth out of the country, Law banned the export of coin and bullion. When this was circumvented by the export of jewelry and other precious objects in lieu of coin and bullion, Law promulgated successive edicts banning transactions in these valuables as well. But he could not stop the erosion of confidence. His "System" was like a leaking bucket full of holes; each effort to plug a particular hole simply forced more water out of the other openings.

Law frantically tried to support the price of Mississippi Company shares near his cherished 10,000-livre level, but was eventually forced to give up. The shares quickly declined to 7,800 livres. Trapped by deteriorating conditions, he announced a plan to phase out gold and silver coins entirely, in favor of paper banknotes. He was condemned mercilessly for his harsh, arbitrary actions. British ambassador Lord Stair, one of Law's fiercest critics, sneered that it was now clear that Law had been sincere when he had earlier converted to Catholicism in order to gain influence at the French court. According to Stair, Law had obviously fully embraced his new faith, since he had established another "Inquisition" and had demonstrated his belief in transubstantiation by turning so much gold into paper.[13]

Law began to crack under the pressure, and perhaps actually suffered a nervous breakdown. Lord Stair relayed the latest gossip back to London, reporting an account he heard from one of Law's footmen. "He [Law] gets out of bed almost every night, and runs, stark staring mad, about the room making a terrible noise, sometimes singing and dancing, at other times swearing, staring and stamping, quite out of himself."[14]

In England, Law's Mississippi Company was seen as a potential rival to the South Sea Company. Thus Law's travails, far from inducing caution in the London stock market, actually fueled a further rise in South Sea shares. In three days (March 19 through March 21) South Sea stock jumped from £218 to £320 on rumors that Law was having nightmares and that he had been dressed down by the regent himself. Perhaps also believing that South Sea and Mississippi Company shares competed for investors' attention, Law is reported to have schemed to undermine the British company, buying South Sea shares in Amsterdam in April 1720 with the intention of suddenly dumping the shares in May to create a panic.[15] If so, the operation never came off. South Sea stock continued to rise.

Shares of South Sea Company were actively traded in Amsterdam as well as in London. Other stocks in Amsterdam, and elsewhere in Europe, soared. Dutch East India stock rose by 25 percent in early 1720, while Dutch West India shares doubled. Insurance and mining company shares in Germany rose smartly, while flurries of speculation hit Bern and Basel. Interest in stocks spread beyond the customary tight circle of wealthy investors, brokers, and dealers in financial centers such as London. A packet stolen from a malter named Isaac Gilpin in the little Oxfordshire village of Warborough contained shares of Pennsylvania flax plantations and an Essex land improvement company, with endorsements showing that the shares had been changing hands among humble rural tradesmen.[16]

In London, all sorts of new joint-stock companies were formed and shares floated. At its peak in 1720, the total capitalization of the London market was over £500 million, roughly one hundred times the amount of 1695.[17] Most of these firms had no intention of seeking charters from the government. One traded in human hair; others dealt in disputed land titles, the manufacture of hats and caps, the importation of broomsticks from Germany, and the extraction of silver from lead. These new flotations were called "bubbles"; the precise origin of this term is unclear, but it stuck in the financial lexicon.

The directors of the South Sea Company saw these proliferating new offerings as undesirable competition, sucking up funds that might otherwise be used to buy South Sea shares. Taking advantage of the political capital they had built up by carefully transferring South Sea stock to important government officials, they pushed through Parliament a law that banned the creation of joint-stock companies not specifically chartered by the government, and required that previously chartered companies only engage in activities explicitly allowed by those charters. Royal assent was eventually given to what became known as the Bubble Act on June 9, 1720, with a proclamation bringing it into force on Midsummer Day. Under the law, unauthorized joint-stock company promoters were guilty of "Praemunire," which carried a penalty of an infinite fine and perpetual imprisonment. This legislation had the desired effect, virtually shutting down the market for new projects.

The South Sea directors sought to squelch competition for investors' funds because the success of the company depended entirely on a rising stock price. By 1720 the company still had no real revenues from trade with the Americas. Its only income came from the interest payments received on the government debt it had taken over, interest which was paid at a lower rate than the prevailing market rate for that debt. The only way the company could generate profits beyond these interest receipts was to sell more stock in the market. (Under the accounting procedures in use at the time, receipts from the sale of new stock above its par value of £100 per share were treated as profits to the company. The higher the price of the stock, the more "profit" the company could make by selling new shares.)

In modern terms this would be called a Ponzi scheme, in which profits for current investors are obtained by taking in more money from future investors. But it was a Ponzi scheme that had the full backing of important government officials, who had personal stakes in the success of the South Sea Company. The passage of the Bubble Act indicated that the company's allies in Parliament had the muscle to eliminate any competitors that might appear. What was developing in the spring of 1720 was an *orchestrated* bubble, controlled by company directors who were in turn closely backed by the authorities.

In April 1720 the company announced an audacious plan to take over more government debt, this time the life annuities that required the state to make large interest payments to annuitants for many years to come. New South Sea shares that could be exchanged for the annuities were authorized. Crucially, the terms of the exchange were not determined by law in advance. If the price of the stock rose, the company would be able to pledge fewer of the then more valuable shares to annuitant holders, allowing the extra shares to be sold off at a profit.

Connected officials in the government were either given shares outright or given the opportunity to buy in at favorable prices. Chancellor of the Exchequer John Aislabie was one beneficiary, secretly buying heavily before the terms of conversion were announced. Aislabie was later described as "a man of good understanding . . . and very capable of business; but dark, and of a cunning that rendered him suspected and low in all men's opinion . . . He was much set upon increasing his fortune and did that."[18]

The conversion of annuities into easily tradable South Sea shares did offer annuity holders a significant advantage beyond simply the vague prospect of participation in future profits from trade with the New World. Annuity contracts were very difficult to resell, since they were denominated in odd amounts that could not be divided or combined and had terms (in the case of the most common life annuities) that would last only until the death of the designated annuitant. In order to receive interest payments from the Treasury, annuity holders were required to submit evidence that the annuitant was still alive. These cumbersome features made annuities unattractive for many potential investors. Because of these limitations, the market for annuities was thin and inactive. It has been estimated that transfers of existing annuity contracts occurred at less than one-tenth the rate of transfers of much more tradable joint-stock shares.[19]

It was thus entirely logical that annuity holders would view the more liquid South Sea shares as a more attractive investment than their awkward annuity contracts. As interest rates declined in a time of peace, the value of outstanding fixed-income contracts (like annuities) should have risen, given that their relatively high fixed-interest payments were now more attractive compared to the lower rates of interest offered elsewhere in the marketplace. But the inability to transact easily in annuity contracts made it difficult, if not impossible, for annuity holders to sell and realize the capital gains lower interest rates should have entailed. South Sea shares, which were easy to buy and sell, held out the possibility of capital gains that annuity contracts did not.

The most rigorous analytical study of the South Sea boom, by Professor Larry Neal of the University of Illinois, focused on the greater liquidity South Sea shares provided.[20] Neal examined early conversions of 6 percent government annuities into South Sea stock and found that the annuities had been trading at a one-third discount from their face value before the conversion was announced, but after conversion, the South Sea stock exchanged for the annuities rose to a one-third premium. Neal concluded that this differential was a *liquidity premium* that investors were willing to pay to swap out of illiquid annuities into a tradable asset that had appreciation potential. Much of the initial rise of South Sea shares in 1720 can thus be attributed to nothing more than this liquidity effect.

But company officials were not content with a moderate increase in share prices; by the spring of 1720 they aggressively conspired to push up South Sea stock far beyond what was justified by liquidity considerations. Consistently optimistic reports were planted in a compliant press. The company itself secretly purchased shares on the open market to drive prices higher. And, most importantly, it offered very liberal credit terms to buyers who bought new stock directly from the company, because every new share the company sold above par caused more profits to be reported, which in turn attracted still more buyers.

The strategy worked; the price of South Sea shares soared. As in France, a noticeable wealth effect spilled over into the broader economy. Land prices near London were observed to be closely correlated to the South Sea stock price, and expensive new carriages that appeared in London were popularly called "South Sea equipages."

Traffic in market news between London and Amsterdam was brisk. By midyear any ship bound for Holland found it worthwhile to advertise an agent "on exchange" who could be engaged to transmit or receive information. In July, regular twelve-hour relays between England and Holland were established. New flotations were offered jointly in Amsterdam and London. When the Bubble Act went into effect in England, offerings still proceeded apace across the Channel in Holland, beyond the reach of the new legislation.

In Paris, conditions could not have been more different. Between January and May 1720, 2.6 billion livres of banknotes were issued, more than doubling the amount outstanding. The resulting runaway inflation destroyed confidence in paper money and in paper shares of stock. Bank runs developed as people frantically attempted to convert unwanted paper banknotes into metallic coins on the few occasions when such conversions were allowed. The panic reached a crescendo on July 17, when fifteen thousand people mobbed the Banque Royale after hearing rumors that exchanges of ten-livre notes for coin would be accepted. A riot broke out, and at least a dozen people were killed, crushed against barricades or trampled to death. The frenzied mob then moved on to John Law's house, from which he had just escaped. Unable to force the heavy iron gates, the mob spent its fury by tearing Law's unoccupied carriage to shreds.

Law attempted to reduce the excess supply of paper by conspicuously withdrawing some from circulation. Shares of Mississippi Company stock belonging to the company itself, and to the Crown, were publicly burned in giant bonfires. Law issued a convoluted edict designed to reduce arbitrarily the value of banknotes, and shares, over time. But such actions, far from stanching the panic and restoring confidence in his "System," simply made matters worse. It was becoming clear that Law's days in power were numbered. He fretted constantly that he was losing the confidence of the regent, and feared that he might actually face execution if that were the only means by which the regent could appease his critics.

Much as would occur in the emerging market crises of the twentieth century, foreign investors in France in 1720 faced disastrous losses, due both to falling share prices and to the rapid depreciation of French currency. In May, one pound sterling was equivalent to 39 paper livres. By September, however, paper livres had declined to the point that it took 92 livres to purchase one pound. After September, there was no real market for paper livres at any price. A few astute foreign speculators actually sold short (both Mississippi shares and livres); the most prominent was a former English associate of Law named Richard Cantillon. Cantillon's sales of shares and currency were of sufficient magnitude to significantly depress the market and thus draw Law's ire. Law summarily told his former friend that unless he ceased such transactions and immediately left France, he would be thrown into the Bastille.[21] Cantillon's "bear raids" anticipated the actions of George Soros and other currency traders two and one half centuries later.

The chaos in France inevitably affected the English market. The glee that had accompanied reports of Law's travails quickly dissipated, replaced by the sobering realization that heavy losses in France were forcing some English investors to retrench by selling London stocks. French holdings of South Sea stock were also being liquidated, in an effort to repatriate desperately needed bullion to France. The flow of precious metals to England that had helped feed the booming London stock market now reversed; each week saw significant quantities of bullion exported. South Sea shares declined under the relentless selling pressure; by late August, South Sea stock had fallen from its briefly attained June peak of £950 to slightly above £700.

Like drowning men, South Sea officials flailed about, desperately seeking some means of reversing the decline. On August 30, the company announced that it would pay a 30 percent dividend (based on a par price of £100 per share) in the current fiscal year and a 50 percent dividend in future years. The hope was that shareholders would be content to hold on to their stock in anticipation of the dividends, but the plan backfired. Speculators realized that a 30 percent return calculated at par was a much smaller return when calculated against a purchase price of many times par. Worse, in order to pay even this dividend, the company would have to earn £15 million per year. That money would have to come either from the sale of even more stock at high prices (now an unlikely prospect) or from actual trade with Spanish America. Unfortunately, Spain adamantly insisted that Gibraltar be returned to Spanish sovereignty before any concessions on trade could be granted. The British government bluntly refused, and placed Gibraltar on a war footing. For the South Sea Company, it was the beginning of the end.

The confused state of affairs spawned a flurry of published attempts to determine the "true value" of South Sea stock. 'Change Alley was awash in pamphlets analyzing the company's financials, which quite often flatly contradicted one another. One of the most cogent works, by economist and Member of Parliament Archibald Hutcheson, concluded that because there were so many unknowns, a value could not reasonably be assigned to the shares.[22]

On September 8, in accordance with the requirements of the company's charter, a General Court of Proprietors of the South Sea Company (something akin to a modern shareholders meeting) was held. Company officials feared a storm of criticism from investors who had been permitted by the company's liberal credit policy to borrow most of the purchase price of shares they had bought from the company, only to see the stock price then quickly collapse, leaving them saddled with debt inadequately collateralized by the greatly depreciated stock. The directors took preemptive action; the meeting was scheduled for noon, but by nine o'clock it had already been stacked with company supporters. The few critics who did get in were shouted down, but to little positive effect. The day after the meeting the stock slid to 575, and it plummeted to 380 by mid-September. Company officials received death threats; one was shot at in the street by a disgruntled investor.

In France the situation was even worse. Rising unrest forced John Law to flee the country in December 1720, leaving most of his remaining wealth behind. He would die nine years later an impoverished and broken man. Conservatives reasserted control, closing down both the Banque Royale and the new Bourse that had just been completed to replace the chaotic open-air market in the rue Quincampoix. Indicative of widespread hostility to the new financial markets, the Bourse was scathingly denounced as "a riotous assembly."[23] An official investigation commenced, which rapidly took on the character of a witch-hunt. More than half a million people came forward to claim losses as a result of transactions in shares and banknotes, and eventually many speculators who were found not to have acted in "good faith" were penalized for a total of 200 million livres. Through forfeitures and confiscations, the number of Mississippi Company shares was reduced form 135,000 to 56,000. Valuable franchises that had been granted to the company (such as administering the domestic tax system and royal mint) were taken away, leaving only the rights to overseas trade. The company would survive until the end of the century, but only as a shell of its former self.

Meanwhile, in London, the South Sea Company directors were forced to seek a rescue package from the Bank of England. Unfortunately, the bank itself faced a potentially devastating run on its own reserves as credit collapsed throughout the economy. It urgently sought to call in loans and acquire bullion, further exacerbating the credit crisis. Conditions were so bad, and distrust of paper representations of money so great, that it was impossible to send even £25 from London to Dublin by means of a bill of exchange. While Englishmen had come to accept banknotes and shares, they had still not abandoned their traditional faith in "hard money," defined by its weight in gold or silver, as the only sound measure of value. In times of crisis, all the paper in the world could not substitute for precious metal.

A tangle of ruined credit threatened to strangle the economy. One gentleman in Exchange Alley admitted that he had bilked his cabman (reneged on his debt) "on account of having been bilked himself."[24] By one estimate, two-thirds of the money in circulation (represented by paper banknotes and shares) disappeared. Urban workmen who depended on the prosperity of the well-to-do lost their jobs, as work abruptly halted on half-finished ships and partly built houses. Tailors, watchmakers, goldsmiths, and other craftsmen saw their business evaporate. Many well-off individuals found their finances shaken even if they had not suffered losses in the stock market. Land prices dropped sharply, imperiling landlords who had borrowed on inflated values.

The South Sea and Mississippi Company bubbles have often been portrayed as a prominent example of the folly of excess speculation, when investors, in a misguided quest for quick riches, abandon all vestiges of common sense. These depictions, based largely on anecdotal accounts of the events of 1720, have a certain intuitive appeal. With the benefit of hindsight, it would appear that many otherwise prudent people made very foolish decisions when caught up in a speculative mania.

But the facts of the South Sea and Mississippi Company debacles lend themselves to other interpretations. For purposes of analysis, Professor Larry Neal and a colleague divided the South Sea Bubble itself into three distinct phases. The first, the period from February through May 19, 1720, encompassed a price rise from £131 to £355. This is roughly from the time the House of Commons accepted the company's proposal to take over the remainder of the government debt to the actual announcement of the terms of the debt assumption. Neal argues that this price rise was not untoward, based on company fundamentals and the aforementioned liquidity considerations. (If the South Sea Company generated profits from trade with the New World anything like the Dutch East India Company had already achieved in trading with the Far East, a price of £355 for South Sea shares would be quite cheap.)

The second phase of the bubble, from May 19 (a price of £355) to June 22 (a price of £765), was clearly, according to Neal's analysis, not justified by fundamentals. Even so, the actions of speculators who bought South Sea stock were not necessarily irrational. The company directors, implicitly backed by the government, were attempting to rig the market, much in the same way that John Law in Paris (although for entirely different reasons) attempted to fix the price of Mississippi Company stock. From this perspective, buyers of South Sea and Mississippi Company shares were not wild-eyed optimists grossly overrating the two companies' profit potential, but were instead simply seeking to take advantage of a scheme by powerful interests to manipulate the market.

The third phase of the South Sea Bubble, in which prices spiked briefly to £950, was, according to Neal, actually an illusion, caused by a misreading of the data. In late June 1720, the South Sea Company closed its stock transfer books in order to straighten out its tangled records so that its annual dividend could be paid to shareholders. While the books were closed, sellers could not deliver shares to buyers because the company would be unable to duly register transactions. Until the books were reopened, the prices quoted were thus *forward* prices, for shares to be delivered in the future, rather than the customary *cash* prices, for shares to be delivered according to normal settlement rules. Because this period was one of great credit stringency, with money increasingly difficult to obtain, forward pur-

chases of shares (which did not require that money be put up to settle the contract until a future date) inevitably were transacted at significantly higher prices than cash purchases of the same shares. Thus,
Neal argues, the final upward spurt in prices in late June that seemed
to provide the most obvious evidence of irrational behavior probably
did not really even occur. It was likely instead simply an artifact of a
forced changeover in the manner in which prices were quoted.

The South Sea and Mississippi bubbles were not simply the product of overly enthusiastic speculators operating in a free market; the
market was rigged, not free. Economic historians have begun to em-
phasize this fact, upgrading their assessments of the performance of
early eighteenth-century stock markets. They cite government actions, not a breakdown of the markets themselves, as the principal
causes of the 1720 debacles.[25]

Modern economists have coined the phrase "rational bubble,"
which at first seems a contradiction in terms. In a rational bubble,
behavior indicative of an irrational bubble can be produced, paradoxically, by investors acting quite rationally. If John Law and the
South Sea Company directors, backed by their respective governments, were blatantly attempting to fix stock prices at high levels,
could investors really be blamed if they sought to go along for the
ride?

Just as the 1719–20 bull market had been international, the collapse in France and England dragged down other European markets.
Holland was hardest hit, with the shares of the Dutch East India
Company and numerous insurance firms dropping precipitously.
There is substantial anecdotal evidence that Dutch investors blamed
their troubles on the South Sea Company, which quickly became a
despised symbol of presumed excesses in the entire London market.
According to contemporary accounts, anything English became a target for investors' wrath. Moses Haasverberg's English Coffee House
in Amsterdam, where English businessmen had been accustomed to
gather and read the English papers while enjoying their favorite English beverages, was sacked and burned by infuriated Dutchmen.

Ultimately the British Parliament stepped in to clean up the South
Sea mess. It arbitrarily revised transactions in South Sea stock,
changing the terms of some and simply annulling others. As had oc-

curred in France, concerted efforts were made to punish those connected with the company (both inside and outside of government) who were blamed for the debacle. Members of Parliament who were also South Sea directors were expelled from the House, and high-ranking government officials (including the chancellor of the Exchequer) were forced to resign and make restitution. Overall a kind of rough justice was done; as an attempt to turn back the clock to the time before the South Sea boom, the Parliament's efforts were reasonably successful. The Exchequer ended up slightly worse off, in terms of the cost of servicing its debt obligations, than it had been the year before. Under the circumstances, however, this was no small triumph.[26]

Numerous pieces of legislation were proposed to regulate the stock market. Most failed to gain enactment, but in 1734 what became known as Sir John Bernard's Act passed both houses of Parliament. The act banned the more exotic speculative practices of trading in options, time-bargains (futures), and the selling of stock that the seller did not actually possess at the time of the sale (short-selling). The provisions of this act, however, seem to have been consistently violated.[27] Additional restrictive bills dealing with the same issues were introduced in Commons in 1745, 1756, 1771, and 1773, but were not passed.

The South Sea Company itself lingered on for over a century, although after 1750 all pretense of engaging in foreign trade was stripped away. The company became, in effect, a mere subsidiary of the Treasury, which paid it to service the government debt. Finally, in 1854 the South Sea Company's capital was converted into government bonds, and it formally ceased to exist.

It is interesting to note the differing effects the punctured bubbles had in England and France. The actions by the British Parliament to deal with the South Sea collapse seem to have been largely effective, minimizing the damage to the economy and to trade. Foreign investors soon returned to the London stock market; one study found that Dutch holdings of Bank of England stock rose from 10.5 percent of the total in 1723–24 to 30.3 percent in 1750, while Dutch holdings of the British East India Company jumped from 1.4 percent to 21.4 percent over the same period.[28] Lord North would estimate in

1776 that fully 40 percent of British government securities were held by foreigners. Economic activity in Britain was unencumbered by capital controls, heavy taxes, or attempts to regulate exchange rates or the money supply. Remarkably modern capital markets were permitted to operate unfettered.

In France, in contrast, the bitter denouement of the Mississippi Company and of Law's "System" created a lingering antipathy to financial institutions that lasted for generations. In October 1722, nearly two years after John Law's forced departure from France, all the registers, journals, ledgers, and minutes of the Mississippi Company were piled into eight large bundles and publicly burned in Paris in a large iron cage specially constructed so that not one article would survive. As one historian put it, "There was hesitation even in pronouncing the word 'bank' for 150 years thereafter."[29] Old antipathies toward speculation and financial markets, typical of the Middle Ages, returned to prominence. While a new stock exchange was formally opened in Paris in 1724, the primary purpose was to concentrate trading in a central location where it could be more closely controlled by the government.

It was at this time that the Industrial Revolution was quietly beginning to transform Britain. The British Bubble Act, with its injunctions against the formation of unchartered joint-stock companies, undoubtedly slowed the pace of development by making it more difficult for entrepreneurs to raise capital. But overall, Britain was far more receptive than France to new ventures, and to financial markets. In 1776 Adam Smith would formally state the case for free markets in *The Wealth of Nations*. Smith disdained the mercantilist tendencies of European governments, arguing instead that the wealth of a nation would be enhanced by removing the encumberances of government from the economy. An "invisible hand," Smith wrote, working through the free interplay of supply and demand, would best allocate resources. It is no surprise that such a landmark work, which would define the development of modern capitalism and markets, was written in Britain rather than France. Such were the sharply divergent legacies of the great speculative bubbles of 1720.

THE NEW WORLD

NATHAN MAYER ROTHSCHILD had carefully assembled a network of trusted associates throughout Europe, who picked up and conveyed to him the sensitive information vital to his family's international merchant banking business. But events in 1815 were too important to trust to subordinates. Rothschild determined that he himself would go to the Continent to witness the battle between Napoleon Bonaparte and the Duke of Wellington that promised to decide the fate of Europe. Near the little town of Waterloo, Belgium, the expected clash occurred. When it was over, Britain was ascendant and Napoleon was finished.

Rothschild hastened back to England with the vital information, paying 2,000 francs to bribe a sailor to cross the Channel in a storm. Upon arriving in London he took up his customary position at the Stock Exchange, but his demeanor did not bespeak the great victory he had witnessed. Instead, his expression was grim. To the exchange members who watched him closely, it appeared that he was the bearer of bad news.

This impression was reinforced as brokers known to be associated with Rothschild moved to sell government funds (bonds) that were the principal instruments traded on the exchange. The market sagged, as other nervous investors sought to follow Rothschild's lead. Waves of selling shivered through the exchange.

But other brokers were buying, quietly, so as not to attract great attention. These men also worked for Rothschild, but were not identifiable as such. They methodically bought up the bonds sold by fearful traders. In a short period of time Rothschild had accumulated a huge position in the funds.

Then his demeanor suddenly brightened. He stepped forward to announce that Wellington had in fact won a great victory, and that England was saved. Prices shot upward. In a matter of a few hours Rothschild had made another fortune.

It is accepted history that the final defeat of Napoleon Bonaparte at Waterloo in 1815 marked a decisive turning point in European military and political affairs. What is less understood is that the events of 1815 also inaugurated a long period of British supremacy in international finance. For most of the nineteenth century, the majority of the world's trading in stocks (and most other securities) would be channeled through London. Nathan Rothschild later described how the City of London had become the indispensable central marketplace of the world. "All transactions, in India, in China, in Germany, in Russia, and in the whole world, are all guided and settled through this country . . ."[1]

In 1815, however, the City of London did not yet have the appearance of a world financial center. The London Stock Exchange had been formally organized by brokers and dealers in 1801, to provide a central location for trading and to set rules for participants. But the market was not really international; only a handful of foreign bonds (and no foreign stocks) were traded. Once war-induced spending halted, a depression set in across England, greatly depressing activity on the exchange.

Trading on the London Stock Exchange, such as it was, was conducted almost entirely in British government securities (funds) and lotteries, and shares of the Bank of England, the East India Company, and the moribund remains of the South Sea Company. A handful of enterprises operating canals, roads, bridges, and waterworks were listed, but traded infrequently. These companies typically obtained their principal funding not through public stock offerings but instead directly from individual investors or regional banks.

There was no financial press to speak of. A biweekly publication entitled *The Course of the Exchange* provided price lists, but no commentary on the markets. Another, called *Lloyd's List*, published exchange rates for foreign currency and a few stock prices from the United States, but little else. What passed for financial news was reported sparingly (if at all) in the traditional press.

Change came rapidly after 1815. Two fundamental decisions taken by the government over the following decade created the conditions in which financial markets in Britain would thrive. First, over initial opposition from bankers and stockjobbers in the City of London, the government determined to return Britain to the gold standard in a process set to begin in 1819. The importance of this decision cannot be overstated. Within a relatively few years the gold standard took on an almost mystical symbolic meaning, and the notion that the British pound was "as good as gold" made sterling the unrivaled medium of exchange throughout the world.

Simultaneously, the displacement of the remaining vestiges of mercantilism by the free markets advocated by Adam Smith opened the way for rapid growth. The strong support for free markets is evident in a public petition signed by nearly two hundred merchants in 1820. The petitioners stated that "the maxim of buying in the cheapest market and selling in the dearest, which regulates every merchant in his individual dealings, is strictly applicable as the best rule for the trade of the nation as a whole."[2] Opponents of mercantilist regulation, such as MP Sir George Colebrooke, had for years been arguing that the stock market should be unfettered by government interference. "The trading of stock," Colebrooke had said in a speech to Parliament, "like every other thing ought to be free of interruption."[3] By the 1820s Colebrooke's reasoning had gained wide acceptance.

Prior to the Napoleonic Wars, Amsterdam had been the leading center of international finance. But French occupation had been cruel to the city's Bourse. Even when the French were forced to withdraw, Amsterdam was unable to regain its earlier status, as the supremacy of English finance and English markets became evident. The first overt sign of the permanently changed circumstances came when the British firm Baring Brothers took the lead in arranging a mammoth bond offering by the French government to fund war reparation payments. Although most of the proceeds were ultimately raised in France and the bonds were denominated in French currency, only a British banking house was capable of handling the deal.

The following year an even more significant bond offering was arranged for Prussia by Rothschild & Company; it was the first time a large loan for a foreign country was denominated not in the currency of that country, but in pounds sterling. Britons could now invest in foreign securities without fear of adverse swings in the value of foreign exchange like those of the chaotic final days of John Law's "System" in France. With this precedent established, Rothschild in quick succession underwrote sterling loans for Russia, Austria, and Spain. The public's appetite for foreign securities was whetted; bigger and more exotic financings were soon to come. Outside of Britain, only Holland provided a significant number of investors for these securities.

By 1822, seven years of peace had improved British finances sufficiently so that the government could refinance its public debt. In March the Treasury redeemed its outstanding 5 percent "stock," called consols (referring to bond issues that had been "consolidated" in earlier years). The consols were to be replaced by a similar issue that paid only 4 percent; any holder unwilling to accept the lower interest rate could get his money back. While the bulk of the £214 million debt was successfully rolled over into 4 percent bonds, many holders refused the exchange. Suddenly a new pool of capital was freed up to seek higher-yielding investment opportunities.

It was at this point that the vicissitudes of politics in faraway lands intervened. Since 1810 various insurgencies opposing harsh Spanish colonial rule had broken out in Latin America. After 1815, Britain, inspired in part by popular support in England for the "liberal" South American revolutionaries seeking freedom from oppressive foreign domination and in part by a hardheaded appraisal of British interests, had begun to support some of the rebel movements with arms and money. By the early 1820s these efforts had borne fruit; several different rebel armies had ousted their colonial masters. The newly independent countries needed money, and turned to the City of London to obtain it.

At the time of the South Sea boom of 1720, British investors had been enthralled by prospects of great riches to be found in South

America. One hundred years after the South Sea collapse, they proved to be equally receptive. The newly formed nation of Colombia was the first to benefit, selling sterling-denominated bonds in 1822. The bonds, carrying an interest rate of 6 percent, were sold to investors at a discount from par so as to yield over 7 percent to maturity. This high rate attracted investors who had been unwilling to accept the reduced yields offered on the new British consols. Promoters claimed that Colombia was at least as sound financially as the United States had been at the time of its creation, pointing out that the United States had carried a foreign debt of £2.5 million and a combined internal debt of £9 million after the War of Independence, while the entire Colombian debt was, in 1822, less than £2.5 million.

Chile and Peru quickly followed Colombia to the London capital market, also selling bonds in 1822. These issues met with a strongly positive reception, even though the British government had yet to officially recognize the new nations that sold them. Popular parodies of the enthusiasm for what today would be called "emerging market" debt appeared in the press. In June 1822, *The Times* printed a facetious account of an overeager investor who was persuaded to buy fictitious "Chinese Turnpike Bonds," only to be subsequently told by the prankster who "sold" them to him that the price of the bonds had collapsed. When the "joke" was at last revealed, the chagrined investor swore to "speculate no more" in the bonds of "the Emperor of China or of the Grand Lama."[4] As *The Times* put it, different types of foreign securities had become so numerous on the Stock Exchange "as to create not a little perplexity to the inexperienced speculators, whose ideas have never wondered beyond three percent consols."[5]

Shortly after the Peruvian loan was launched, the "inexperienced speculators" in the City of London must have been even more perplexed by an improbable character with the impressive title General Sir Gregor MacGregor. MacGregor had not distinguished himself in his previous Latin American endeavors; fighting as a mercenary employed by anti-Spanish rebels, he had commanded a disastrously mismanaged expedition to attack the Spanish in Panama, infuriating the rebel leadership to the point that he was forced to flee to escape execution. But MacGregor was not finished with Latin American intrigues. He proceeded up the Central American coast from Panama, arranging to meet the "king" of the Mosquito Indians along what is now the coast of Nicaragua. After many glasses of rum, the intrepid MacGregor persuaded the Indian leader to grant him a concession of eight million acres carved out of the Indian's vast domain. MacGregor then returned to England, where he styled himself as Gregor I, the Cazique of Poyais, and sought to raise money to finance his new "country."

MacGregor announced a £200,000 bond issue, ostensibly to finance the colonization of Poyais. Pamphlets were printed and distributed, describing Poyais as a rich land offering easy opportunities for wealth. The capital city of St. Joseph was pictured with broad avenues, elegant houses, and cultural accoutrements such as an opera house. MacGregor quickly sold parcels of his land to prospective immigrants, who eagerly set sail to make their fortunes in the New World.

Enthusiasm for foreign securities was so great that the *Morning Herald* wrote, "anything in the shape of a bond will find a purchaser in the foreign market."[6] MacGregor's Poyais issue was immediately snapped up. But when the unfortunate would-be colonists eventually arrived in Poyais, they found only a few ramshackle huts in a sweltering, insect-infested jungle. The local Indians soon turned hostile, and many of the immigrants succumbed to native attacks or tropical diseases. A few drowned attempting to escape to nearby Belize. Most never saw Britain again.

MacGregor absconded from England, taking with him most of the proceeds of the Poyais bond issue. Surprisingly, however, the revelation of the full extent of the fraud did little to dampen investor enthusiasm for Latin American securities. To handle the heavy volume of trading in foreign issues, a Foreign Stock Exchange was created in 1823. The new exchange initially dealt in foreign sovereign debt, but within a few months a new investment vehicle—joint-stock companies organized to exploit the fabled wealth of the New World— became the rage.

In colonial times, Spain had prevented foreign nationals from investing in or working its colonial mines, jealously guarding its imperial prerogatives. Now that Spanish control had been removed, however, the field was wide open for British entrepreneurs. Promoters of mining shares were not shy about extolling the potential of their new ventures. One prospectus stated that "lumps of pure gold, weighing from two to fifty pounds, were totally neglected" in Spanish America, and claimed that the company's mines would produce "considerably more than the quantity necessary for the supply of the whole world."[7]

Deeply ingrained beliefs about the innate superiority of British management led most Britons to believe that British businessmen, backed by British engineers and British capital, could work wonders in mines that the Spaniards had failed to fully exploit. The prospectus offered by the Anglo-Mexican Mining Association, one of the new joint-stock companies, proclaimed, "It is believed that by the introduction of English capital, skill, experience and machinery, the expenses of working these mines may be greatly reduced and their produce much augmented."[8] Another prospectus claimed that by "uniting the scientific and mechanical improvements of the Old World with the already attained practice and experience of the established mines," great profits could be produced.[9]

Unlike MacGregor's Poyais scheme, most of the Latin American operations were legitimate business ventures. New Central and South American issues were brought to market at a furious pace in 1824 and 1825, coinciding with a boom in all stock offerings. During this period, nearly six hundred companies were organized or projected to operate in Britain or abroad. These included agricultural ventures in Canada and Australia, a sugar-refining firm in Bengal, and ice-making, canal-construction, and steam-navigation companies in Britain itself. The Metropolitan Bath Company was organized to pipe in salt water from the coast for discriminating bathers who preferred to swim in seawater, a Metropolitan Fish Company was set up to provide low-cost fish to the London poor, and the Patent Steam Washing Company was formed to steam clean clothes.

One of the more interesting foreign ventures was the Colombia Pearl Fishery Association, formed in October 1824, the first nonmining joint-stock company established to operate in Latin America. The company's directors included two earls, one MP, and a Royal Navy captain. The prospectus noted that pearl fishing, once highly prof-

itable, had been discontinued because of "the presence of certain destructive fish" (presumably sharks). To get around this problem, the
firm intended to employ diving bells to protect workers harvesting
the abundant pearls, allowing the men to stay underwater for up to
eight hours in perfect safety.

Investors were only required to put up £2 for each £25 share, with
remaining capital to be called when needed. This common type of
subscription plan enabled investors to purchase shares for relatively
small amounts of money. The theory was that the companies would
call on shareholders periodically for more money when the expansion of operations required it. By late 1824, most Latin American
stocks, like Colombia Pearl Fisheries (and particularly the mining
companies), commanded substantial premiums over their original issue prices.

The frenetic pace of new projects created a tremendous strain on
Parliament, which was required under the old Bubble Act of 1720 to
authorize each new corporation. Some promoters evaded the Bubble
Act requirements by forming "trusts" in lieu of corporations, with
"trustees" managing the assets of the businesses. Other operators
took advantage of the lengthy delays involved in getting parliamentary approval by forming and publicizing new ventures and issuing
stock while the charter application was still pending. When the stock
price rose, they sold out and disappeared before Parliament ever
acted on the charter request.

In 1825 Parliament finally repealed the Bubble Act. Henceforth
any group of seven or more individuals could start up an unchartered
joint-stock company, with transferable shares. Importantly, however,
these unchartered firms would not have independent legal status,
separate from their principals. Shareholders would be fully liable for
any losses their companies incurred, even if those losses exceeded the
amount of money the shareholders had invested. It was widely believed that limiting shareholder liability (as is now done in modern
corporations) would encourage shareholders and managers to take
irresponsible risks. Parliament also enacted a requirement that shareholders of companies previously chartered by the government be "individually liable, in the extent of their persons and property, for the
debts . . . of the corporation."[10]

The enthusiasm for Latin American investments in 1824 occurred in spite of the fact the British government had not yet officially recognized any of the newly independent South and Central American nations. This situation was rectified in dramatic fashion at the turn of the new year, 1825, when Foreign Secretary George Canning announced commercial agreements with three of the new Latin American states. This was widely (and correctly) interpreted as de facto recognition. Canning moved in response to French military intervention in Spain; in a famous remark he said that he had "called the New World into existence, to redress the balance of the Old."

The effect on Latin American mining stocks was immediate and dramatic. Prices soared. In late January the United States ambassador in London, Richard Rush, wrote that "nothing was ever like it before, not even the days of the South Sea scheme . . . Shares in some of the . . . companies have advanced to seventeen hundred per cent within a few months, and are bought with avidity at this price. I have heard it said that noblemen of great estates, and directors of the Bank Of England, participate; also that princes of the blood press forward to obtain shares."[11]

Mining enterprises were being formed so frequently that *The Times* wrote, "a new day seldom passes without the arriving at maturity of some great project, requiring a large amount of capital, independent of numerous minor undertakings which escape notice in the crowd."[12] Another newspaper noted, "the jobbers at the Stock Exchange are bewildered with the variety of new schemes brought forward."[13] As the boom continued, investors became less discriminating. Unlike the companies formed in 1824, by early 1825 many new mining ventures did not actually own or have leases on mines at the time of formation. Instead, the proceeds of the stock issue were to be used to acquire mines the companies would then operate.

In speculative ventures such as these, accurate information is extremely important. Unfortunately, such information was often woefully lacking in the primitive stock market of the 1820s. Most prospectuses for Latin American mining companies in 1824 and 1825 relied almost entirely on data compiled by the Prussian baron Alexander von Humboldt, who traveled extensively in South America between 1799 and 1804. Humboldt's journals contained a vast compendium of information on subjects ranging from geography to botany, and included sanguine assessments of possible mineral wealth and commercial opportunities in Spanish America. Excerpts of Humboldt's journals were published in a London magazine between 1815 and 1821. These outdated accounts, written by a man possessing no real expertise in commercial affairs or mine engineering, provided the analytical basis on which substantial investments were made.

Where hard information was lacking, eager proponents of the boom stepped in to provide confident appraisals of future opportunities. These included Benjamin Disraeli, a young man destined to lead an extraordinary life. As biographer Jane Ridley describes him, Disraeli was both a thoughtful observer and a man of action, a self-made politician in a time when birth and social rank were all-important, and a man of ideas, an adventurer, a philanderer, and a speculator. It was this latter attribute that caused Disraeli to get caught up in the Latin American market boom in 1824, even before he attained the age of twenty.

The son of a distinguished literary critic of Jewish birth and grandson of one of a select group of Jews permitted to act as stockjobbers, Disraeli had dutifully taken a position his father had secured for him in a solicitor's office. But young Benjamin did not think he could become a "great man" through the law. Stock speculation, on the other hand, seemed a much more promising method of obtaining the wealth he needed to overcome his lack of social rank so as to achieve a position of influence. Referring to the speculative environment of 1824, Disraeli later wrote, "It immediately struck me that if fortunes were ever to be made this was the moment and accordingly I paid great attention to American affairs."[14]

Possessing limited personal resources, Disraeli borrowed from friends and associates to finance his speculations. He made his first purchases in November 1824. His timing was propitious; when Canning effectively recognized the new South American republics at year-end, Disraeli's stocks skyrocketed. One of his largest holdings, Anglo-Mexican, leaped from £33 on December 10 to £158 on January 11.

Disraeli had become acquainted with John Powles of J. A. Powles

& Company, a merchant bank that was promoting three Latin American mining firms, including Anglo-Mexican. When public charges of fraud were made against Anglo-Mexican and another company sponsored by J. A. Powles, Disraeli was hired by Powles to compose a pamphlet refuting the criticism. Disraeli's piece, which ran to one hundred pages, attacked critics who drew parallels with the South Sea debacle a century earlier. Three editions were eventually published; in them, Disraeli, writing anonymously, claimed to be a disinterested observer, falsely implying that he did not own shares in the companies he commented on. Not everyone took the bait. One reviewer commented, "Whoever wrote it is an ugly customer."[15]

But Disraeli, whatever his ethics, was a true believer. He told a friend, "I have read every book on the subject and conversed with secret agents of the Companies in which I am interested and I have come to the conviction that the 100 pound shares in the Mexican mining companies will in a very few years be worth upwards of 1000 pounds apiece." Later he went so far as to say, "I actually feel dizzy. It is truly a work for life," adding, "On the Mexican mines I rest my sheet anchor."[16]

Some observers disagreed with Disraeli's boundless optimism. Alexander Baring, whose banking firm had studiously avoided any association with the mining companies, stated that he saw little difference between gambling "in the hells of St. James Street" and the merchants on the stock exchange. The Latin American mining companies, he believed, would prove to be "delusions."[17] Comments like these did not go unnoticed; by April, unease spread slowly through the market, with a gradual decline in prices for South American debt issues becoming more pronounced as spring passed into summer. New stock offerings continued to come to market, but did not trade immediately to the substantial premiums that speculators had come to expect.

In August, what would prove to be the last Latin American bond issue of the boom—an offering for the United Provinces of Central America—was announced. It received a lukewarm response and quickly slipped to a discount from its initial price. Like a canary in a mine, this performance sounded a warning of imminent peril. In short order, the financial markets were swept downward in what would come to be known as the Panic of 1825. The cause of the collapse was much broader than simple overspeculation in foreign securities. Agricultural prices in Britain had fallen sharply under the weight of an influx of imports. Several large northern England trading houses, caught by the market downdraft, failed, dragging under other firms with which they did business. At the same time the Bank of England, concerned about its declining gold reserves, began to call in loans and to purchase bullion, further tightening credit conditions.

The rickety structure of English banking was painfully exposed by the credit stringency. To preserve the monopoly position of the Bank of England, so-called country banks had not been permitted to organize as joint-stock companies, meaning that their capital base was small. In many cases they did not have the wherewithal to withstand the financial tempest that swept across Britain in late 1825. By the end of the year more than seventy financial institutions had collapsed.

Even the venerable Bank of England itself was in jeopardy. At the last minute it was saved by a large deposit of gold sovereigns that Nathan Rothschild shipped across from Europe. Nevertheless, the bank came in for harsh criticism for having contributed to the credit crisis. The *Morning Chronicle* condemned it for "having issued paper money heretofore so freely . . . [inducing] extensive speculations in merchandise, in foreign funds and in shares, and by now having limited . . . their issues in such a sudden manner." But another London paper, the *Courier*, dissented, reminding readers that it was not the bank's function to regulate the economy or the money supply. The Bank of England had not yet fully evolved into a modern central bank; it did not act as a lender of last resort. In its haste to protect itself, the bank exacerbated an already bad situation.

Stock prices dropped precipitously during the panic. Real Del Monte, the leading South American mining company, fell from a high of £1,550 to below £200; lesser outfits fared even worse. By late November, most trading in foreign stocks had ceased, as a market for those stocks no longer really existed. Disraeli's investments were wiped out, leaving him deeply in debt. He did not turn twenty-one until December 21, 1825, when the worst of the panic had passed, so he was technically not liable for debts incurred while he was a minor.

But creditors pursued him nevertheless; for the next twenty years, his debts defined his life. Ruin and disgrace were never far away, and several times he had perilously close scrapes with bankruptcy and debtors' prison. He became quite skillful at deceiving his creditors and in acquiring wealthy patrons (particularly women). The stress took a toll, however; he suffered from several mysterious illnesses and probably had a nervous breakdown shortly after the market collapse.

Disraeli turned to writing as a means of supporting himself. By the time he entered Parliament in 1837, he had published eight novels, five pamphlets, an epic poem, several satires, and a constitutional treatise. Incredibly, in spite of his precarious financial position and occasional vicious anti-Semitic attacks, he eventually became the leader of the Conservative Party, chancellor of the Exchequer, and, ultimately, prime minister. But his painful experience as a speculator in foreign stocks would always be with him. Writing years later, he glumly admitted, "We have no hope for Del Monte: we try to forget such things."[18]

While the market collapse did expose some outright frauds, the real problem with most of the foreign ventures was a pronounced lack of reliable information. Investors (and most company managers) had little if any specific knowledge of the countries in which their new firms were to operate. In one particularly egregious case, a company was formed to make butter from the milk of the many cattle that grazed on the Argentine pampas. Scottish milkmaids were sent to Buenos Aires, where they diligently churned milk into butter, only to discover that the butter was unmarketable because it would not keep in the warm climate and because the local populace preferred to cook with oil.

When actual engineering reports began to come in on the Latin American mines, they were quite disheartening. The lack of roads and ports, combined with problems of climate, geography, and the debilitating effects of fifteen years of civil war against the Spanish, meant that far greater capital would be required than had been anticipated. Only two of the mining associations had been capitalized at as much as £2 million, and of the total paper capitalization of £24.5 million for all the mining companies, only £3.5 million had actually been paid in by shareholders, who had been permitted (as was customary) to initially put up only a small portion of the face value of their investments. The tight money conditions of late 1825 and early 1826, combined with newfound caution on the part of shareholders, meant that little additional money would be forthcoming. Calls on shareholders to make good on their remaining obligations were ignored.

In October 1825, excerpts from a study by Francis Head, chief engineer of the Rio Plata Mining Association, operating in what is now Argentina, were reprinted in the press. The Rio Plata prospectus had claimed that gold on the company's property "appeared in sight when the rain washes away the dust which covers the surface."[19] Head's report flatly contradicted this rosy picture. He concluded that the mines were too far removed from supplies, transport, and water; that they were much less rich than described; and that the local authorities were corrupt and difficult to deal with. As he put it somewhat sarcastically, Argentina was a country that produced "only horses, beef and thistles."[20] The mining ventures failed because of ignorance on the part of the organizers; in their haste to promote their grandiose schemes, the promoters never took the time to understand local conditions.

After his report was made public, Head's salary was promptly cut off by furious Rio Plata directors. It was a futile gesture. Head's revelations simply confirmed conclusions that most market participants had already been forced by events to accept.

As 1826 progressed, many mining companies were dissolved. In most instances, shareholders recovered little if any of the money that they had invested. *The Times*, commenting on the demise of the Chilean Mining Association, wrote that it had "committed suicide and agreed to bury itself in the mines wherein its property had already been swallowed up."[21] The demise of many Latin American mining ventures had the side effect of further depressing the market for the Latin American debt issues. Buyers of South and Central American bonds had calculated that revenues from successful mining operations would benefit the economies of the newly independent countries, helping them service their debt. When the illusion of mining profits faded, so did the perceived creditworthiness of new nations.

By spring 1826, Latin American bonds had, on average, tumbled by 40 percent from their original offering prices. The first actual default occurred when Peru failed to meet an interest payment on April 15. In quick succession, all of the Latin American countries (with the exception of Brazil) defaulted. Amazingly, not one of these countries ever made even a single interest payment, other than those payments made from proceeds of the bond sales that had been specifically held back for that purpose. Throughout much of the remainder of the nineteenth century, the various South and Central American countries would restructure the debts (often several times). The real winners in this sorry process were the British investment bankers who had underwritten the bonds and then collected fees for advising on the restructurings. The typical Latin American government issuer received only about 60 percent of the actual proceeds of a given debt offering, with the remainder going for various discounts, fees, and deductions. (Not all of these amounts went to the bankers, but the underwriting spreads and fees earned were huge.)

In January 1827 the first comprehensive analysis of all the new equity offerings brought to market during the 1824–25 boom was compiled by a writer named Henry English, entitled *A Complete View of the Joint Stock Companies formed During the Years 1824 and 1825.* According to English's figures, there had been only 156 joint-stock companies in existence, with about £48 million in capital, when the company formation boom began in 1824. With the exception of 25 insurance companies, these were all infrastructure concerns (canals, bridges, waterworks, etc.). But in 1824 and 1825, a staggering total of 624 joint-stock ventures were formed or projected, including 74 mining companies (26 in Latin America), totaling £372 million in capital at face value, on which £17.6 million had actually been paid in by stockholders.[22]

By 1827, 118 of the companies with a total capital of £50.6 million had been abandoned, including some major Latin American mines. Their shareholders lost £2.4 million in paid-in capital. No information could be obtained on a further 236 firms capitalized at £143 million, meaning that they had also disappeared. Only 127 companies of those created in 1824 and 1825 were still in existence, with an aggregate face capitalization of £103 million, of which only £12.2 million had been paid in. Based on these surviving firms' share prices at year-end 1825, this £12.2 million investment was now worth £9.3 million.[23]

English noted that in 1824 and 1825 a total face amount of £32 million in bonds issued by foreign states (Latin American nations plus Austria, Greece, Portugal, Naples, and Denmark) had been brought to market in London, on which £25.3 million had actually been put up by investors. English calculated that combined with the amounts paid into joint-stock companies during this period, the total amount of capital British investors had placed in speculative ventures was a staggering £42.9 million.[24]

By December 1828, of the twenty foreign loan issues still trading on the Foreign Stock Exchange, only seven (all of which, except Brazil, were European nations) were being serviced and repaid. By 1829 most of the Latin American mining associations had either ceased to exist or curtailed operations greatly. *The Times* called the collapse "one of the most extraordinary instances ever known of the depreciation of property . . . "

Writing in the 1830s, the economist Charles McCulloch provided explanations for the failures. McCulloch said that British entrepreneurs had had little understanding of the true extent of the damage done by Latin American civil wars and were unaware of how few skills the natives possessed, since most managers had been Spanish and had either died in the wars or been expelled. McCulloch noted that since gold and silver mines did not exist in England, English engineers often lacked the necessary expertise to replace their Spanish predecessors. And finally, McCulloch admitted, many of the Spanish mines had been operated with slave labor, an advantage not available to the British companies.

Of all the Latin American mining ventures, only Real Del Monte could be called a long-term success. The company spent three years after its formation in 1824 repairing and developing its mines, finally commencing production in 1827. Despite chronic mishaps and cash flow difficulties, the mines, which had yielded their first silver in

1521, still operate today. Unfortunately for the original shareholders, including Benjamin Disraeli, several financial reorganizations wiped out their equity. They would never recover their investments.

What were the consequences of the crash? It is impossible to estimate the total damage done to individual investors because the debt instruments were usually bearer bonds,* and registers and certificates listing stockholders have long since vanished. Anecdotal accounts abound, however. In one example, the *Morning Chronicle* in December 1826 described an auction where shares and debentures belonging to "a highly respectable" ham-and-provision merchant were sold off for the benefit of his widow. The merchant, said the *Chronicle*, had "destroyed himself [committed suicide] in a fit of temporary derangement caused by the depreciation in value . . . of some Spanish bonds." While suicides were rare, there is no question that the effect of market losses on many individuals was devastating.

Despite woeful references to "Spanish bonds," what was really significant about the Latin American boom and bust of the mid-1820s was the degree to which equity investment, not debt, was preeminent. Far more Britons owned Latin American shares than owned Latin American bonds. Between 1823 and 1825, at least forty-six companies were formed or projected to invest in Latin America, with a nominal capitalization of over £36 million; the face value of Latin American bond issues was £20 million. The minimum bond denomination was £100, and the bonds were usually sold on offering at discounted prices of between 75 percent and 89 percent of par, while the par value on shares could be as low as £25, making them much more accessible to small investors. Although data is not available to estimate the percentage of Britons who actually owned stocks (certainly only a small fraction of today's much more widely distributed ownership), there can be little question that the number of shareholders in the mid-1820s was far greater than ever before.

Even so, it would be a mistake to exaggerate the importance of the early nineteenth-century stock market to the broader economy. Most

---

*A "bearer" security is one whose ownership is not registered with the issuing entity. It must be presented to agents of the issuer when interest or dividend payments are due, so that those payments can be made to the "bearer" of the security.

of British industry had little to do with the financial markets in the City of London. This was due in part to the way wealth was distributed in British society. Because Britain, unlike France, had not experienced a violent revolution that wiped out much of the upper class and their accumulated wealth, there existed in Britain in the early nineteenth century a sufficient number of wealthy individuals to finance business ventures independently, without resort to the sale of shares in joint-stock companies. Furthermore, many people believed that the separation of management and ownership that joint-stock companies implied was an inherently bad way to run a business. Adam Smith himself had written in *The Wealth of Nations*, "The directors of such [joint-stock] companies, . . . being the managers of other people's money than of their own, it cannot well be expected, that they should watch over it with the same anxious vigilance . . ."

This criticism of joint-stock firms was frequently repeated, in many different forms. Most businessmen relied on internally generated funds and local lending, and remained very suspicious of the machinations of London stockjobbers. Evidence of the deep-seated antipathy to the markets of Exchange Alley can be found in Malachy Postlethwayt's *Universal Dictionary of Trade and Commerce*, which listed twelve reasons why stockjobbing was detrimental to society. Postlethwayt concluded that "the domestic traffic in the stocks of companies, so engrosses the thoughts of proprietors, that the national commerce often suffers, for want of that money being employed in a free trade which might prove much more to the advantage of the Kingdom, as well as to that of the stockholders themselves, if they employed the same property in general trade."[25]

Reflecting the extent to which the British economy was divorced from the nascent stock market, the collapse of the stock market boom of the mid-1820s had less impact on the overall economy then the bursting of the South Sea Bubble, even though more individuals were involved in the emerging market boom of the mid-1820s than had been active in the South Sea boom of 1720. The South Sea collapse had required massive parliamentary intervention to essentially rewrite hundreds of transactions in order to put the economy back together again. No such action was taken (or contemplated) in 1826.

A severe recession hit Britain that year, but it was due to a banking crisis that was only tangentially related to the stock market break.

The Panic of 1825–26 did not have serious long-term consequences. International investment by Britons did not cease after the Latin American debacle, but poured into other areas, notably the United States. Stocks and bonds were issued by private American developers to build canals and roads and to establish banks. Individual state governments also were frequent issuers of debt. European (primarily British) investment in state and corporation stocks and bonds in the United States jumped from $12.8 million in 1820 to $26.5 million in 1830 to $200 million in 1840.[26]

Surprisingly, it was not long before Latin American investments again became acceptable. One country, Brazil, never really lost access to City of London capital markets because it, alone among the South American countries, never defaulted on its debt. Brazilian enterprises (such as the Brazilian Gas Light Company) were able to sell stock in London throughout the 1830s. By midcentury, money again flowed into Latin American countries other than Brazil; one historian estimates that these investments, on average, were profitable, yielding a 6 percent rate of return, far above that available on consols.[27]

Given the dearth of information available to both stock promoters and investors, the large number of novice market participants, and the fact that the very idea of overseas equity investment was new, it should not be surprising that wildly erratic price movements occurred. But the boom and bust of the mid-1820s apparently did not discourage investors from continuing to purchase joint-stock company shares or from investing in overseas equity projects. It can best be seen as a rather messy, but nevertheless very important, first step in the development of an international market for equities.

4

THE RAILROADS AND THE MIDDLE CLASS

IN 1825 AN ODDLY SHAPED CONTRAPTION chugged across the English countryside on tracks linking the towns of Stockton and Darlington. This first passenger steam railroad was regarded as little more than a curiosity; within two decades, however, the economies of Western Europe and North America would be irrevocably altered by the new mode of transportation. The railroad industry's unprecedented need for capital would transform primitive stock exchanges into the vibrant markets essential to a modern economy.

Initially, the Stockton-Darlington line received little attention from the markets, preoccupied as they were with giddy enthusiasm for Latin American schemes. Early rail transport met with a great deal of skepticism and frequently outright hostility. Farmers feared that locomotives would prevent cows from grazing and hens from laying eggs and would blacken the wool of sheep. Landlords worried that the noise and smoke would detract from their enjoyment of their estates. And some physicians even questioned whether the human body could withstand the great speeds (up to fifteen miles an hour) at which the new trains traveled.

Soon after the Stockton-Darlington line opened, six additional railways were authorized by Parliament, but any prospect of a railroad boom was snuffed out by the financial crisis of late 1825 and 1826. It was only after the Liverpool and Manchester Railway began operating in 1831, and was quickly able to pay a 10 percent dividend, that investors began to focus on the new technology. Liverpool and Manchester shares soon doubled in value, and other railway companies were hastily organized.

The man who best personified the British railroad industry in its early years was George Hudson. The heavyset son of a Yorkshire farmer, Hudson had worked as a linen draper until he inherited a substantial sum that enabled him to begin investing in railroads. Unlike many other money men who would come to run great rail combines in France, Germany, and the United States, Hudson thrust himself enthusiastically into the day-to-day management of the rail enterprises in which he invested; he was a railroader first and a financier second. By 1844 Hudson controlled over one thousand miles of track, more than one-third the trackage in operation in Britain. The press crowned him as the "Railway King" and the "Railway Napoleon."

Hudson recognized that the railroads were creating the need for broad-based financial markets that could raise capital from nontraditional sources. The money needed to build the new lines did not come from the great merchant banks, like Barings or Rothschilds, that had financed entire nations. Instead, financing was typically provided by merchants and landowners who lived along the routes of the new lines, and by middle-class tradesmen.

Benjamin Disraeli, still licking his wounds from the collapse of the Latin American share boom, described the public enthusiasm for railway investment in his novel *Endymion*. "One or two lines of railway, which had long been sleepily in formation, about this time were finished . . . Suddenly, there was a general feeling in the country that its capital should be invested in railways; that the whole surface of the land should be transformed, and covered, as by a network, with these mighty means of communication." In a subsequent passage Disraeli wrote: "What is remarkable in this vast movement in which so many millions were produced, and so many more promised, was, that the great leaders of the financial world took no part in it . . . All seemed to come from the provinces, and from unknown people in the provinces."

Another contemporary observer commented, "In every street in every town, persons were to be found who were holders of Railway Shares. Elderly men and women of small realized fortunes, tradesmen of every order, pensioners, public functionaries, professional men, merchants, country gentlemen—the mania had affected all."[1]

Hudson carefully stage-managed the openings of new lines, ostentatiously promoting the ventures with an eye to raising more capital in the future. One of his new companies, the York and North Midland Railway, announced an extremely generous dividend of 9 percent (three times the rate paid by government bonds) while the line itself was still under construction.[2] The fact that the dividend was paid out of capital, not profits, did not seem to concern him.

Hudson also made use of a new financing device—what became known as "vendor" shares—issued, in lieu of cash, to pay firms that supplied the new railroads during the construction phase, before revenues were received. Not unlike the use of stock options by present-day start-up companies to pay key employees, landlords, and suppliers, these "vendor" shares enabled the new rail lines to pay expenses in stock during the construction phase, before revenues started to come in. Since (as in the case of modern stock options) there were usually restrictions that prevented vendor share owners from selling out before a predetermined future date, the arrangement had the added benefit of minimizing the actual number of shares in circulation in the company's early years, creating a scarcity value. Hudson (and other railroad promoters) took full advantage of this lack of supply, using various stratagems to push market prices higher. Hudson recognized, as did the managers and investment bankers for start-up technology companies in the late 1990s, that a strong performance of newly issued shares could provide invaluable publicity.

Grateful shareholders of one of Hudson's companies went so far as to collect money to erect a statue of him; the incredible sum of £20,000 was reportedly raised.[3] Hudson was a celebrity. John Francis wrote of Hudson in his *History of the Railways*, "The press recorded his whereabouts, the draughtsmen penciled his features . . . He wielded an influence in England unparalleled and unprecedented."

The new share offerings from Hudson (and other British railroad promoters) greatly expanded the size of the British stock market. Similar growth, however, did not occur in the bourses of Continental

Europe. In most European countries, the government took a much larger role in developing railroads. In Belgium, the first railroads were actually built by the government itself, while Holland contracted with private companies to build lines along routes laid out by the state. In France, the government acquired the right of way and built the roadbed for the early lines, while private companies laid the rails, provided rolling stock, and operated the roads.

Because the French capital markets could not provide the necessary funds for even this limited private role, most new French railroad companies turned to London. One company that sought to sell 150,000 shares in London was inundated with requests to purchase 400,000, while another French railway brought to market shortly thereafter raised more than half its total capital from British investors. In one year alone, more than fifty railways were organized in France, for which over £80 million were provided by the London stock market.[4]

The railroad boom spread to Germany, albeit a few years later than Belgium and France. Prior to the 1840s German joint-stock companies had been rare; wealthy Germans kept their money in land, mortgages, and government bonds. Since Germany was a patchwork of separate states and principalities, not yet a single entity, there was no uniform German corporate law. Until Prussia, the largest German state, passed a joint-stock law in 1838, such companies could only come into existence by an "act of grace" on the part of the local ruler. After Prussia moved, pressing demands to finance railroads quickly forced other states to follow. Karl Marx wrote, "The urge to . . . build new railroads, and above all to invest in corporations and speculate with stocks, gripped all classes from the peasants to the prince . . ."[5] One historian claimed that the evolution of financial markets (which had occurred over more than two hundred years in England) was telescoped into a fraction of that time span in Germany.[6]

More recent analysis suggests, however, that German enthusiasm for the new equity markets was not very deep; the stock market was an inherently alien idea grafted onto more traditional German economic structures. The short German experience with equity markets inevitably meant the breadth of public participation in new issues was considerably less than in Britain. With a few highly visible exceptions, the German public shied away from presumably "risky" new railroads and industrial ventures, preferring the relative safety of government bonds.

One prominent economic historian observed that Germany suffered from a "shortage of entrepreneurs" and an "insufficiency of previously created wealth . . . to be placed at the disposal of entrepreneurs."[7] As a result, a peculiarly Germany institution—called the *Grossbank*, or credit bank—grew up to provide needed funding for the new railroads and other industrial entities. Combination investment banks, commercial banks, and brokerage firms, the *Grossbanken* were large joint-stock banks specifically established to make long-term financing available to industrial firms. They did not have any parallels in British or American capital markets. One historian aptly described the *Grossbanken* as "the most important stimuli to German industrialization."[8]

Gustav von Mevissen, founder of the first of the *Grossbanken* in 1848, made the financing of new companies the primary objective of his bank. The bank organized the formation of the first German mining corporation, the Kölner Bergwerksverein, as well as the first steel and machine companies.[9] German credit banks also provided crucial funding for the construction of early railroads. The banks underwrote securities issues that were to be sold to the public, or, when (frequently) the public market for those securities was not large enough, the banks bought a substantial portion of the issues themselves. In many cases the banks became the controlling shareholders of the companies they financed. The large credit banks, not the German stock market, became the principal financing mechanism for German industry.

It would be in the vast United States, not Continental Europe, that railroad financings created a rollicking stock market unparalleled in history. American railroads, while they often received substantial public subsidies from the states and cities to be served, were conceived, financed, and built by the private sector. British capital financed much of the American railroad boom; by 1836 over $90 million had been raised for investment in railroads in the northern American states, with over half of that amount coming from Britain.

As George Hudson had so presciently recognized, these large sums could not be raised through traditional investment channels. Efforts by Hudson and others to entice middle-class investors into buying railroad shares had been generally successful, but by the middle of the century they were increasingly impeded by a previously overlooked fault in the joint-stock organizational structure. Joint-stock shareholders were technically liable for all actions and debts of the companies they invested in; the limit of that liability was not restricted to the amount of money they had actually invested, but could in theory extend to all the personal assets of individual shareholders. In the worst case, an individual investor, who had no role in the management of the firm, could be bankrupted by liabilities passed through to him. As this risk became more widely publicized, it had the effect of noticeably dampening middle-class interest in stock investing.

During the initial period of rapid growth in the British stock market in the late seventeenth and early eighteenth centuries, little attention had been given to this issue. It wasn't until the later decades of the eighteenth century that corporate charters even included clauses making reference to shareholder liability, with the treatment of shareholders varying substantially from case to case. Some charters sought to specifically exempt investors from any liability beyond their investment, while others did precisely the opposite. In some instances, corporate directors were given immunity from personal liability but shareholders were not.

In practice, there were few attempts by creditors to pursue individual shareholders when companies found themselves unable to meet their obligations. But since most companies had the ability to make "calls" for more capital from their stockholders, company creditors could (and sometimes did) sue the company itself in an effort to force it to issue such calls in order to raise the funds necessary to pay off debts. By the 1850s the entire question was a legal muddle.

This was a crucial issue upon which the future development of the stock market would stand or fall. A modern market requires the participation of large numbers of middle-class investors, not just a few wealthy individuals. Only in this way can it access the capital necessary to fund large industrial enterprises. But potential middle-class investors were reluctant to participate in investment schemes that exposed them to unlimited liability. If the joint-stock laws were not altered to address this issue, the future growth of the equity market would be severely constrained.

Ironically, France, which in most respects lagged behind Britain in the development of financial markets, had an advantage when it came to the matter of limiting shareholder liability. The Napoleonic Commercial Code of 1808 had ratified the previous practice of allowing partnerships with silent—or "sleeping"—members, as long as those partners did not take an active role in the management of the business. These partnerships were called *sociétés en commandite.* In addition, the code had also created an entirely new entity—the *société anonyme*—which was the first true limited-liability corporation. *Sociétés anonymes* issued shares that were transferable, and limited the liability of shareholders to the amount of money they had invested.

Because the idea that investors could not be held personally responsible for the actions of their firms was so revolutionary, the government kept tight control over the number of *sociétés anonymes* that were authorized. An advisory opinion issued to the Council of State spelled out the reason for concern. "Because Societies anonyme[s] have no agent who is personally liable," the opinion stated, "in the best interest of commerce they cannot be authorized without the greatest of caution."[10] New *sociétés anonymes* could only be created with the direct approval of the government, for fear that the companies would become "a snare for public credulity." A great deal of emphasis was placed on assessing "the status and morality of the subscribers of shares."[11]

The companies approved to operate as *sociétés anonymes* included a number of insurance companies, a foundry, a coal mine, a canal, three theaters, a coach company, bridges, a sawmill, a producer of vegetable dyes, a firm that extracted sugar from beets, and a secondary school. Shares were held in large denominations by relatively small groups of people. Even though many of these enterprises were successful, an ingrained distrust of them remained. The government rejected many applications to form *sociétés anonymes*; in one instance, a mining engineer advised against the creation of a *société anonyme* because he felt it would be "slow, incoherent, and without guarantees."[12]

To get around limitations placed on the formation of *sociétés anonymes* in France, capitalists began to use the *société en commandite* partnership structure to operate larger businesses. Most investors could thus secure limited liability as silent partners, making them more willing to invest. This trend accelerated after 1832, when a French court decision allowed *sociétés en commandite* to issue bearer shares—shares that were not specifically registered to any individual but were the property of whoever held them. Men who were supposed to be "silent" partners could thus hide their identity through the bearer shares and get away with exercising a role in management.

Unfortunately, the rapid growth in the number of *sociétés en commandite* was accompanied by high-profile scandals. It has been estimated that one-third of all *sociétés en commandite* floated in France during the 1850s were fraudulent, operated by unscrupulous general partners.[13] The French bureaucracy was innately suspicious of speculation, dating back to the French Revolution and before that to the experience of John Law's failed Mississippi Company. Inevitably, pressure to halt the perceived abuses of speculative *sociétés en commandite* grew more intense.

In 1856 both Britain and France enacted defining pieces of legislation dealing with the formation of new corporations. They moved in opposite directions. Henceforth, general incorporation with limited liability was to be permitted for British nonfinancial joint-stock companies. Any group of seven or more persons could form a limited-liability corporation simply by registering it and stating that it was "limited." (Because of fears about irresponsible speculation, such advantages were not extended to insurance and banking companies until years later.) But simultaneously, in France tight new restrictions were imposed that drastically curtailed the rate of formation of large *sociétés en commandite*.

As is usually the case with political acts, there were a number of factors involved. In France, prevailing attitudes in the bureaucracy and among the public were hostile to business, and thus made the government much more willing to enact restrictive regulations in the heat of scandal. In Britain, however, public sentiment was much more pro-business, and the powerful British Christian socialist movement, far from opposing limited-liability legislation, actually supported it as a means of facilitating investment by workingmen in the companies that employed them. Furthermore, advocates of limited-liability protection argued that limited-liability laws in the United States (where rules for corporations were set by the individual states) were causing British companies to seek charters overseas.

The restrictive French legislation of 1856 set back the development of the Paris stock market. Between 1860 and 1867 only a few *sociétés en commandite* were formed, and, on average, fewer than thirteen *sociétés anonymes* were created each year. It soon became clear that the rules were badly hampering the ability of French businesses to raise needed capital. Much as had earlier occurred in Britain, demands were raised that the government make it easier to finance the new railroads and other large industrial entities that a modernizing economy required.

In 1867 the French government reversed itself, enacting legislation permitting general incorporation with limited liability. France was followed by Spain in 1869, Germany in 1870, Belgium in 1873, and Italy in 1883. The delay in opening the French market to new limited-liability enterprises proved critical, however; combined with the disruptive effects of the Franco-Prussian War of 1870, the restrictive policies of the government delayed the development of the French stock market and ensured that the Paris Bourse would not rival the London Stock Exchange as the central financial marketplace for the world.

While limited-liability legislation removed a major impediment to mass participation in the stock market, it did nothing to ameliorate another growing concern—financial instability that led to periodic market collapses. In the early 1840s two important pamphlets were published in England, presenting opposite viewpoints on the source of the problem and how to deal with it. One, by Horsley Palmer, blamed the travails of the markets on excessive speculation in railroad securities, particularly those associated with American railroads. Palmer was one of the first writers to explore the notion that periodic speculative booms inevitably lead to economic "busts." (At roughly the same time, Charles McKay published a book entitled *Popular Delusions and the Madness of Crowds*, which described so-called speculative bubbles, particularly emphasizing the South Sea episode. McKay's book was enormously influential, anticipating many other similar works, and is still in print today.) What was really important about Palmer's pamphlet, however, was that Palmer put forth a means of dealing with recurring boom/bust crises. Palmer proposed that the Bank of England stop acting narrowly as a private for-profit institution and become instead a bona fide central bank, pursuing countercyclical monetary policies (easy money in times of commercial distress) to offset the impact of the speculative market cycle.

Samuel Jones Loyd, a leading banker of the day, took issue with Palmer in a lengthy broadside that was widely circulated in the City of London. According to Loyd, the difficulties plaguing the economy had little to do with any intrinsic speculative cycle; rather the source of the problem was the Bank of England itself. The bank, Loyd charged, had alternated back and forth between easy money and tight money policies based solely on its own parochial concerns. To prevent this, Loyd called for rigid restraints on the bank's ability to issue banknotes, which served as money in circulation in the British economy. Loyd and his supporters succeeded in persuading Parliament to pass the Banking Act of 1844, which specifically forbade the Bank of England from attempting to manage the supply of money. A fixed limit was set on the number of notes that the bank could issue, and a fixed ratio between the value of the notes and gold bullion was established. Palmer and his allies warned that the rigidity of the new regime could prove disastrous in a financial crisis, preventing the Bank of England from providing badly needed liquidity.

Those who feared an economic crisis didn't have long to wait. In January 1847 an outflow of gold from England to pay for food imports during the Irish potato famine forced the Bank of England to raise its discount rate to 4 percent in order to ration credit. Because the Bank Act severely restricted the bank's ability to grant credit (issue notes) that was not backed directly by gold, the supply of money and credit contracted when gold was sent out of England. Disraeli later described the period as one of "commercial distress of unprecedented severity. Private credit was paralyzed, trade was more than dull, it was almost dead—and there was scarcely a private individual in this kingdom, from the richest and the noblest in the land down to the most humble among the middle classes, who was not smarting under the circumstances of commercial distress . . ."[14]

By early October, with the gold outflow unabated, the Bank of England was forced to cease lending altogether. On Monday, October 17, what became known as the Week of Terror began. The market for stocks, and even for British government bonds, virtually disintegrated. Several major banks failed. George Norman of the Bank of England recalled, "Everyone seemed afraid of his neighbor."[15] On Saturday, October 22, a group of City bankers arranged an emergency meeting with the prime minister and the chancellor of the Exchequer, pleading that the Bank Act of 1844 be suspended. After much indecision, the government finally relented, reluctantly suspending the act and thus allowing the bank to resume lending.

As soon as the temporary suspension was announced it became unnecessary. Once money market participants realized that an infusion of credit from the Bank of England would be available, they were reassured, and the panic ceased. For the first time, a central banking institution, acting as a lender of last resort, had intervened to prevent a market collapse.

Although the British banking system weathered the crisis, a long bear market depressed stock prices. Between 1846 and 1849 the Newmarch index of leading railroad securities fell from 1,175 to 444, a decline of 62 percent. To make matters worse, many shareholders were hit with additional assessments on their shares just when money was the most difficult to obtain. (It was common practice for railroad investors to initially put up only a fraction of the par value of the shares they purchased; the railroad companies had the right to "call" on the investors for more money when needed, up to the full par amount.) This led to the apparent oddity of some rail stocks trading at negative prices, where the buyer was paid by the seller to take the shares off his hands, so that the seller could avoid paying upcoming capital assessments.[16]

George Hudson, as the personification of the British railway boom, quickly became the goat of the market collapse. Increasingly unstable, by 1848 he often appeared to be drunk in the House of Commons (where he had earlier won a seat), and reportedly lost his temper when another member suggested he "join a temperance society."[17] Hudson and two of his railroads were specific targets of a scandal sheet published in August 1848 entitled *The Bubble of the Age, or, the Fallacies of Railway Investments.* The author criticized Hudson's practice of promising extravagant dividends to push up share prices, and was harshly critical of insider trading by railway directors.

Hudson admitted that his personal affairs and those of his companies had unfortunately become intertwined, but claimed that this had not been to the detriment of the public shareholders of his railroads. (He had, for example, several times personally guaranteed the debts of companies he controlled.)[18] Many of the practices that Hudson engaged in were quite common at the time, and had been ignored when railway shares were rising. Hudson's friends felt that he had been made a scapegoat for the market collapse, and repeated investigations never did find grounds for criminal charges. Hudson eventually paid back much of the money he was accused of taking from his railroads, but was ultimately arrested for debt in the 1860s and vanished into obscurity. At his death in 1871 he left an estate of only £200.[19]

Critics were quick to blame the crisis on a capital shortage resulting from extravagant speculative investment in railroads. They cited a *Times* survey of October 1845 that listed over twelve hundred railroad projects (under construction or planned) with a projected cost of £560 million as an indication of the degree of railroad overbuilding. The entire annual gross national product of Great Britain at the time was estimated to be about £550 million.

Even S. J. Loyd, one of the principal advocates of the Bank Act restraints on Bank of England lending policies, seemed to come around to the view of Horace Palmer and others that the root of the problem was overspeculation. Loyd described the speculative cycle this way: "First we find it [the markets] in a state of quiescence,—next improvement,—growing confidence,—prosperity,—excitement,—overtrading,—convulsions,—pressure,—stagnation,—distress,—ending again in quiescence."[20] After the 1847 debacle, he was quick to blame "the extraordinary diversion of capital from trading purposes to the construction of railways." Alexander Baring ascribed the crisis to "the extravagant circulation of railroad paper by which much of our present difficulties has been caused."[21] The *Economist* argued that heavy railway expenditures had swallowed capital that would have been available for normal trade and so had forced up the interest rate from 2.5 percent in 1845 to almost 10 percent in October 1847.

Many observers agreed with the *Economist* that excessive speculation in railroads was diverting needed capital from other enterprises. In fact, this was one of the most frequently voiced critiques of nineteenth-century stock markets, which were often seen as institutionalizing unproductive speculation. Legitimate businesses suffered because they had to compete for capital with imprudent "speculative" ventures.

There is a very significant flaw in this argument. Despite specific crises, such as that of 1847, in which tight money conditions forced interest rates sharply higher, the general trend in interest rates and in dividend yields paid on British stocks was one of steady decline over time. If capital had indeed been scarce, sucked up by unproductive speculation, the interest rates and dividends necessary to attract capital should have risen. This did not happen; a capital shortage most certainly did not exist in Britain at midcentury.

Later economists have strongly disputed the notion that overspeculation in railroads was the principal cause of the 1847 crisis, instead pointing to the rigidity of a monetary system based exclusively on gold. In the first half of the nineteenth century, the supply of gold did not keep pace with the growth of the world economy; one leading index of prices shows that the general price level in Britain declined from an index value of 130 (before the gold standard was reinstated) to 91 by 1830, to 84 by 1843, and to a low of 79 in 1849, about the time the gold discovery in California began to reinflate a gold-based world economy.[22] The monetary system was particularly vulnerable to bad harvests (such as the Irish potato famine), which required Britain to unexpectedly import large quantities of foodstuffs to feed its burgeoning population. Payment for these imports drained gold from Britain, forcing a contraction of credit that could hit the economy hard. Just this seemed to happen in 1847, and was probably far more important than any hangover from excess speculation in railroads.

Whatever the precise causes of the 1847 panic, the Bank of England's steps to stabilize the banking system, and thus the financial markets, set an important precedent for the future. Its willingness to act as a lender of last resort was again evident in its response to the Overend Gurney crisis of 1866. Overend, Gurney & Company was one of the premier British banking firms, but lax management had allowed it to stray into many ventures beyond its traditional areas of expertise. By 1866, it had overextended itself to the point where it could not meet its obligations in the face of simultaneous business reverses, and was forced to "suspend" payments, meaning that it was effectively bankrupt. The shock waves resulting from the failure, according to financial historian Leland Jenks, shot out in "concentric waves from Hong Kong to Buffalo."[23] Overend Gurney's international presence was so extensive that the British Foreign Secretary felt compelled to send assurances to the nation's embassies around the world that the finances of Britain itself remained sound.

The Bank of England briefly considered providing direct aid to Overend Gurney, but an inspection of the ailing firm's books quickly dispelled any notion that such a rescue was feasible. Instead, the bank aggressively made funds available to other, more financially sound firms, pumping a record four million pounds of new notes into the banking system on the worst day of the crisis. The bank's governor, Lancelot Holland, boldly stated the new policy. "We will not flinch," he asserted, "from the duty which we conceived was imposed upon us of supporting the banking community, and I am not aware that any legitimate application made for assistance to this house was refused."[24]

The most compelling intellectual basis for Bank of England intervention was provided seven years later by Walter Bagehot. Bagehot was described as "the most Victorian of the Victorians . . . whose influence, passing from one fit mind to another, could transmit and can still impart, the most precious element in Victorian civilization, its robust masculinity and sanity."[25] In May 1873, six years after the publication of his epic treatise *The English Constitution*, Bagehot wrote *Lombard Street*, which was subtitled *A Description of the Money Market*. Bagehot argued that crises such as that of Overend Gurney, and the sheer volume of the City's assets and liabilities, meant that "we must examine the system on which these great masses of money are manipulated, and assure ourselves that it is safe and right."

As Bagehot put it, "Money will not manage itself, and Lombard Street has a great deal of money to manage." The only institution capable of such management—the Bank of England—had never been given any sort of official mandate to do so. "We have placed the exclusive custody of our entire banking reserve in the hands of a single board of directors," Bagehot observed, "who have never been told by any great statesman or public authority that they are so to keep it or that they have anything to do with it."

Bagehot applauded the bank's decision to make credit readily available during the Overend Gurney crisis. Writing in the *Economist*, he called the bank's action a "welcome" acceptance of the notion that the bank was a lender of last resort, and thus responsible for maintaining the "sole banking reserve of the country."[26] This idea was not by any means universally accepted; one prominent critic denounced Bagehot's proposal as "the most mischievous doctrine ever broached in the monetary or banking world of this country." In his view, it was most certainly not "the proper function of the Bank of England to keep money available at all times to supply the demands of bankers who have rendered their own assets unavailable."[27]

Bagehot's views were clearly controversial at the time they were voiced. But looking back, economic historians view the Bank of England's response to the Overend Gurney failure and Bagehot's subsequent intellectual justification for it as harbingers of a concept that would become widely accepted in the future. The Bank of England now had an obligation that stretched beyond that of simply another private bank. By acting as a lender of last resort, the bank would attempt to cushion the credit crunches that precipitated market panics. This was a crucial step toward creating a more stable stock market that could appeal to the great mass of potential middle-class investors.

Unfortunately, the bank could do little to deal with another deterrent to middle-class investing—the scandalous misuse of shareholder funds by unscrupulous corporate officials. One of the most egregious such instances, on either side of the Atlantic, was the looting of the Erie Railroad by New York market operators. The American Civil War and the completion of the transatlantic telegraph had made possible an unprecedented boom in European investment in the American "emerging market," as very low yields on British government bonds (approximately 2 percent) caused yield-hungry investors to look to America for superior returns. By the late 1860s the New York stock market had become the second largest in the world, and while the par value of securities listed on the London Exchange was still more than three times greater than that of the New York Stock Exchange ($10 billion to $3 billion), the New York market was growing much faster. But the lack of an established body of rules of corporate behavior inevitably meant that abuses would occur.

Speculative New York stocks were called "fancies"—usually highly volatile rail stocks with uncertain prospects. The fanciest of all the fancies was the Erie Railroad, a debt-ridden line stretching across southern New York State that was often the most actively traded stock in the postbellum period. The man whose name was most closely associated with the Erie Railroad was the "speculative director," Daniel Drew. A former cattle drover, Drew once said that trading stocks without access to inside information was like buying cattle by candlelight. Drew's lanky build and bony cheeks gave him a cadaverous appearance, accentuated by the black suits he invariably wore. He was deeply religious, always carrying a Bible and frequently quoting Scripture, but somehow his religious beliefs existed on a very different plane from his Wall Street dealings. Drew would belt out hymns with deep-felt emotion from the pews of church on Sunday, but come Monday morning, in his Wall Street office, he would not hesitate to swindle any unwary victim who had the misfortune to stray across his path.

"Uncle Daniel" Drew served several terms as a director and as treasurer of the Erie, making frequent use of the inside information he gleaned to manipulate Erie shares. Brokers were fond of saying of Drew and Erie:

Uncle Daniel says up, Erie goes up.
Uncle Daniel says down, Erie goes down.
Uncle Daniel says wiggle-waggle, Erie bobs both ways.

Drew delighted in taking advantage of uninformed speculators, particularly foreigners, whom he contemptuously referred to as "greenhorns." He is said to have remarked that he "loved to burn 'green' wood, because it had more sap in it."

Drew was first aided, then betrayed, by two notorious market operators, Jay Gould and Jim Fisk, who could not have been more different from each other. Gould was a small, shy man who possessed a brilliant analytical mind, while Fisk was a big, flamboyant showman who rollicked through life (and Wall Street) as if it were one large circus. The two men finagled their way onto the Erie board of directors in later 1867, as part of a compromise between railroad magnate Cornelius Vanderbilt and Drew, who had battled for control of the line.

The arrangement did not last, and within months a vicious struggle broke out between the Vanderbilt forces on one side and Drew, Fisk, and Gould on the other. Before it was concluded, the "Erie War" would witness the wholesale bribery (by both sides) of the New York judiciary and of much of the New Jersey and New York State legislatures. Armed conflict nearly broke out, as Vanderbilt thugs organized to storm the fortified headquarters of the Drew forces in New Jersey, only to be convinced at the last minute that Drew was not there. Vanderbilt, who had been snookered into buying up millions of dollars' worth of Erie shares run off on a printing press by Fisk, finally sued for a peace that enabled him to get his money back. The settlement effectively turned the Erie over to Gould and Fisk.

The two men then proceeded to secretly sell huge additional quantities of new Erie stock, increasing the number of shares outstanding from slightly more than 200,000 to nearly 800,000. They used the proceeds of the sales to finance various other schemes, including an audacious plan to corner the market in gold in 1869 that involved an attempt to bribe President Ulysses S. Grant. When the scheme collapsed, it plunged the entire nation into a recession.

When the new Erie shareholders (many of them British) attempted to exercise the control of management that their ownership interest implied, Gould employed several devices to obstruct them. He changed the company's bylaws, requiring stockholders to appear in person at shareholder meetings to vote their shares, and staggered the terms of his directors so that they could not be challenged all at once. When all else failed, he simply refused to register the shares held by the British holders in the Erie record books, and made use of the corrupt New York judiciary to forestall legal efforts to force such registration. Ever since the advent of the corporation, Adam Smith and others had warned about the dangers of divorcing corporate governance from ownership. Gould's high-handed actions provided hard evidence that those concerns were justified.

The well-respected *Times* of London observed that Gould's machinations "seem likely to create distrust as to the possibility of any legal, equitable control being exercised for the protection of investments in American corporations."[28] The *New York Times* concurred, opining that "England and France have had their speculative bubbles, their gross violations of trust, their robbery of confiding stockholders by men high in position, with riches in abundance. But neither England nor France presents a parallel with the infamies of the Erie railroad."[29]

In late 1869 a committee representing the British owners of 190,000 Erie shares was formed, with the intent of wresting control of the railroad from Gould and Fisk. But when the group's attorneys presented share certificates at the Erie offices in Manhattan, Gould flatly refused to register them. Recognizing that the corrupt local courts were firmly in Gould's pockets, the attorneys took the case to the federal judiciary.

Fisk pretended to be unperturbed by the new legal twist. Upon being served with a subpoena by a federal marshal, Fisk shrugged and said, "If these Britishers prefer that their share of the earnings of the road shall be eaten up in lawsuits instead of being distributed as dividends, I can't help it."[30]

The stockholder representatives also moved on another front, attempting to persuade the New York State legislature to change the laws that allowed corporate managers like Gould to run roughshod over shareholder interests. The *Commercial and Financial Chronicle* supported the efforts, fearing that if they were not successful, foreign investors would stay away from the American stock market. Stating succinctly that "the letter of the law is very deficient in its regulation of the management of corporate interests," the paper urged the legislature to take the steps necessary to protect the "legitimate" owners.

Gould was not to be bested in the arena of New York politics, which he had, through the copious use of bribes, rigged to his advantage. Testifying before a legislative committee, he made a blatant appeal to antiforeign (and anti-Semitic) prejudice. If the legislature acted on the urgings of the British, Gould warned, "Bona fide owners [will] have no voice, and the board of directors to manage the affairs and administer to the wants of this great corporation [will] be made up in the dingy office of a Jew banking house in London."[31] Legislators sympathetic to Gould used fear of foreign ownership to justify their actions, but in a moment of honesty one assemblyman admitted to a British representative that he might have done better had he brought "$20,000 to smooth the way."[32]

In July 1871, more than a year after legal action commenced, the British shareholders committee received a favorable ruling from a U.S. district court. Major newspapers declared war on Gould, with the *New York Herald* commenting that corporate officers like Gould "virtually say to foreign investors [that] if they send their money to the US they must run the risk of confiscation."[33] Perhaps most important, Gould's allies in Tammany Hall were on the run, as reformers pressed to root out widespread municipal corruption. Stripped of protection from a corrupt local judiciary, the other Erie directors, who until this point had condoned Gould's actions, now feared that they could be held personally liable if they failed to guard shareholder interests. After a tense confrontation between federal marshals and thugs hired by the Erie management, Gould was forced to relinquish control.

Erie stock jumped five dollars when Gould's departure was announced. In the days that followed, large buy orders, particularly from London, sent the price even higher; within two weeks it had spiked 60 percent, to a level not seen since the earliest days of the Gould-Fisk regime. The *New York Herald* took note of the heavy foreign buying, observing, "One thing seems certain, that Erie has been restored to its old pinnacle of fame as the great speculative medium of the Stock Exchange, with the modification that henceforth, with a cable across the Atlantic and the shares distributed over the two continents, its field of patronage will embrace a much wider world."[34] Financial historian John Steele Gordon, writing more than one hundred years later, went even further when assessing the importance of the Erie to the world market. The "scarlet woman of Wall Street," commented Gordon, referring to the Erie, "quite unintentionally, had brought forth a child, and the global capital market had been born."[35]

Most importantly, the "Erie Wars" triggered important changes that would make the American market more investor-friendly. The brokerage community, which depended on commissions from investors' orders, pressed the New York Stock Exchange to promulgate rules to prevent the worst abuses. In response, the exchange issued regulations that required companies to provide a public registry of all shares issued and to give advance notice of any new share offerings. Rules for the election of corporate directors were tightened. Significantly, these reforms were not the product of government action; rather, it was the New York Stock Exchange that imposed the new standards.

The New York Stock Exchange, like the Bank of England and the London Stock Exchange, was developing into a quasi-public institution, gradually assuming many of the regulatory responsibilities that governments, in an age of liberal laissez-faire economics, would not take on. It was in the self-interest of exchange members to make the market attractive to the middle-class investors needed to provide funding for capital-intensive businesses like railways. While by modern standards the early reforms in New York and London seem trivial, and certainly did not prevent serious scandals from occurring in the future, they did establish an important precedent that would lead to additional incremental improvements. Both Wall Street and the City of London recognized that markets that were not perceived as "fair" could not hope to satisfy the demand for capital of modern industrial economies.

A GLOBAL STOCK MARKET

IN 1886 Baron Edward Revelstoke (Edward Baring), managing partner of the prestigious firm of Baring Brothers (Barings), sensed a major opportunity. His firm's arch rival, the house of Rothschild, had passed on a chance to underwrite the first public offering of shares in the Guinness breweries. The family of Sir Edward Guinness had been brewing its thick brown beverage since the middle of the eighteenth century, and Guinness was a familiar brand name throughout much of the world. Like many other privately held companies, Guinness had concluded that the capital necessary to run a large industrial concern could best be obtained through the device of the limited-liability corporation. In fact, the 1880s marked a turning point in the history of equity markets, as major industrial firms began to embrace the modern corporate structure. In less than a decade, from 1884 to 1893, the total amount of capital represented by British limited-liability firms more than doubled, from £475 million to £1.1 billion.[1]

"Ned" Revelstoke, recognizing the fundamental shift that was occurring, jumped in when Rothschild held back, offering to underwrite Guinness shares with a par value of £6 million, of which the Guinness family would retain £800,000 worth. The gamble paid off handsomely. When Barings invited applications on Saturday, October 23, the offering was met with overwhelming demand. The London *Daily News* reported, "Barings' place was literally besieged.

Special policemen kept back the pushing crowd of clerks, agents, messengers and City men, and pains were taken to have one of the swing doors only partly open, so none but . . . clerks and Stock Exchange men . . . could squeeze in."[2] Some applicants wrapped forms around stones and hurled them in through the windows. Orders totaling £114 million were submitted for the £5.2 million worth of shares to be sold. By Monday morning, the £10 ordinary shares were trading above £16, a premium of more than 60 percent above the offering price.

It was widely believed that Baring Brothers made a profit of £1 million on the Guinness deal. This estimate was probably too high, but there was no doubt that the Guinness underwriting was a tremendous coup for Baring Brothers, and for Revelstoke himself, made even sweeter because it had come as the result of an embarrassing misjudgment by the Rothschilds. The house of Rothschild was still the leading merchant banking firm in England (and hence the entire world), but Barings was rapidly closing the gap, aided by a fundamental shift in the focus of British overseas investment.

By the end of the nineteenth century, the economies of Western Europe had caught up with Britain in industrialization and were able to generate needed investment capital internally. The proportion of British foreign investment that went to Europe fell steadily, from 66 percent in 1830 to 25 percent in 1870, and to only 5 percent by 1900.[3] British (and European) foreign investment shifted to developing countries, particularly in the Americas. The Rothschilds dominated the European financial markets, but conspicuously lagged behind Barings in exploiting opportunities in the New World. The changing flow of overseas investment thus worked to benefit Barings.

Between 1865 and 1890 Barings handled 28.7 percent of North American railroad stocks issued through London, worth £34.7 million. Drexel, Morgan & Company (later to become simply J.P. Morgan & Company) was next, underwriting 21.6 percent, or £26 million. The Rothschilds underwrote only £800,000 worth of North American railway stocks during this period. No other competitor had as much as 10 percent of the market.[4]

Looking beyond the United States, Edward Revelstoke saw great potential in Latin America, particularly in Argentina. Political stability, combined with a program of monetary reform, had greatly enhanced investor confidence. Total British investment in Argentine joint-stock companies jumped from £25 million in 1880 to £45 million in 1885, and reached a staggering £150 million in 1890.[5] In 1889 Argentina alone absorbed nearly 50 percent of all British funds invested overseas. Between 1870 and 1890 Argentina imported capital equivalent to 18.7 percent of its GNP; these figures dwarf by comparison the 4 percent of GNP Argentina imported during the so-called emerging market boom of the 1990s.

The Baring Brothers' aggressive efforts in Argentina and elsewhere were not universally acclaimed. In December 1888, the *Statist* magazine published a tough critique of Barings' underwritings. Noting that all but two of the thirty-two issues Barings had brought to the London market since 1882 had been foreign, the *Statist* complained that investors who purchased these issues were given little to rely on beyond Barings' reputation. The "prospectuses," the magazine noted, "were too frequently . . . not merely meager, but quite insufficient to judge the character of the security." Furthermore, the magazine complained, "The Messrs Baring . . . never state the compensation they receive for bringing out either a loan or a company, though surely this is a material circumstance." The *Statist* worried that Baring Brothers had failed to exercise "a restraining influence upon borrowers . . . particularly Argentine borrowers, when it became evident that they were piling up debt too fast."

Such criticisms, however, did not prevent Revelstoke, and Barings, from plunging into a huge deal to finance a waterworks and sewage system for Buenos Aires. The plan called for a total investment of £21 million, payable in several installments, far larger than any similar previous transaction.[6]

The new issue flopped. Of the £2 million initial offering, only £150,000 worth of shares were actually sold to investors. Meanwhile, conditions in Argentina deteriorated. The government reneged on a commitment to sound fiscal and monetary policies, allowing inflation to spiral out of control. Violence broke out in Buenos Aires, and the water company was denounced as a feeding trough for corrupt politicians and rapacious foreign capitalists. Revelstoke, writing in mid-1890, was forced to admit that "the accounts we get from

B. Ayers are not very satisfactory. It seems to us that a crisis is almost inevitable and the consequences may be serious. Our money market is getting tighter daily . . . Argentine securities of all kinds are depressed and practically unsalable in any quantity and are likely to remain so for the present."[7]

In what must have been a profoundly humiliating experience, Revelstoke was forced to go hat in hand to Nathan Rothschild for assistance. Rothschild declined, and privately told associates that he thought Baring Brothers was doomed because of its large Latin American commitments. Revelstoke's last option was to seek aid directly from the Bank of England. On November 11 the Russian government planned to withdraw £1.5 million it had on deposit at Baring Brothers. Unless something was done quickly, Barings would be unable to meet the withdrawal.

After much agonizing, the Bank of England decided to organize a syndicate of British banking firms to rescue Barings. At first Nathan Rothschild was openly skeptical of the bank's plan, noting that it would require a large number of competing banks to work together, in the process making clear to everyone the dire straits in which Barings found itself. Barings had £15 million in notes outstanding, and Rothschild doubted that any hastily organized syndicate could possibly hope to raise the money required to meet these obligations if panicked holders presented Barings paper for payment all at once. But he also recognized the disaster an uncontrolled collapse would precipitate. He admitted to the prime minister that if the "catastrophe" played itself out, it would bring down many other firms and could destroy London's position as the financial center of the world.[8]

The Barings panic quickly spread across the Atlantic, slamming the New York stock market. The speed of telegraphic communication and the relative liquidity of many American rail stocks meant that nervous British investors could sell stocks in New York quickly to raise money. The *New York Times* described what happened: "London, caught loaded with unmarketable rattletraps from the furthermost ends of the earth, has been forced into a great financial liquidation; and the result has been long felt here—for finding the readiest market for their American stocks, the Europeans have sold back to us the greater portion of the United States railway stock investments." The panic in London quickly became an international panic, affecting investors in the United States not even remotely connected with Barings.

A meeting of leading London bankers was arranged by the governor of the Bank of England, who announced that the bank would contribute to a rescue fund if other major firms would also do so. The head of one of the largest London banks offered to contribute £500,000 if Rothschild would come up with a like amount. After some temporizing, Rothschild gave in and agreed to participate; the funds necessary to bail out Barings were quickly assembled. Later, one of the bankers in attendance claimed that Rothschild had been "shamed" into participating.

The rescue plan worked; once again the Bank of England had intervened to provide liquidity in a time of crisis. Part of the price of the Barings bailout was that the old Barings partnership was dissolved, to be eventually replaced by a limited-liability company. The financial losses (as well as the professional embarrassment) suffered by the original partners were acute. Ned's brother Tom Baring described the outcome bitterly: "The name and the glory and the position and everything is gone. Ned would have it all—glory and wealth. He might at least have guarded our good name. But it has all gone, offered up to his insatiate vanity and extravagance."[9]

Barings' essential cross-Atlantic position fell not to Rothschild but to the house of Morgan, befitting the greatly increased importance of the American capital markets in the world economy. At the beginning of 1895, the firm name of Drexel, Morgan & Company was shortened to just J.P. Morgan & Company, to reflect the true reality of control. John Pierpont Morgan also ran the London investment banking firm J.S. Morgan & Company.

A large, physically imposing man with a piercing glare, Morgan brought a sort of august dignity and respectability to a Wall Street community that had been dominated by the likes of Jay Gould, Jim Fisk, and Daniel Drew. Morgan made judicious use of his good name to certify the worthiness of American stocks and bonds, assuring foreigners that they could invest their money without fear of chicanery; it was not uncommon for American railroads to have 40–50 percent foreign ownership. The *Commercial and Financial Chronicle* noted,

"Many new issues are listed almost simultaneously in New York and London," and added that this was also increasingly true for Amsterdam, Berlin, and Frankfurt.

As a young man, Pierpont had witnessed firsthand the near-collapse of the Morgan family fortune in the Panic of 1857. That experience left him wary of the chaotic excess inherent in unrestrained markets, and he would seek to tame that excess whenever possible. Much of Morgan's career was devoted to restructuring American corporations (particularly railroads) with an eye toward reducing "wasteful" competition and financial instability. Ultimately, his objective was to make the market safer for investment capital, particularly foreign capital, which he saw as essential to the development of the American economy. By the 1890s the term "Morganization" found its way into the common lexicon. As broadly defined, it referred to massive reorganizations/mergers of railroad (and later industrial) corporations, to improve profitability and financial stability.

The need for restructurings was particularly acute in the railroad industry, where high fixed costs combined with low marginal costs encouraged ruinous competition. In Morgan's view, overbuilding of railroads, often funded by debt, had created excess capacity. Once the capacity was in place, the actual cost of operating trains on the rail lines was relatively low. This situation inevitably encouraged vicious rate wars, as railroads slashed fares in a frantic effort to win more business. In any sort of economic downturn, disaster resulted, as the railways were unable to earn enough money to pay their heavy debt charges. Morgan sought to provide a much more solid financial footing for the surviving companies.

Implicit in "Morganizations" was an enhanced role for equity financing that would have a dramatic impact on the nature and importance of the stock market. Morgan sought to reduce debt in restructured companies to manageable levels; this inevitably meant that equity capital would replace debt capital in the financial structures of the surviving entities. Debt required fixed interest payments that could be quite burdensome in periods of weak economic activity. Equity, on the other hand, required only that discretionary dividend payments be made when profits allowed. If railroads, and eventually other businesses, could be financed more by equity rather than debt, they would be much better prepared to survive periods of economic uncertainty.

Equity financing would be extremely important to the new industrial corporations that would within a few decades supplant the railroads as the primary engines of economic growth. Until the final decade of the nineteenth century, most such industrial concerns had faced great difficulty in obtaining outside financing. The bond market was closed to them because the volatile nature of their businesses (compared to relatively more predictable railroad revenues) was too risky for lenders, and the stock market was not sufficiently developed to raise large amounts of equity capital for industrial ventures. Large industrial enterprises like Guinness in Britain and Standard Oil and Carnegie Steel in the United States had originally been privately funded, financing expansion from retained earnings, not from accessing the capital markets. Many investors remained deeply skeptical of investing in industrial concerns. The prevalent view was voiced by Erasmus Pinto in his 1877 book *Ye Outside Fools! Glimpses inside the Stock Exchange*. Referring to stocks trading on the London Stock Exchange, Pinto advised, "Take no shares in industrial companies, unless fully acquainted with the concern."[10] As late as 1896, when Charles Dow created the Dow Jones Industrial Average to complement his index of rail stocks, there were only twelve industrial stocks listed on the New York Stock Exchange that he deemed worthy of inclusion.

The success of the Guinness offering, and others that followed, began to erode investor antipathy toward industrial companies. New publicly held industrial corporations were created in the United States and Britain at an accelerating pace; often these giants were created by merging several smaller competitors together. By 1900, 185 such amalgamations had occurred in the United States, valued at over $3 billion, nearly one-third of the total capital invested in American manufacturing enterprises. Even more massive creations followed, with huge numbers of new shares sold to the public. The greatest of them all was J. P. Morgan's gargantuan U.S. Steel, created in 1901 with a total capitalization of $1.4 billion; the federal government, with an annual budget of about $350 million and a national debt of slightly more than $1 billion, seemed small by comparison.

Equity financing, and the stock market that went with it, had truly become indispensable to the modern industrial economy.

New York was fast emerging as a competitor to London's dominance of the world financial markets, in large part because the industrializing American economy was now larger than that of Britain. The London Stock Exchange retained a substantial edge over its Continental rivals, however, because of the head start it had in developing capital markets, and also because of the consistently noninterventionist policy of the British government that allowed those markets to function freely. After the repeal of the Bubble Act in 1825, the British Parliament had stepped away from any real effort to interfere in the stock market, resisting periodic pressures that ran counter to its prevailing laissez-faire ideology.

This was not the case elsewhere in Europe. In France, concern over excessive speculation led to enactment in 1893 and 1898 of laws that restricted stock exchange activity and foreign ownership of securities. Similar concerns caused Germany to pass several restrictive acts, including the Bourse Law of 1896, which became (with later modifications) the fundamental legislation regulating the stock market in Germany. In both countries, much of the agitation against "speculation" originated in the agrarian sector. Farmers were perplexed, and often enraged, by sharp swings in the market prices of agricultural commodities. It was assumed (correctly in some instances) that speculators were manipulating the market. Since stocks were usually traded on or near the same exchanges that dealt in commodities, the stock market was tainted by association.

The sweeping German Bourse Law of 1896 prohibited the purchase on credit of most agricultural commodities as well as shares of industrial and mining companies. The law also established a Stock Exchange Register, which all so-called speculators were required to sign when they engaged in transactions. The intent of the law was to distinguish between the activities of these "speculators" and those of legitimate investors and businessmen. Unfortunately, the term "speculator" was poorly defined, leading to a great deal of uncertainty that stifled activity.

The net effect of these restraints was to drive business away from the organized stock exchanges. Within a year, over seventy branches of foreign brokerage firms were set up in Germany to channel orders outside the country for execution. Individual jobbers, who up until 1896 had been important factors in providing liquidity for trading on German exchanges, were squeezed out of the market. The big German banks benefited because only they had sufficient capital to continue to operate in the market without using credit, and also because they could take much of their trading in-house (away from the moribund stock exchanges) simply by matching up buy and sell orders from their clients.

Thus, unintentionally, the Bourse Law further strengthened the already dominant universal German banks. As described by one historian, the large German corporate banks in the late nineteenth century "monopolize[d] the financial arrangements of industrial concerns," serving them "from cradle to grave."[11] Entrepreneurs seeking financing would not think of going to the stock market; instead they would approach one of the credit banks. These banks maintained "a distinct staff of . . . industrial experts usually drawn from industry itself, and a highly developed department of information," for the purpose of examining new business opportunities and making long-term commitments to business enterprises.[12] The approach was very different from that of British banks, which would generally only make short-term loans, leaving the provision of long-term (equity or debt) financing to the public capital markets.

German banks developed very intimate relationships with German industry, often making substantial long-term loans or even taking direct equity ownership in client firms. (The fact that banks were allowed to vote the proxies for shares held on deposit for individual clients further enhanced their ability to influence corporate managements.) In effect, the banks substituted for the active capital markets that existed in Britain and the United States. Although some of the most onerous provisions of the Bourse Law of 1896 were repealed in 1908, the paramount role of banks in buying and selling stocks and in providing capital to business was never challenged.

Unlike the United States and the United Kingdom, both France and Germany placed restraints on the trading of foreign securities. The dubious rationale was that foreign investments somehow drained off needed capital from domestic markets. The cumulative effects of all the restrictive French and German legislation took their toll; by the turn of the century the volume of stocks traded on the London Stock Exchange exceeded that of all French and German exchanges (and all other Continental bourses) combined.

Outside of Europe, North America, and a few areas settled by Europeans, stock markets were virtually nonexistent. Organized equity markets were an exclusively Western institution. That was to change, as Japan, in one of the most remarkable transformations in history, sought to westernize itself at a breakneck pace. The impetus for reform was provided by the arrival in the 1850s of the "black ships," foreign warships that shocked the Japanese elite into the harsh realization of just how weak and backward Japan was. In an impressive example of collective will, the Japanese determined that it was necessary to push through a wholesale adoption of Western ideas in order to make Japan competitive, to create, as one popular slogan put it, "a rich country and a strong army."[13]

It was a very tough task. Japan was a primitive, almost feudal society; there was no system for the accumulation of capital or for the investment of capital in commercial enterprises. The economy had to be built from the ground up. Inevitably, the role of the government in effecting this transformation was paramount. The government provided funds, owned and operated major industrial concerns, and promulgated a series of new laws to regulate the modernizing economy. The intensive involvement of the Japanese government in all sectors of the economy, which persists to this day, originated during this period.

By 1880 the heavy financial burden caused the authorities to put up for sale most industrial enterprises other than those associated with railroads, telegraph and telephone systems, and military arsenals. These entities were sold for relatively low prices payable in installments. Even so, given the primitive state of the Japanese economy, the only parties capable of purchasing the new business firms were the wealthy families that already dominated the Japanese economic order. These family groupings would later evolve into the peculiarly Japanese organizations called *zaibatsu*, which literally means "financial cliques." Each *zaibatsu* house was headed by a family patriarch, usually a man of samurai descent. These large concerns, comprising banks and industrial enterprises controlled by the families Mitsui, Iwasaki (Mitsubishi), Sumitomo, and Yasuda, among others, would come to dominate that new industrial Japan.

Japan adopted the gold standard in 1871. The first Japanese joint-stock companies were formed in the 1870s; rules that limited shareholder liability were fixed in law in 1879, making possible the sale of government enterprises beginning in 1880. Early stock exchange regulations were promulgated in 1878 and frequently revised in succeeding years. Authorities sent out emissaries to inspect foreign exchanges and government regulations drew heavily on examples from both Berlin and London. Many of the new rules were quickly abandoned, however, as Japanese bourses reverted to patterns established by existing rice and commodity exchanges.

The Exchange Law of 1893, which remained the basic legal code for stock exchanges until 1943, ignored abuses such as secret transactions, wash sales, price rigging, and corners. Virtually no effort was made to protect individual investors, given the domination of the market by large family organizations. Soon, probably inevitably, a peculiar opprobrium became attached to the profession of *kubuya* (stock dealer).

The poor reputation of stockbrokers did not deter ambitious young men from seeking to make their fortune in the nascent Japanese stock market. One such man was Tokushichi Nomura, who had become fascinated by the stock market while working as an apprentice in his father's money-changing business. In spite of an unimpressive record in his early attempts at speculation, in 1904 Tokushichi persuaded his father to put up half the family fortune to bankroll an expansion of the family business into stockbrokerage. The younger Nomura's judgment proved to be correct; the market boomed in the midst of a strong economic expansion powered by the Russo-Japanese War. But Nomura was not content simply to act as a broker for clients buying and selling shares; he wanted the firm to be actively involved in buying shares itself. His timing was perfect; in the midst of what would prove to be one of Japan's greatest bull markets, virtually every purchase he made produced large gains. By the end of 1906, while still in his twenties, he was a very rich man.

Nomura carefully studied accounts of stock markets outside Japan and became convinced that the Japanese market would eventually collapse. Never one to hesitate, he abruptly reversed his position in the market, selling out the stocks he owned and then going short, selling shares he did not possess in the anticipation that they would decline. He eagerly awaited the market collapse he felt was inevitable.

Instead, the market rise continued, and actually accelerated. A distressed Tokushichi Nomura took out a large newspaper advertisement, warning investors that the market was badly overpriced. He sold still more stock short, with borrowed money. But nothing seemed to halt the market's inexorable upward movement.

Nomura was now desperate. He later recounted how at one point he hid under his desk and furtively rode through the streets in an enclosed ricksha to avoid creditors.[14] Forced to seek financial assistance, he approached a friend who was an officer at the bank that had already loaned him much of the money he had plunged into stock speculation. Nomura's plea for still more money was a calculated appeal on both a personal and a business basis. He was a man of honor, he said, and would certainly repay the loans once the inevitable market break occurred. But if he did not receive the additional loan, he warned, his firm would fail, most likely dragging the bank down with it. "I am betting my life that I am correct," Nomura stated. "If someone considers the matter thoroughly and does nothing, the outcome is the same as if he had considered nothing at all. I have never been wrong."[15]

Nomura got his loan. The market surged for two more days, then suddenly reversed. In two weeks in late January 1907, stocks plunged by more than one-third. By the end of the year the Japanese market had lost a staggering 88 percent from its January high. Nomura made three million yen from his short sales and became a legendary figure among market participants. But even Nomura himself could not possibly have anticipated that his young firm, Nomura Shoten (Nomura Securities), was, more than half a century later, to become the largest stockbrokerage in the world.

Tokushichi Nomura was acutely aware that the Japanese stock market was insignificant compared to the markets in New York and London. In 1908 he visited Wall Street and later wrote, "All the wealth of the world gathers here and is distributed outwards."[16] By comparison, the Japanese market looked like a petty collection of "rice dealers." Even though Nomura was a preeminent figure in the Japanese market, he was treated like an obscure Japanese tourist in New York. When he requested a meeting with J. P. Morgan, he was turned away at the door.

From Japan to Europe, equity markets at the turn of the twentieth century had become important institutions, playing an influential role in the world economy. Surprisingly, virtually no rigorous academic research had been done on those markets until 1900, when a young doctoral student at the Sorbonne in Paris named Louis Bachelier published his dissertation entitled *The Theory of Speculation*. Bachelier was the first to employ mathematical techniques to explain stock market behavior.

Bachelier's work was revolutionary. He was the first to make the argument that the stock market is "efficient"—meaning that prices set on stock exchanges, through the actions of many different market participants, represent the best possible valuation of individual stocks. As he put it, "Clearly the price considered most likely by the market is the true current price: if the market judged otherwise, it would not quote this price, but another price."

Bachelier observed that stock price fluctuations grow larger over time, and devised a mathematical approach to analyzing this behavior that is similar to the formula used by physicists to describe the random collisions of molecules in space. Much later, this process would come to be described as a "random walk."

As if this were not enough, Bachelier also developed early elements of probability theory, derived a formula that anticipated Einstein's research into the behavior of particles subject to random shocks in space, developed the now universally accepted concept of stochastic processes (the analysis of random movements among variables), and made an attempt to provide a mathematical valuation of futures and options.

Bachelier concluded that stock price movements were essentially unpredictable, and often could not be explained even after the fact.[17] Describing how prices were set in the market, he wrote, "Past, present and even discounted future events are reflected in the market price, but often show no apparent relation to price changes . . . . artificial causes also intervene: the Exchange reacts on itself, and the current fluctuation is a function, not only of the previous fluctuations, but also of the current state. The determination of these fluctuations depends on an infinite number of factors; it is, therefore, impossible to aspire to mathematical predictions of it . . . the dynamics of the Exchange will never be an exact science."[18]

Bachelier recognized the significance of his findings, stating, "It is evident that the present theory resolves the majority of problems in the study of speculation by the calculus of probability."[19] Six decades later, leading scholars agreed; one said, "So outstanding is [Bachelier's] work that we can say that the study of speculative prices has its moment of glory at its moment of inception."[20]

Regrettably, Bachelier never received much recognition during his lifetime. His dissertation was awarded "honorable mention" instead of the "very honorable mention" that was a prerequisite to securing academic employment. Part of the problem was that his research topic—stock speculation—was so unorthodox. One of his professors commented, "M. Bachelier has evidenced an original and precise mind." But he added, "The topic is somewhat remote from those our candidates are in the habit of treating."[21]

The stock market may have seemed "remote" to members of the French academy, but it was attracting increasing attention—and criticism—elsewhere. This was true even in the United States, which, like Great Britain, had adopted a laissez-faire attitude toward the market in the nineteenth century. In 1912 a Congressional subcommittee headed by Representative Arsène Pujo of Louisiana took up an investigation of what had come to be known as the "money trust," defined as a small, incestuous network of bankers and businessmen that presumably controlled the American economy. The committee counsel, Samuel Untermeyer, described this "money oligarchy" as a "system [that was] vicious and dangerous beyond conception."[22] No one doubted that J. P. Morgan was the committee's principal target.

The *Washington Post* urged the committee to "settle once and for all the question of whether a small group of men control the financial and business destiny of the nation." Many leading bankers and businessmen ducked the hearings, finding excuses for not testifying.

Morgan, however, agreed to appear, even though he was physically exhausted in what would prove to be the last year of his life.

The hearings quickly turned into an inquisition rather than an inquiry. But the aging Morgan held his own. Ultimately, his testimony, and those of other witnesses, did not elicit much information, but this did not prevent the subcommittee from condemning the activities of stock market operators and concluding that "the facilities of the New York Stock Exchange are employed largely for transactions producing moral and economic waste and corruption." The subcommittee also made specific recommendations, calling on Congress to mandate the incorporation of stock exchanges so that they might be regulated, to empower the government to determine the percentage of a stock's purchase price that could be borrowed by the buyer (margin requirement), to make manipulation illegal, and to mandate federal supervision of new issues of securities. In the end, however, none of these proposals was enacted.

Instead, the efforts of Congressional reformers were focused on the need to create a central bank to manage the supply of money and credit in the economy. In 1913 Congress established the Federal Reserve System, a central national bank disguised for political purposes as a system of regional banks ostensibly operated by private bankers. The impetus for creating the new institution had been provided by the Panic of 1907, when J. P. Morgan had acted as a "lender of last resort," organizing emergency loans to troubled banks and brokers to prevent an uncontrolled chain reaction of bankruptcies. The stark reality that the fate of the American economy had been so dependent on one man finally forced Washington to take action.

Much as the Bank of England had done in Britain, the purpose of the new American central bank was to prevent the monetary instability that had in the past precipitated financial panics. Charles Hamilton, the first governor of the Federal Reserve System, predicted that stock market panics "generated by the distrust of our banking system" would be relegated to "the museum of antiquities."[23]

The "progressive" reformers in the United States, who sought to restrain the concentrated power of large financial institutions, had no real counterparts in Germany and Japan. At the time of the Pujo hearings in America, the German system of universal banking (dominated by a few large institutions) that had begun with the *Grossbanken* in the 1850s was already well entrenched. Likewise, the *zaibatsu* in Japan were steadily consolidating their hold over the Japanese industrial economy. Non-Anglo nations, lacking the lengthy experience with free financial markets that characterized British and American capitalism, developed along very different paths, marked by much more concentrated economic power.

Whatever the character of different national economies, however, as the twentieth century opened, no one could argue that the stock market was not a thoroughly international institution, albeit with London as the indispensable center. Virtually no part of the globe was left out; it was possible to trade almost continuously around the clock, shifting with the sun from London to New York to San Francisco to Melbourne. Railroads still dominated the list of publicly traded stocks, with many American railroads raising as much capital overseas as in the United States. (One Canadian railroad, Canadian Pacific, was 80 percent owned by Europeans.) But by the end of the century investor interest was by no means restricted to railroads. New companies virtually anywhere in the world with intriguing prospects could tap into substantial amounts of capital.

A South African gold mining boom in the 1890s attracted feverish interest on all European exchanges, including lesser centers in Constantinople, Vienna, Madrid, Moscow, and Cairo, as well as Johannesburg. Even after the boom collapsed, some major companies like Rand Mines and Central Mining Corporation continued to be traded internationally and held in large quantities by non–South Africans. Other mining ventures developed large cross-border stockholdings; British companies like Rio Tinto and Tharsis, formed to exploit Spanish copper, attracted substantial interest outside of Britain, while Australian and American mining firms such as Broken Hill Properties and Anaconda also became international investment vehicles. Nobel Dynamite Trust of Sweden became an international stock, as did a number of Dutch, French, and German industrial concerns.

While the equity market could truly be said to be a global phenomenon by the beginning of the twentieth century, it still had a decidedly European tinge. Of the eighty-nine principal stock exchanges in the world, fifty were located in Europe, primarily Western Europe. Of the remaining exchanges scattered outside of Europe, most were in areas of European settlement, such as the United States and British Commonwealth nations like Canada and Australia, as well as in colonial regions (such as India). It has been estimated that by 1910 there were £32.6 billion of public securities held worldwide, owned by approximately 20 million investors. Of this total, Britons held 24 percent, Americans 21 percent, Frenchmen 18 percent, Germans 16 percent, Russians 5 percent, and Austro-Hungarians 4 percent, with 2 percent each held by Italians and Japanese.[24]

In spite of the restrictions placed by the French and German governments on foreign stock listings, there was a significant foreign presence even in these markets. Between 1893 and 1913 the percentage of foreign securities listed on the Paris Bourse rose from 25 percent to 34 percent, while in Berlin foreign listings rose over the same period from virtually nothing to nearly 20 percent. These numbers still paled in comparison to London. In 1913, 52.3 percent of all securities quoted on the London Stock Exchange were non-British.

Individual investors were the principal players in the stock markets in the early years of the twentieth century, but the role of private "institutional" investors (banks, insurance companies, etc.), which would come to dominate the markets at the end of the century, was beginning to be felt. There were no pension or retirement funds that invested in stocks; the idea that long-term investments in stocks were a suitable means of saving for retirement was still decades away. But banks had begun to invest some of their reserves in stocks as the market became more liquid, making it possible for the banks to easily raise money by selling their stocks when the need arose. More importantly, insurance companies (particularly life insurance companies) greatly increased their investments in publicly traded securities. The first such investments by insurance companies had been made at the time of the South Sea boom in 1720; by the beginning of the twentieth century it had become a standard practice, with the portion of life insurance company assets invested in securities rising from 24.4 percent in 1870 to 50.6 percent in 1913. Because the life insurance companies were themselves also growing rapidly at the same time, their holdings of shares and bonds, in absolute terms, actually went up by a factor of ten times over this period.[25]

In 1850, financial assets such as mortgages, bank deposits, government bonds, and corporate stocks and bonds made up 39 percent of all the assets owned by the British public. By 1913 the proportion had risen to 64 percent. Over the same period, the total amount of household assets, in real terms, also tripled, so effectively financial assets now formed a much larger share of a much larger pie. The most rapidly growing component of household financial assets was transferable securities, traded in public markets. Of these, the share taken by foreign stocks and bonds jumped from 8 percent to 28 percent.[26]

Because of the very unequal distribution of wealth, however, the average shareholder owned a very small number of shares; the bulk of British shareholdings was still concentrated in the hands of the wealthy. The percentage of the population that held a substantial percentage of their assets in stocks and bonds quadrupled between 1870 and 1914. But that represented an increase from only 0.8 percent to only 3.2 percent.

By 1913 international financial markets, including equity markets, had reached an apogee. Capital moved freely across international borders; Great Britain exported capital equivalent to 7 percent of its GNP in 1913, a figure that would never again be attained by a developed nation. The ratio of stock market capitalization to GNP in 1913 was higher for developed countries than it would be until the 1980s. The globalization of the early twentieth century fostered an optimistic belief that growing interdependency among nations would reduce, and eventually eliminate, the possibility of war, leading to a permanent era of peace and prosperity.

The case for early twentieth-century globalization was eloquently stated by the British writer Norman Angell in a book published in 1911, which was immediately made available in fourteen countries and eighteen languages. Angell's reasoning—that trade between nations and mutual dependence on financial markets would make military conflicts obsolete—bears an uncanny resemblance to the arguments of those today who advocate improved economic ties with states like China, so as to draw them firmly into the family of nations.

Regrettably, Angell's optimistic vision was to prove illusory. Just as global markets seemed to have triumphed over the vestiges of nationalism and mercantilism in 1914, the world war that many observers believed to be impossible exploded into reality. The war would take countless casualties, one of which would prove to be the flourishing new stock markets. The new international economic order that had seemed so promising would be swept away in the conflagration.

A NEW ERA

"IT CAME UPON US like a thunderbolt from a clear sky."[1] That is how one London Stock Exchange member described the advent of the Great War, now known as World War I. Even though there had been periodic war scares, virtually no contingency planning for the outbreak of war had been done by officials of the world's major stock exchanges. As a result, the immediate reaction to the sudden onset of the conflict was confusion, uncertainty, and fear. All major exchanges quickly determined that they had but one choice: to shut down.

Abruptly, the widespread buying and selling of stocks across international borders ceased, not to be restored for generations; the promising birth of a truly global stock market was brutally aborted. Paradoxically, the war would also set in motion other entirely unanticipated changes, initiating a process that would ultimately democratize the stock market, beginning the market's transformation into the modern, broad-based institution that it is today.

Panic began first in Vienna on July 25, 1914; by July 31 waves of selling had engulfed bourses from Berlin to Paris to London to New York. In Germany, major banks hastily organized a syndicate to support stock prices, without success, as selling quickly overwhelmed the syndicate's resources. In Paris, no real effort was made to stem the free fall that resulted from a complete absence of buyers. Stocks also fell sharply in New York, even though the United States was not

directly involved in the European conflict. New York market participants anticipated forced sales by European investors seeking to repatriate funds, and feared that hurried withdrawals of gold from the
United States by citizens of the belligerent nations could undermine
the financial health of American banks.

In London, where the stock market was the most internationalized, the potential for damage was greatest. German (and to a lesser
extent Austrian) banks and individuals were major participants in the
London market; suddenly they were "enemies," and monies owed by
them to British banks and stockbrokers were uncollectible. The London exchange, like most major European bourses, operated on a
fortnightly settlement system, meaning that transactions could be
outstanding for as much as two weeks before they were paid for.
London brokers and dealers faced the very unpleasant fact that thousands of trades they had executed for "enemy" nationals could now
not be settled. London Stock Exchange brokers and dealers routinely financed their business with bank loans; if the banks called in
their loans while the exchange members were unable to collect from
foreign clients, many exchange members would fail. Such a series of
bankruptcies might set off a chain reaction of other collapses, becoming a full-blown panic.

The unsettling reality was captured by a candid admission from
leading stockbroker Paul Nelke. Like most jobbers, Nelke had "always traded on credit." Before July 1, he said, he "had been a rich
man." But now, he conceded ominously, he "could not say."[2]

After the Stock Exchange suspended trading, the British government stepped in, freezing in place the bank loans that exchange
members used to finance themselves. From this point on, the London exchange and it members were to be entirely dependent on decisions of the government; without the moratorium on the repayment
of bank loans, many members would fail. All parties recognized,
however, that the moratorium was at best only a stopgap measure.
Eventually the viability of the banks themselves might be called into
question if they were unable to recover monies they had lent to
stockjobbers.

The Treasury, the Bank of England, and the Stock Exchange
hastily cobbled together a plan in which the settlement of all transac-

tions with "enemy" nationals would be frozen until after the war. In order to preserve the collateral backing bank loans made to stockjobbers, minimum prices for stocks were established, below which trading was to be prohibited. This effectively meant trading could not occur in many securities, where buyers were unwilling to pay the minimum prices. But at least the brokers and banks could maintain the fiction that the securities in question were of sufficient value to collateralize existing loans. Under these tight restrictions, the London Stock Exchange hesitantly reopened for business on January 4, 1915.

Elsewhere in Europe the situation was even more grave, with exchanges remaining closed indefinitely. The Berlin Stock Exchange did not finally reopen until late 1917, although "unofficial" trading resumed, off the exchange, in 1915, with tacit government approval. Even when the Berlin exchange reopened, no trading was allowed in bonds or preferred shares, on the grounds that such instruments would drain funds desperately needed for government war loans. The publication of stock quotes was banned throughout the war, so as not to incite speculation.

The New York Stock Exchange resumed severely curtailed trading in late 1914. It was soon discovered, however, that the war, far from being a threat to business in America, was to be a boon. While gold did flow out of the country in the first month after the war began, that flow soon reversed as foreign investors realized that the United States was a haven, safe from the rapidly expanding conflict. Demand for American exports by the Allied powers, as well as by nonbelligerent nations, rose dramatically. Trading restraints were found to be unnecessary as the market stabilized on its own and then began a sustained rise.

The Allied powers in Europe were quickly forced to suspend the hallowed gold standard, meaning that they would now have to deal with unstable foreign exchange relationships that were anathema to fixed-rate orthodoxy. Tight controls were clamped on to prevent destabilizing flows of funds. Citizens of the belligerent powers were effectively prohibited from buying foreign securities, because they could not obtain foreign currency for the countries they might want to invest in. Even purchases of securities issued by Allied states attempting to finance their war efforts were blocked. When it was pointed out that British exchange controls prevented Britons from investing in French and Russian bonds sold to finance the joint war effort against Germany and Austria, British authorities turned a deaf ear. Preserving the value of the British pound took precedence even over the desperate financing needs of Allied governments.

Bans were quickly imposed on stock market transactions by enemy nationals. It was well known that many Germans held American securities that traded in London, and it was feared that they would attempt to raise much-needed dollars by selling those securities. Soon the ban on trading was extended to all foreigners who had not lived in Britain for at least ten years or been naturalized for at least five. In a matter of a few months, the traditional acceptance of unrestricted capital flows that had made London the center for foreign investment flows was shattered. It would never be fully restored.

Even Britons of German or Austrian descent who were respected members of the Stock Exchange faced overt hostility. On the morning after the passenger liner *Lusitania* was sunk, the *Financial Times* reported that "few German or Austrian members had the temerity to enter the Stock Exchange, but those few who did put in an appearance were promptly surrounded by a hostile crowd and hustled out again."[3] The exchange went so far as to post a notice requiring members of German or Austrian birth to "keep away from the house at present."[4] Many of the banned members drew up and published elaborate declarations of loyalty, but this was often not enough.

Over one hundred exchange members banded together to form an "Anti-German Union," calling for the removal from the exchange of all members of enemy birth. When one broker, himself of impeccably English ancestry, wrote to protest the group's activities, he was scathingly denounced by a participant in the Union. "When your own wife, daughters and female relations have been raped to death by the huns," wrote the enraged Union member, "when your sons have been slaughtered by them, your house burned and your disgusting person driven into the ignominious slavery you so richly deserve, I hope you will see no occasion to change your views."[5]

Even the high and mighty felt the wrath of militant patriots, if only through innuendo and veiled criticism. Sir Ernest Cassel, who from the 1890s until his retirement in 1910 had been "the greatest financial operator since Nathan Rothschild after the Napoleonic Wars," was not immune, having been born in Germany decades earlier. Cassel had kept an active interest in the stock market after his retirement, and issued a public letter to the press after the commencement of hostilities testifying to his "unfailing loyalty and devotion to this country."[6] Questions about his patriotism were not stilled, however, and after the Battle of Jutland it was widely rumored that he had sought to exaggerate the adverse implications of the battle to profit in his market dealings.

Throughout Europe, investors systematically dumped their holding of overseas securities in the early months of the war. This trend was soon to be accentuated by government action on the part of the belligerent powers to requisition domestic holdings of foreign stocks and bonds, so that those securities (particularly those that were dollar-denominated) could be sold to gain needed foreign exchange. Domestic holders were compensated for the value of their securities with government bonds. This wholesale liquidation meant that the quantity of American securities held abroad fell from $5.4 billion in 1913 to less than $1.6 billion after the war, with most of the remaining amount consisting of U.S. government bonds.

To finance the war effort, Allied governments raised taxes and sold bonds. Total British government indebtedness jumped from £700 million in 1913 to a staggering £7100 million by 1919. Of that, £1.4 billion was raised abroad, primarily in the United States. Fully two-thirds of the $32.8 billion the American war effort cost was financed through the sale of bonds. The cost of the war was greater than the total amount spent by the federal government in the entire prior history of the United States, from 1789 to 1916.

Because belligerent governments did not want any competition in raising these huge amounts, new securities issues by business were prohibited unless they specifically aided the war effort. With very few new stock offerings coming to market and with rigid restrictions imposed that stifled activity, the importance of stock markets to the overall economy declined dramatically. In Germany, for example, new stock issues were brought to market in 1917 at only one-tenth the rate of 1913.[7] The vastly enlarged presence of government in the capital markets harkened back to the days, before the development of railroads, when government securities dominated the financial markets.

The massive intrusion of government into the capital markets was bound to have serendipitous effects; the most pronounced impact was the introduction of millions of middle-class people to the notion of purchasing securities. Large-scale public relations campaigns were mounted in the warring nations to encourage individuals to buy government bonds. One estimate of the number of British investors stood at 13 million in 1918, up from a mere 1 million in 1914. Virtually all the new investors had first been induced to buy war bonds. In the United States, broad-based appeals to small investors were made for Liberty Loans, the official title given to the war finance campaign. A nationwide network of Liberty Loan committees was set up, to be assisted by organizations ranging from local Chambers of Commerce to Boy and Girl Scout troops. Liberty Loan posters, which appeared everywhere, became something of a new art form. Impassioned pleas were made in theaters and other public forums. The first campaign raised money from 4 million separate individuals. The second was subscribed to by 9.4 million, the third by nearly 18.4 million, and the fourth received support from almost 22.8 million. Most of the subscribers had never invested in any type of security before.

The British historian Hamilton Whyte, commenting on the effect of wartime finance on middle-class Britons, wrote, "The effects of the war have been to enlarge the interest of the public in the movements of the prices of stocks and shares, and many of the smaller sums which previously lay dormant in current accounts, or which were allowed to remain on deposit or in savings banks accounts, are now finding their way into stocks and shares."[8] By the 1920s shareholding in Britain was far more widely dispersed than ever before, albeit it now consisting of holdings of domestic, as opposed to foreign, firms. One study of the seven largest British companies showed that they were owned by a collective total of 385,000 shareholders, with an average holding of only £311. Eighty-five percent of shareholders owned less than £500 worth of stock.[9]

A similar pattern emerged in the United States. Not only did the number of Americans who owned shares rise dramatically, but the distribution of shareholding in the United States shifted significantly from higher-income to middle-income individuals. One of the scholars who complied the data, Gardiner C. Means, wrote, "This represents a shift of almost revolutionary proportions, and of great social significance."[10] In 1917, when the United States entered the war, according to Means's survey people with annual incomes over $20,000 received 79 percent of all dividends; by 1921 the percentage of all dividends received by these "high income" individuals had fallen to 47 percent. Big increases in the share of dividend income were shown by taxpayers in the $1,000–$5,000 income group; in 1917 this group had received 9.5 percent of all dividends, but by 1921 they took in almost 23 percent.[11]

France, among the eventually victorious Allied powers, was affected the least. At the time of the war most Frenchmen, unlike Britons and Americans, did not even have bank checking accounts, preferring instead to hold cash. While significant quantities of French war bonds were sold to individuals, corporations and institutions purchased a proportionately greater percentage of the government debt than was the case in Anglo nations. French public acceptance of financial markets and investing continued to lag well behind that in the United States and Britain.

The fates of other Continental stock markets were even grimmer. The hyperinflation that devastated Germany in the early 1920s wiped out the savings of the German middle class; wholesale prices rose from an index value of 101 in July 1922 to an incredible 750,000 sixteen months later.[12] Even routine consumer transactions were badly disrupted; the price of a kilogram of sugar jumped from 474 marks in May 1923 to 5.6 *billion* marks a mere six months later. A story was frequently told of a worker who took a wheelbarrow full of marks to buy a loaf of bread. After reaching a bakery, he parked the wheelbarrow outside while he checked to see if any bread was available. When he came back out, he found that the money had been dumped in the street and the wheelbarrow stolen. Even had they wanted to, under these conditions most Germans did not have the resources to become significant investors.

German companies seeking equity financing were forced to go

abroad, and those few individual investors who still held foreign stocks had their shares requisitioned by the government to pay off the heavy reparations levied on Germany by the Allies. The Vienna exchange ceased to be a major market after the Austro-Hungarian Empire collapsed, and the nascent Russian exchanges were squelched by the Bolshevik Revolution. Across the continent of Europe stock markets withered and died.

Where equity markets survived, they were now largely national, not international, in nature. Nowhere was this change more evident than in London. In the period 1910–13, 71 percent of all capital raised in London was for foreign entities; this activity abruptly halted during the war years and never recovered. The proportion of British national wealth invested in domestic stocks rose from 23 percent in 1913 to 36 percent in 1927. As might be suspected, the proportion of national wealth invested in British government debt also jumped dramatically, from 5 percent to 18 percent over the same period. These gains came largely at the expense of overseas holdings.

In fact, the British government actively tried to restrain investment in foreign stocks in the postwar period, for fear such investment would put pressure on the value of the pound; Britons investing overseas would have to sell pounds to acquire the foreign currency necessary to pay for the foreign securities. Montagu Norman, the governor of the Bank of England, wrote to the Stock Exchange to this effect in 1925: "It seems essential that for the present all moneys available for investment shall, as far as may be possible, be retained in this country for the purposes of reducing the strain on the Exchanges."[13] The Stock Exchange complied, acting to block most new issues of foreign securities. The exchange, like the Bank of England before it, was now a semipublic institution. Government policy could be (and was) implemented through Stock Exchange actions without requiring specific legislation or official edicts.

It would be a mistake, however, to conclude that government policy alone was responsible for the decline of London as a center for international equity investment. The market itself dictated the suspension of British foreign investment. In the nineteenth century, relatively low interest and dividend rates in Britain had made the higher returns available overseas (particularly in the United States) attractive. But this relationship had reversed by the 1920s; interest rates and dividends were now generally higher in Britain than in the United States. In an era in which stocks were still evaluated on the basis of their current dividend rate (rather than on future earnings prospects, as today), there was little incentive for British investors to seek out foreign opportunities.

New York was now home to the largest stock market in the world, having surpassed London's during the war years. The New York Stock Exchange was mainly a market for domestic American securities, not a truly international exchange as the London exchange had been; the booming American market of the 1920s would be driven almost entirely by Americans, buying American companies. As in Britain, large numbers of middle-class investors, introduced to financial markets through war bond purchases, had entered the stock market for the first time. But otherwise the market itself had changed relatively little. In many ways it was still largely a primitive insider's game, shackled by conservative standards of valuation that appear hopelessly anachronistic today.

Dividends were all-important. The price an investor was willing to pay for a stock reflected what he would receive directly from his investment—his share of the company's earnings in the form of dividends paid out to him from those earnings. Since stocks were presumably riskier than bonds (which had fixed interest rates and guaranteed the return of principal on maturity), investors demanded dividends on stocks that were greater than the interest rates available from bonds, so as to be compensated for the extra risk. Dividend rates in all stock markets in the 1920s were higher than interest rates paid on government and high-quality corporate bonds, and had *always* been so.

The tool most commonly used today to value stocks, the price-earnings (P/E) ratio, had its origins in this analysis, although in a way that would now be considered backward. Appropriate P/E ratios for stocks were derived from dividends. As a standard rule of thumb, it was assumed that a mature industrial company should pay out between 50 and 60 percent of its earnings in dividends. In the early 1920s, dividends on industrial stocks listed on the New York Stock Exchange averaged between 5 and 6 percent. Therefore, if a company's annual dividend was between 5 and 6 percent of its price and was to represent between 50 and 60 percent of its earnings, the earnings per share must equal 10 percent of the stock price. Put in the form of the price-earnings ratio, the price of a share of stock should be ten times the company's earnings per share—a P/E ratio of 10 to 1. By 1920, the 10-to-1 P/E ratio had become a well-accepted rule of thumb for valuing industrial stocks.

Because it was not believed feasible to forecast future earnings accurately, price-earnings ratios were calculated on the basis of the *current* year's earnings. Richard Schabacker, financial editor of *Forbes* magazine, described the accepted methodology this way: "Since it is generally impossible to prophesy what earnings the stock will show in any future time, it is necessary to base this [P/E] ratio on the probable earnings for the current year."[14] Anything else was regarded as speculation, not investment.

The arbitrary derivation of appropriate P/E ratios from current dividend payouts resulted in relatively low stock prices. Since stock prices fluctuated with dividends, and dividend rates were relatively high, stock prices had to be relatively low to produce the required high dividend rates. (The dividend rate is simply the dividend per share divided by the price per share of the stock—hence the lower the share price, the higher the dividend rate.)

Some authoritative voices were beginning to question this conservative orthodoxy, however. Speaking in late 1920, Charles Schwab, the energetic president of Bethlehem Steel, posed a rhetorical question, "What's wrong with the market?" Schwab argued that stock prices did not adequately reflect the expansive potential of American industry. A self-appointed spokesman for the business community, Schwab never passed up an opportunity to proselytize on behalf of big business and his belief that the scientific management of large, modern corporations would bring a revolution in living standards for the entire population. Attributing much of the then-current economic malaise to the high tax rates introduced during the war and not yet repealed, Schwab vigorously voiced the Wall Street consensus that if the federal government would only get out of the way, business would bring about a quick return to prosperity and, inevitably, much higher stock prices.

Schwab was prescient, recognizing that changes were occurring in the economy that were not yet reflected in stock prices. The traditional methods of valuing stocks based on current dividend rates assumed that a mature company would pay out the majority of its earnings in dividends to its shareholders each year. Yet even by the time Schwab spoke, many companies were moving to abandon that practice. During the war some utility companies had adopted a policy of constant dividend payments, with any "surplus" earnings to be retained for future contingencies. This practice spread to industrial companies after the war and in a few years would be generally accepted. The "retained earnings" of the company would be used to finance expansion rather than be automatically paid out to shareholders in the form of dividends.

The idea that traditional, conservative approaches to valuing stocks were no longer valid was the central conclusion of a landmark book published in the United States by Edgar Lawrence Smith in 1924 entitled *Common Stocks as Long Term Investments*. Smith assembled empirical data to show that a diversified portfolio of common stocks had consistently outperformed bonds over long time horizons, explaining that the increasingly common practice of retaining earnings to finance future expansion created a "compounding effect" that gave the stocks of modern corporations an "upward bias." His book caused something of a sensation, both among academics and the financial press. Prominent economist Irving Fischer commented: "It seems, then, that the market overrates the safety of 'safe' securities and pays too much for them, that it underrates the risk of risky securities and pays too little for them, that it pays too much for immediate and too little for remote returns . . ."[15] In a nutshell, Fischer encapsulated the radical conclusion implicit in Smith's results—that investors, in a misguided quest for safety, were paying too little attention to future returns relative to current income. This idea had been slowly crystallizing for a number of years; now Smith's book provided a solid foundation for the new theory of stock valuation. Obviously Smith's work did not, by itself, cause the spectacular rise in the American stock market in the years following its publication. The market would have risen anyway, given the growth in the economy and in corporate earnings. But without doubt the rate of increase in American stock prices during the 1920s was greatly accelerated by the growing acceptance of new, forward-looking standards of valuation.

Why did the new, more aggressive, growth-oriented standards of valuation catch on first in the United States? Why were Americans more receptive to stocks as investments, and more willing than Europeans to embrace "riskier" strategies for stock investment? Edward Chancellor suggests that the history and culture of the United States make Americans much less risk-averse than other peoples. In *Devil Take the Hindmost*, Chancellor writes that the experience of colonizing a wild continent, pushing the frontier of civilization ever westward in the face of very real dangers, fostered a willingness to take chances. A people who would uproot themselves from their homes and travel long distances to settle in a hostile wilderness would presumably think nothing of risking mere money in speculation.

A pro-business entrepreneurial spirit did pervade America in the 1920s. President Harding, before dying unexpectedly of apoplexy in 1923, had openly called for "less government in business and more business in government." His successor, "Silent Cal" Coolidge, went him one better, stating bluntly that "the business of America is business." In keeping with the times, Bruce Barton, a consummate salesman and pioneer of modern advertising techniques, published a book entitled *The Man Nobody Knows*. Barton's subject, surprisingly, was none other than Jesus Christ. Barton argued that Christ, far from being a dreamer only interested in spiritual affairs, had been "the first businessman," whose parables were "the most powerful advertisements of all-time." Christ was, according to Barton, a man who "picked up twelve men from the bottom ranks of business and forged them into an organization that conquered the world." *The Man Nobody Knows* became the best-selling book in the United States in 1924.[16] It is inconceivable that such ideas would have received widespread acceptance in France or Germany.*

By the mid-1920s the United States found itself in a dominant po-

---

*Interestingly, a book entitled *Jesus CEO* made the *Wall Street Journal* business best-seller list in 2001.

sition in the world. Relatively low interest rates and relatively high stock prices (compared to non-American markets) meant that foreign investments often looked cheap to American investors. When British chancellor of the Exchequer Winston Churchill restored the pound to the gold standard in 1925, the potential for exchange-rate instability that had deterred foreign (American) investment in England was eliminated. American investors no longer risked losses that would result from a depreciation of the pound relative to the dollar. It was now possible to focus on the relatively cheap British stock valuations without worrying about exchange-rate shifts.

The extent of the difference in valuations between the American and British stock markets in the 1920s can be seen by comparing dividends and price-to-earnings ratios for American and British industrial stocks. As the American stock market boomed, P/E ratios for industrial stocks rose, from 10.5 to 1 in 1926 to 15.8 to 1 in 1929, while dividend yields in percentage terms fell from 5.3 percent in 1926 to 3.5 percent in 1929. In Britain, however, while price-earnings ratios rose and dividends fell over the same period, the magnitude of the moves were not nearly as pronounced. P/Es on the London industrials rose from 9.5 in 1926 to only 11.4 in 1928, when they peaked, declining slightly in 1929. Dividends remained high by American standards, slipping only from 6.17 percent in 1926 to 5 percent in 1928 before rebounding to 5.47 percent in 1929.

In the second half of the 1920s, meaningful amounts of money flowed from the United States to Britain, attracted in part by these cheaper prices. American investors acquired significant ownership in several major British firms; one of the largest was the (British) General Electric Company, which by 1929 was 40 percent owned by American investors. A new form of share ownership, called American Depository Receipts (ADRs), was created to facilitate investment by small investors in overseas stocks. An American broker in London, acting for an American client, would purchase shares in a British company but then issue an ADR against those shares rather than send the actual certificate to the American owner. The broker would hold the underlying shares and assume responsibility for the collection of dividends due and other bookkeeping matters, thus freeing the investor from those onerous chores. The ADRs traded freely in the market as a substitute for the underlying shares. By 1929 over fifty ADRs issued against shares in British companies were actively traded in New York.

ADRs were needed because of the increasing importance of middle-class investors to the stock market. Large investors could rely on personal brokers to deal with the intricacies of foreign investing; small investors did not have that luxury. Paul M. Warburg, a managing partner of Kuhn, Loeb, commented on how Wall Street had been changed by the influx of new participants. "Where heretofore investment banking addressed itself primarily to the comparatively few possessed of large incomes . . . successful distribution of large volumes of new securities can only be carried on by following wealth into the millions of small rivulets and channels into which it now flows."[17]

Clarence Hatry, a brash newcomer to the City of London, recognized how the small investor was changing financial markets. In 1926 he founded Corporation and General Securities, the vehicle by which he would become famous (or infamous). To win more business, the firm irritated established investment bankers by cutting the underwriting spreads (fees) charged by bankers to handle new issues of stock.[18] It also pioneered mass advertising techniques aimed at small investors. Hatry used his earnings to finance an extravagant lifestyle, sailing in a $112,000 yacht and outfitting his wife with $1.4 million in jewelry. His rambling house included an upstairs swimming pool, a glass-floored winter garden, and nine bedrooms.[19] The ostentatious display of wealth served a business purpose, however. As the New York Times later put it, Hatry's "amazing flair" "inspired confidence . . . in investors."

Hatry was not content simply to act as an underwriter and broker for mid-sized businesses seeking to tap the newly available pool of middle-class savings. He became directly involved in a number of the businesses he underwrote, including photography equipment, industrial machinery, retailing, and steel. In early 1929 he devised an ambitious plan to merge several British steel companies, seeking to increase their efficiency. He committed a substantial portion of his firm's (and his own) capital to the endeavor. The effort was ill-timed, as a general economic downturn set in. By June Hatry was in a bind. The sources of financing for his new venture were drying up, and it was obvious that competing London bankers (who still resented his newfound prominence) would do nothing to assist him.

It was at this point that Hatry stepped over the line. When Hatry's Corporation and General Securities, Ltd., underwrote securities for a client corporation, it would customarily give scrip* to buyers until the actual new securities were issued and delivered. But to cope with his cash flow crisis, Hatry covertly issued more scrip than was required to facilitate the steel merger. That extra scrip was then used as collateral for bank loans. Hatry clearly believed that he needed only bridge a short-term financing gap, after which point he would be able to make good on the loans before any damage was done. He was badly mistaken.

As the British economy worsened, the financial markets continued to fall, and money became even tighter. Unable to come up with the funds to make good on the scrip loans, Hatry was exposed. Bankers holding the scrip realized that their "collateral" was worthless; the revelation shocked the City of London. The Hatry affair touched off several investigations in Britain and led to vocal calls for government-mandated reforms.

Hatry himself was eventually convicted of forgery and conspiracy. One observer friendly to him later wrote that while there had been "serious irregularities," Hatry was not inherently criminal. He was, instead, "a man of high quality and notable achievement, who was caught in a world depression and hoped, by taking risk, to win through, not for himself but for his enterprises."[20] The justice who sentenced Hatry had a slightly different perspective. Hatry's explanation for his actions, the justice noted, "was the defense of any office boy who robbed a till to back a winner."[21]

Although Hatry's business career reached an unpleasant conclusion, his basic insight—that the stock market was no longer an institution of interest only to the very wealthy—was valid. Rising markets

*The term "scrip" refers to a provisional certificate entitling the holder to receive new stock when it is issued.

in both Britain and the United States in the 1920s were driven by expanded middle-class participation. In America, for the first time, the stock market became part of the common culture.

The man who best personified the market to millions of Americans was a veteran trader named Jesse Livermore; a new phrase, "If only I had Livermore's money," entered the common lexicon in the 1920s. A popular (albeit highly sanitized) biography of Livermore appeared in 1924, and was quite influential in shaping the views of many persons who would later themselves be major players in the market. Edward Crosby Johnson II, who would establish the extremely successful Fidelity mutual funds, first became interested in the stock market when he read Livermore's biography. Years later Johnson said, "I'll never forget the thrill. Here was a picture of a world in which it was every man for himself, no favors asked or given."[22] Livermore "operating in the market," Johnson exclaimed, "was like Drake sitting on the poop of his vessel during a cannonade. Glorious."[23]

In reality, Livermore made his reputation by manipulating the press as well as stocks. Several times over his career he lost millions and was wiped out. But each time he would return chastened to what he really did best—persuading wealthy backers to give him another chance. To Jesse Livermore, Wall Street was a "giant whorehouse," where brokers were "pimps" and stocks "whores" on which customers threw their money away. Livermore—a "madam" who for a percentage arranged it all—wanted only a chance to play the game.[24] But to many small investors Livermore was a visible example of a poor farm boy who had made a fortune in stocks. Others could, presumably, do the same.

Stock prices, as measured by the Dow Jones Industrial Average, rose by more than 400 percent from their 1921 low to the eventual 1929 high. In 1927 President Calvin Coolidge declared that America "was entering upon a new era of prosperity"; immediately the phrase "New Era" was picked up by commentators, who used it as a catchword for what many believed promised to be a period of permanent prosperity. According to New Era advocates, the scientific management of business and the implementation of sound economic policies by government would eliminate the troublesome boom-and-bust cycles of the past, generating steady growth and rising wealth for all Americans.

Economic statistics buttressed the New Era case. Revolutionary new technologies were reshaping the American economy and American business. In 1919, for example, only 32 percent of the machinery in American factories had been powered by electricity. By the late 1920s that figure had risen to nearly 50 percent and was continuing to climb, with concomitant increases in productivity. The replacement of horse-drawn wagons by trucks and automobiles traveling a network of newly built highways was revolutionizing transportation. And other, still newer industries based on radical new innovations (such as broadcasting and aviation) held out the prospect of even greater gains in the future. The statistics on productivity for the decade reflect these technological advances; in the ten-year period beginning in 1919, productivity grew at an annual pace of 3.7 percent, one of the highest rates on record. In the face of this undeniable progress, who could really dispute the optimistic outlook of the New Era proponents?

Not only were corporate profits growing rapidly, valuations (as expressed in P/E ratios) were also expanding. P/Es for New York Stock Exchange industrial stocks, which had routinely languished below the traditional standard of 10 to 1 prior to the 1920s, expanded to 13.9 to 1 in 1927, to 14.2 to 1 in 1928, and to more than 16 to 1 in 1929. While these ratios still appear quite conservative by modern standards, in the late 1920s they inevitably raised the concern that the market was overvalued, presumably due to "excessive speculation."

The stock that best symbolized the presumed speculative excess of the late 1920s was Radio Corporation of America (RCA). RCA was the leading player in the glamorous new broadcasting industry; it manufactured radios and operated radio stations, and was aggressively pursuing the new technology of television. The stock shot up from $32 per share in 1926 to $127 in 1927, and to an astounding $574 (adjusted for a split) in 1929. In a graphic demonstration of how standards of valuation had changed, this huge gain occurred even though the company had never paid a dividend.

But critics of excess speculation—who focused most on the absence of a dividend—failed to appreciate the growing importance of earnings growth to stock market valuations. In 1925, RCA had earned $1.32 per share. By 1928 it was earning $15.98 per share. Even though the stock price jumped from $32 to $420 over this period, the P/E ratio hardly expanded at all. Was a P/E ratio of 26 to 1 excessive in 1928, given the company's record of success and potential for future growth? By the standards that would consistently prevail in the future, it most certainly was not.

According to accepted wisdom, the last years of the 1920s bull market blur together into one long, exuberant binge. Investors were carried away with enthusiasm for New Era innovations and growth, losing all sense of perspective. But a careful reading of the financial press at the time does not support this monochromatic interpretation. There were many voices sounding cautionary notes in 1928, warning that the market had advanced too far too fast.

The respected financial editor of the *New York Times* Alexander Dana Noyes consistently expressed words of caution. He was not alone. A major brokerage firm ran prominent ads asking, "Will You Overstay the Bull Market?," while Moody's Investment Service warned that prices were too high, having "overdiscounted anticipated progress." Bernard Baruch advised friends to watch economic statistics with care; he was concerned that a crash might be in the making.

Herbert Hoover, as Secretary of Commerce in the Coolidge Administration, also worried about the ebullient stock market, although he did not actively publicize his views. He wrote in his memoirs that he first became concerned about the "growing tide of speculation" in 1925, condemning it as a crime "far worse than murder[,] for which men should be reviled and punished." Hoover claimed he had requested that "the editors and publishers of major newspapers and magazines . . . warn the country against speculation and the unduly high price of stocks," and that he had asked Federal Reserve Board governor Roy Young and Treasury Secretary Andrew Mellon "to strangle the speculative movement."[25]

Congressional critics of speculation spoke out as well. In early 1928, the Senate Committee on Banking and Currency held hearings on the subject. Senator Carter Glass, who had been instrumental in creating the Federal Reserve System, questioned whether "the public speculating in stocks on the stock exchange" understood "the real intrinsic value of the stocks" they traded. He cited the sharp decline in price of a particular stock and asked, "What is that but gambling?" Senator Robert La Follette went further, decrying "the great American evil of stock exchange speculation."[26]

It is thus clearly not correct to suggest that there were no voices of caution during the market boom. But the American stock market shrugged off these views, rising more than 40 percent in 1928, including a significant jump after Hoover was elected President in November. The P/E ratio of the Dow Jones Industrials increased from 12 to 1 to 14 to 1, and the market closed on the last trading day in December at its high for the year. American investors, growing more accustomed to aggressive standards for valuing stocks, began to seek out cheap stocks in other markets, much as British investors had searched the world for attractive opportunities in the nineteenth century. A "New Era" truly seemed at hand.

CRASH

IN A STOCK MARKET COMMENTARY on September 9, 1929, the *New York Times* warned: "It is a well-known characteristic of 'boom-times' that the idea of their being terminated in the old, unpleasant way is rarely recognized as possible." In fact, the American stock market had already peaked on September 3, a day that at the time appeared to be of little note. An erratic downward trend commenced, continuing into early October, but it did not elicit much concern. Most observers expressed optimism, both about the stock market and the economy. One of the most prominent New Era believers, Yale economist Irving Fischer, proclaimed on October 15 that "stocks have reached what looks like a permanently high plateau."[1]

Fischer's timing could not have been worse. Little more than a week later, on October 24, the accelerating decline turned into a rout. The stock ticker, which disseminated prices to brokerage offices around the world, could not keep pace. Worried investors could not find out what was happening; uncertainty inevitably incited fear. By 11:30, the market had disintegrated in panic.

The New York Stock Exchange closed its visitors' gallery but could not prevent a crowd from gathering on the street outside. Rumors were rampant, and policemen arrived to prevent any disturbances. When a workman appeared atop a nearby building, many in the crowd assumed he was preparing to jump. One observer thought that the faces in the crowd showed "not so much suffering as horrified incredulity."[2]

Reporters scrambled to cover the unfolding story, and soon ascertained that leading Wall Street figures were assembling at the offices of J.P. Morgan & Company to deal with the crisis. Their purpose was to organize a consortium to support the market. The senior Morgan partner, Thomas Lamont, presided over the meeting, causing the press to draw comparisons to the successful effort by J. P. Morgan, Sr., to halt the panic of 1907.

When the meeting concluded, Lamont told the assembled journalists that the bankers had decided to pool their resources and use the money to stabilize stock prices. In what Frederick Lewis Allen later called one of the most remarkable understatements of all time, Lamont said, "There has been a little distress selling on the stock exchange,"[3] but added that the decline was "due to a technical condition of the market," and was "susceptible to betterment."[4]

The agent for the banker's pool was Richard Whitney, acting president of the New York Stock Exchange and a leading light of New York society. Whitney appeared on the Exchange floor at 1:30, going first to the post where U.S. Steel stock traded. He entered a bid of $205 per share (the price of the preceding trade) for 10,000 shares, then proceeded methodically to place similar bids for other major stocks. The effect was immediate; prices jumped up almost as violently as they had fallen earlier in the day. In many cases, Whitney did not actually have to buy much stock, the psychological effect of his bids being sufficient to stem the collapse.

A record volume of nearly 13 million shares traded on October 24, and the bankers and brokers who organized the pool were, for the moment at least, heroes. The market rose the following day, and held steady in the short Saturday session. Even the normally cautious *New York Times* opined that Wall Street could now be "secure in knowledge the most powerful banks in the country stood ready to prevent a recurrence." President Hoover declared that "the fundamental business of the country . . . is on a sound and prosperous basis." He reportedly declined, however, to make a positive remark about stock prices.[5]

Most of the press commentaries over the weekend were positive; the consensus seemed to be that the worst was over. But shockingly, the market broke badly again on Monday. Even rumors that Charles Mitchell, chairman of National City Bank, was meeting with Morgan partners did not stem the slide. (If Mitchell did in fact meet with Morgan partners, it was likely to obtain a personal loan to cover his own losses, not to organize another pool to support the market.)

By coincidence, Winston Churchill had been present in the visitor's gallery of the Exchange before it was closed during the Thursday panic. On Monday evening he attended a dinner party in his honor organized by Bernard Baruch. Charles Mitchell, and several other bankers who had participated in the effort to stabilize the market, were also present. Mitchell made light of his travails, offering a joking toast to "my fellow former millionaires."[6] Most of the attendees were cautiously optimistic, hoping the market had seen its bottom.

The following day—Tuesday, November 29, to be forever known as "Black Tuesday"—wiped out those hopes. A crushing 16.5 million shares traded in a precipitous drop that erased all the gains of the previous year. The men behind the bankers' pool gave up all pretense of further intervention; Thomas Lamont tried to argue that it had never been the intent of the bankers' pool to maintain a specific level of stock prices. Chagrined, he was forced to deny reports that the bankers had actually been selling stocks short (conducting a bear raid) to profit from the distress of others.

The slide continued until mid-November, when a recovery of sorts finally began. At its November low, the market (as measured by the Dow Jones Industrial Average) had dropped nearly 50 percent from its early September high. The ferocity of the decline stunned most observers, but surprisingly, despite its magnitude, there was little immediate spillover into foreign markets. Indicating how the international connections so important to the pre-1914 stock market had withered by 1929, the *Economist* noted during the worst of the New York rout that the "role of the London Stock Exchange during the past week has been largely that of an interested but passive spectator."[7] Other European bourses, while generally falling, did not experience the panicky selling witnessed in New York.

British stocks had in fact been declining for some time in the face of slower economic activity brought on by the Bank of England's tight money policy. In the sobering new environment that now prevailed on both sides of the Atlantic, the antics of operators like Clarence Hatry and Jesse Livermore, which had often been a source of bemusement when stock prices were rising, took on a more sinister character. The British Parliament, in a direct response to the Hatry affair, passed the Company Act of 1929, requiring greater disclosure by companies issuing shares to the public. There were bitter after-the-fact denunciations of the London stock market "boom" of 1928, which, according to one writer, "foisted a great deal of worthless trash on the public, and very few securities of permanent worth."[8] A more rigorous analysis, looking at the subsequent performance of 1928 stock issues, found that by 1931 additional issues of stock by established companies had fallen only 18 percent, while issues by companies entirely new to the market had tumbled 83 percent. Many critics blamed the London Stock Exchange authorities for accepting so many new listings of such dubious quality. Significantly, the critics, both in and out of government, were increasingly unwilling to rely on the Stock Exchange to regulate itself.

In the United States, where the bull market of the late 1920s had been more ebullient than in Britain, public perception of the market changed even more radically. Prominent Wall Street bankers and leading market operators, who had only months before been lionized in the press as titans of finance, now suddenly seemed impotent at best or mendacious at worst. Even the recently retired president of the New York Stock Exchange, E.H.H. Simmons, denounced the imprudent speculation widely believed to have led to the crash. Referring to the events of 1929, he noted, "Every serious break in the stock market is always attributed to over-speculation . . ."[9]

Some critics went further, arguing that the problem lay not simply in occasional periods of speculative excess, but in the nature of stocks themselves. In 1931 Lawrence Chamberlain and William Hay wrote *Investment and Speculation*, implicitly attacking Edgar Smith's landmark 1924 work *Common Stocks as Long Term Investments*, which had provided a rationale for the 1920s boom. "Common stocks," according to Chamberlain and Hays, "are not superior to bonds as long-term investments, because primarily they are not investments at all. They are speculations." The new standards of valuation—emphasizing future earnings projections rather than current dividends—that had characterized the "New Era" of the 1920s bull market were now widely discredited. Worse still, excesses resulting from the acceptance of the new standards were blamed for the severity of the crash in the United States, which in turn was seen by many critics as a cause (or at least a precursor) of the Great Depression.

The notion that a dangerous instability was inherent in free-market capitalism itself, and not just in the American stock market, gained rapid acceptance after 1929. In 1928, at the height of the decade's prosperity, Joseph Schumpeter had published an article entitled *The Instability of Capitalism*. In it, he referred to "the tendency toward self-destruction [in a capitalist economy] from inherent economic causes . . ."[10] Schumpeter's article had received little attention outside of academia when it was first published. But in the early 1930s, as financial crises seemed to spawn still other crises in rapid succession, his ideas received a great deal of exposure and growing acceptance.

"Speculators" whose activities were presumed to contribute to the destabilization of markets (and entire economies) became targets of opprobrium. Deeply ingrained beliefs that had antecedents in early religious thought came to the fore, as the Depression of the 1930s was blamed by many on the excess speculation that had preceded it. One prominent U.S. senator declared that the stock market was "evil," a "great gambling hell" that should be "closed down and padlocked." Unwittingly, he was echoing views expressed earlier by Karl Marx, who had written that speculation played about the same role in economics as did "original sin in theology."[11]

The evil speculator was already a stock figure in literature, transcending national boundaries, from Augustus Melmotte in Anthony Trollope's *The Way We Live Now* (1875), to Friedrich Spielhagen's Philipp Schmidt in *Sturmflut* (1877), to Frank Algernon Cowperwood in Theodore Dreiser's *The Financier* (1912).[12] In an introduction to a twentieth-century biography of Swedish speculator Ivar Krueger, John Kenneth Galbraith warned that "no one should imagine" that financial crimes were confined to any one place or one time. Speculative excess, and financial frauds associated with speculation, were ubiquitous.[13] In the harsh environment of the 1930s, popular animus toward "speculators" mixed together with serious academic critiques; British economist Lionel Robbins placed the blame for the market crash and subsequent depression on "the proliferation of fashionable fraud" and excessive "speculation."[14]

To some prominent Americans, the market crash and its aftermath represented a kind of rough punishment for the sins of excess. Treasury Secretary Andrew Mellon thundered, "Let the slump liquidate itself. Liquidate labor, liquidate stocks, liquidate the farmers, liquidate real estate . . . it will purge the rottenness out of the system. High costs of living and high living will come down. People will work harder, live a more moral life. Values will be adjusted, and enterprising people will pick up the wrecks from less competent people."[15]

The search for scapegoats was on. Market operators like Jesse Livermore in the United States and Clarence Hatry in Britain were obvious candidates. One leading American newspaper declared, "Livermore, formerly one of the country's biggest speculators, [was] the leader of the bear clique" that drove down stock prices.[16] The *New York Times* observed that "the ascendancy of Livermore to the position he once held as a leading market operator on the bear-side after years of eclipse is one of the most intriguing developments of the market." The *Wall Street Journal*, while not specifically identifying Livermore, complained that there had been "a lot of selling to make the market look bad."

Many analysts also believed that the misbehavior revealed by the sudden collapse of Clarence Hatry's financial empire helped trigger the disastrous events on Wall Street in October 1929. Charles Geisst, in his well-received 1997 history *Wall Street*, wrote that "Hatry's failure sent reverberations straight across to Wall Street in the autumn of 1929, just when the market was at its most vulnerable point." Contemporary press accounts discussed possible selling in New York by British investors, with the *Financial Times* observing, "Wall Street heard reports that London speculators were selling heavily [in New York] in order to raise funds to meet settlements in connection with the Hatry collapse." The *Economist* cited "several indications of 'protective selling' [in New York] and of the transfer of funds to London as a result."

Unfortunately, although the likes of Livermore and Hatry made appealing villains, their influence on events was greatly exaggerated. While Livermore made about $6 million selling stocks short during the crash, he apparently lost about the same amount on stocks he owned. Financially, he was no better off than before. In fact, none of the major market operators (including Livermore) possessed the wherewithal to have caused the crash, even if they had desired to do so. The market was simply too big to be manipulated by a single individual.

The Hatry failure occurred in September, more than a month before the New York market crash. The affair made headlines in the New York press, but with no noticeable impact on the stock market. There were additional minor articles in the *New York Times* and the *Wall Street Journal* in October, but they dealt with mundane matters like the denial of bail to Hatry and after-the-fact synopses of Hatry's difficulties. The articles were very brief, and could hardly have had a significant effect on the American market.

There simply were not enough European investors left in the American stock market for their actions to have precipitated the 1929 crash. The great American bull market of the 1920s was almost exclusively a domestic affair. Most European investors had thoroughly divested themselves (or been forced to divest themselves) of American stocks during or shortly after World War I. But the press (and many historians) were still caught up in an earlier (prewar) era, in which international capital flows were the norm. Nearly two months after the worst of the New York crash, the *New York Times* published a scathing denunciation of Hatry, blaming him in part for the collapse. "Our Ponzi's," the *Times* wrote of Hatry, "simply are not in a class with the long succession of modern British adventurers and buccaneers of whom Clarence Hatry is the latest and, in terms of the havoc he has wrought, the greatest . . . the enormous Hatry vacuum compelled the withdrawal of London money from Wall Street and helped precipitate our own October panic."

Overall, criticism of speculation was strongest in the United

States. Undoubtedly this was because the stock market crash and subsequent depression were more severe than in other industrialized countries. But was the stock market boom of the 1920s really the product of irresponsible speculation, which ineluctably, almost as in a biblical morality tale, was followed by a crash and depression?

Recall Charles Kindleberger's defining conditions for a speculative bubble, described in Chapter 2. First, something new occurs, which appears to have revolutionary implications. This can be a decisive change in the political environment (such as South American countries' gaining independence from Spain in the early nineteenth century) or it can be the appearance of radical new technologies that seemingly hold out great profit potential. These exogenous "new" events impact the markets by creating expectations of rapid economic growth and large profits.

Such an exogenous shock alone, however, is not enough to inflate a speculative bubble, according to Kindleberger. It is also necessary that an ample supply of ready credit be available to facilitate speculation. Easy money provides the fuel that ignites the boom. Then, as interest in the market increases, new participants are attracted to the game, and the bubble inflates at a rapid rate until it inevitably bursts.

Do the events in the American stock market in 1929 conform to this model? At first glance, there are important similarities. New technologies, ranging from electricity to automobiles to aviation to broadcasting, were creating the rapid productivity gains glowingly cited by New Era advocates. The Federal Reserve appeared to loosen credit, pumping up stock prices. And anecdotal accounts of the period make frequent reference to large numbers of inexperienced speculators, enticed into the market by skyrocketing stock prices, who by their actions pushed up stock prices more and more until shares were trading at "irrational" levels.

There is no question that new technologies provided much of the rationale for the New Era bull market. But beyond that "exogenous" event, the applicability of the speculative bubble model to the 1920s market is dubious at best. According to conventional wisdom, the Federal Reserve created the conditions for the speculative orgy by cutting interest rates at the wrong time, thereby providing easy credit to fuel the stock market boom. These ill-advised easings had been the result of efforts to halt the flows of gold into the United States in the mid-1920s that had destabilized foreign currencies, notably the British pound. By reducing American interest rates, the Fed made dollar-denominated investments less attractive to Europeans. Adolph Miller, a member of the Federal Reserve Board who opposed the interest rate cuts, later said that the decision to reduce rates represented "the greatest and boldest operation ever undertaken by the Federal Reserve System . . . [which] resulted in one of the most costly errors committed by it or any other banking system in the last 75 years."[17] Lionel Robbins of the London School of Economics agreed, stating that "from that date, according to all the evidence, the situation got completely out of control."[18] In this view, the stock market boom of the late 1920s (and thus the subsequent crash) was given impetus by a mistaken Federal Reserve monetary policy driven by foreign exchange considerations.

But was Federal Reserve monetary policy really all that easy during the 1920s boom? In their classic work *A Monetary History of the United States: 1867–1960*, Milton Friedman and Anna Schwartz calculated that "the stock of money . . . failed to rise and even fell slightly during most of the expansion—a phenomenon not matched in any prior or subsequent cyclical expansion. Far from being an inflationary decade, the 1920s were the reverse." (U.S. consumer prices actually declined over the decade at a rate of 0.9 percent.) The stock market boom of the late 1920s could not have been caused by easy money, because money was not easy.

What of Kindleberger's third requirement—that large numbers of inexperienced speculators flood into the market, forcing prices ever higher, to ever more unreasonable levels? Popular accounts of the period portray an American public caught up in an orgy of speculation. A British correspondent in the United States wrote how the stock market invariably dominated conversations at social affairs he attended: "You could talk about Prohibition or Hemingway, or air conditioning, or music, or horses, but in the end you had to talk about the stock market, and that was when the conversation became serious."[19] A familiar story, variously attributed to Joseph Kennedy or Bernard Baruch, describes how even shoeshine boys were dispensing tips on the market in the summer of 1929. John Brooks, in

Once in Golconda, describes scenes of brokerage offices packed with amateur speculators who had quit their jobs to devote full time to the market.

Unfortunately, this popular conception of 1929 does not conform to observable reality. It is estimated that between 4 and 6 million Americans (15–20 percent of American households) owned stock by 1928. Most of these people, however, owned very small quantities, often purchased through plans where customers of public utilities were allowed to buy shares in the utility companies that served them, or through limited employee stock-purchase plans where employers sold small amounts of stocks to their employees. The number of Americans who regularly traded stocks was far smaller. In 1929 there were approximately 1.5 million active brokerage accounts in the country, out of a population of 120 million consisting of between 29 and 30 million households. Of these 1.5 million accounts, 600,000 were margin accounts, in which borrowed money could be used to buy stocks. Since some investors maintained more than one broker-age account, the total number of people holding accounts was un-doubtedly significantly less than 1.5 million, and the total number of individuals maintaining margin accounts less than 600,000. From this data it appears that only 3–4 percent of American households were actively engaged in stock trading in 1929, with less than half that number investing on margin.

More recent analyses of the American stock market crash and the Depression of the 1930s refute the notion that the crash was the re-sult of "overspeculation" or that the crash in any way caused the De-pression. While P/E ratios in the late 1920s were certainly higher than they had been at the beginning of the decade, this was due more to the fact that ratios had been extremely low earlier rather than that they were inordinately high in the late 1920s. (The average P/E ratio for New York Stock Exchange–listed industrial stocks in 1929 was only about 16 to 1, which is fairly conservative by standards that would prevail for most of the second half of the twentieth century.)

Writing in the *Business History Review* in 1975, Gerald Sirkin cited data going back to 1800, from which he identified a major change in the nature of the growth process in the American economy beginning early in the twentieth century. According to Sirkin, before

1900 most growth in the economy was generated by providing more capital to business. After 1900, however, much of the economy's growth resulted from increases in productivity, which enhanced the return on capital earned by business and accelerated the rate of increase in corporate earnings. This evidence provides statistical justification for the arguments of New Era proponents like Irving Fischer.

Specifically analyzing market valuations in 1929, Sirkin concludes the market P/E ratios were justified by the growth of earnings in the late 1920s. While some stocks were overvalued, he found that the overvaluation was concentrated in only approximately 20 percent of stocks, leaving the overall market fairly priced. Sirkin writes that the data do not present a picture of "speculative orgy" in "a time of madness." Instead, in his words, most stocks were "cold sober," although a few did show signs of "over-indulgence." His conclusion: "not much of an orgy."

Several other studies have confirmed Sirkin's view.[20] But regardless of what subsequent research would show, it was widely accepted in the 1930s—both among academics and the general public—that excess speculation and the consequences thereof were instrumental in bringing about the economic collapse of the 1930s.

Sirkin's work came much too late to salvage the reputation of New Era proponents such as Irving Fischer of Yale, whose widely publicized remark just days before the crash—that stocks were on a "permanently high plateau"—would be used against him again and again. In 1930, Fischer attempted to defend himself in a book entitled *The Stock Market Crash—and After*. He did not back away from his belief that science-based productivity gains and growing economies of scale had permanently increased the profitability of American business. Corporate earnings, Fischer showed, rose at an annual rate of 9 percent from 1922 to 1927, and increased even more rapidly after that. (Profits for the first nine months of 1929 were 20 percent above profits for the comparable period in 1928.) Fischer concluded: "This record is eloquent in justification of a heightened level of common stock prices during 1929."

Unfortunately, *The Stock Market Crash—and After* received a hostile reception. As *The Commercial and Financial Chronicle* commented, "The learned professor is wrong as he usually is when he talks about the stock market." Critics attacked Fischer personally, noting that he had lost most of his own wealth in the market. It was also alleged that Yale's endowment fund, which Fischer advised, was hit hard by the crash, but this was untrue. The "conventional wisdom" that New Era advocates were hopelessly misguided would dominate economic thought and public policy for decades.

Whatever the cause of the American stock market Crash of 1929, by 1931 it was the Great Depression, not the lingering aftereffects of a speculative orgy, that wreaked havoc on world financial markets. As the Depression deepened, a financial crisis swept through Europe; bank runs in Austria and Germany were touched off by fears that high-profile business failures would pull down major commercial banks that had lent money to the bankrupt entities. On July 13, 1931, the large German Danat Bank failed, forcing the government to declare a two-day "bank holiday" and close the Berlin Stock Exchange.

Britain now found itself vulnerable because of its overpriced currency. Sterling had in fact been under pressure for most of 1930, with the Bank of England requiring support from the Bank of France and the Federal Reserve to maintain its value. The pronounced slump in British exports associated with the Depression, and the loss of earnings from shipping and overseas investments, created imbalances in the supply and demand for sterling that could not be sufficiently mitigated even by strict exchange controls. In early 1931 John Maynard Keynes referred to "an extraordinary nervosity about [the pound] in the London market," which led to "more or less open talk about the devaluation of sterling and the abandonment of the [gold] standard."[21] In just over two months after July 13, Britain lost over £200 million in gold reserves trying to support the pound.

In a frank memo to the prime minister, Keynes wrote: "when doubts as to the prosperity of a currency, such as now exist about sterling, have come into existence, the game's up."[22] In fact the game was up. On September 20, 1931, Britain was forced to abandon the gold standard, effectively devaluing the pound. Interestingly, reflecting the diminished importance of the stock market, London Stock Exchange officials were not even consulted about the decision, ex-

cept to ascertain if they intended to close the exchange in the immediate aftermath of the announcement. The exchange did in fact close
for four days. When it reopened, the following ominous notice was
posted for all members to see: "The Chancellor of the Exchequer
wished it to be stated that any British Citizen who increased the
strain on the Exchange by purchasing Foreign Securities himself or
assisting others to do so was deliberately adding to the country's difficulties."[23] The chancellor of the Exchequer, Neville Chamberlain,
warned that "this country is in no position to invest large sums at
long-term in foreign countries."

The climate of opinion in the United States was even more fore-
boding, perhaps because the decline in stock prices was so much
more severe. The London market eventually regained its 1928 peak
level by 1935, and moved higher thereafter. The American market,
however, as measured by the Dow Jones Industrial Average, dropped
a calamitous 87 percent from its 1929 high to its 1932 bottom, and
would not again reach its 1929 level for twenty-five years, in 1954. By
March 1933, when newly elected President Franklin Roosevelt took
office, the nation's financial system was on the verge of collapse. To
deal with the crisis, the President declared a "bank holiday." As part
of the "holiday," all stock exchanges were closed from March 6 to
March 14. Many bankers and brokers spoke openly of the possibility
of revolution. Joseph P. Kennedy, himself one of the leading market
operators, wrote three years later that "I am not ashamed to record
that in those days I felt and said I would be willing to part with half
of what I had if I could be sure of keeping, under law and order, the
other half."[24]

The federal government moved overtly to intervene in the economy and the financial markets as never before. The first area the
Roosevelt Administration targeted for regulation was new stock
offerings; the President asked that such regulation be based on "the
ancient truth that those who manage banks, corporations and other
agencies handling other people's money are trustees acting for others."[25] He insisted that "the burden of telling the whole truth [be
placed] on the seller."[26] Congress quickly passed the Securities Act of
1933, requiring that most new stock issues be registered with the

government and that investment banking firms underwriting those offerings adhere to strict standards of disclosure.

Next, the Administration proposed and Congress enacted the Banking Act of 1933 (the Glass-Steagall Act). This legislation separated commercial and investment banking activities by prohibiting commercial banks from underwriting or trading equity securities. In effect, it forced commercial banks to divest themselves of their investment banking and brokerage operations. The legislation also established the Federal Deposit Insurance Corporation to insure private bank deposits, on the theory that if these deposits were protected by a government agency, panicky withdrawals of deposits in times of stress on the banking system would be prevented. The FDIC would go on to become a remarkable success, making runs on banks a thing of the past.

This reform legislation was largely unopposed by Wall Street. Most of those in the financial community recognized that serious problems did exist, and that some new regulation was inevitable. But when the Roosevelt Administration proposed what would become the Securities and Exchange Act of 1934, which directly regulated stock market trading, it ran into fierce resistance. Richard Whitney, president of the New York Stock Exchange, complained that such a law would cause "the nation's securities markets [to] dry up."[27]

Whitney and other critics were ignored. The sweeping act banned insider trading, defined as trading based on "material non-public information." It prohibited various schemes that were commonly used to manipulate stock prices, and forbade the deliberate dissemination of false information. A Securities and Exchange Commission was created to enforce the new regulations. Its powers were so broad that, as one observer noted, "there is scarcely a single aspect of the operations of a securities exchange which is beyond the commission's reach."[28]

The Securities and Exchange Act also empowered the Federal Reserve to set margin requirements regulating the percentage of the purchase price of a stock an investor was required to put up, without borrowing, to finance the purchase. Low margins were widely assumed to have exacerbated the crash of 1929. Reformers believed that requiring investors to come up with more of their own money to purchase stocks in the first place would make forced selling less likely during market declines.

By contrast, relatively little legislation to reform the stock market was enacted in Britain in the 1930s. "Share pushing"—whereby promoters sold questionable new issues to the public—was a continuing concern, and resulted in an official government inquiry in 1937. The investigation concluded that the main victims of such scams were inexperienced investors who demonstrated a "curious reluctance to seek any advice before parting with money or securities."[29] The "Share Pushing" investigation did lead to the Prevention of Fraud Act of 1939, a comprehensive piece of legislation designed to clean up abuses in the new issue market. But the government never seriously considered, much less enacted, a far-reaching system of market regulation similar to that in the United States.

Despite new regulations designed to protect individual investors, stock markets around the world were thoroughly discredited by the mid-1930s. Thus it is surprising, and perhaps ironic, that one of the most important books ever written about the stock market was published in 1934. Given a title—*Security Analysis*—that made it sound like a textbook, the book outlined a systematic quantitative approach to valuing stocks. The authors were David Dodd and Benjamin Graham. Graham is today generally conceded to be the father of modern security analysis.

Born Benjamin Grossbaum, Graham changed his name during World War I because "Grossbaum" sounded German. He was described by a friend as "a funny little guy, sort of ugly,"[30] and his interests as a youth ran toward classical literature and Spanish poetry. He considered a career in academia, but a fascination with the stock market ultimately led him to take a job on Wall Street after he graduated from Columbia in 1914.

When Graham arrived on Wall Street, little research was available on stocks. The traditional practice of evaluating shares was based almost exclusively on current dividends, and required relatively little in the way of analysis other than a judgment that the dividend was secure. But Graham sought to do more. He attempted, through a detailed examination of a company's financial statements, to find opportunities that the market was overlooking, usually companies whose assets were not properly valued in their stock prices. Because few other investors engaged in such analysis, Graham was able to find and exploit many instances of misvaluation.

Graham was very successful during the 1920s but lost a lot of money in the early 1930s after the crash, when his conviction that prices had fallen too far caused him to buy heavily just at the onset of the Great Depression. But this experience did not cause him to adopt the Chamberlain-Hay view that stocks were by definition speculative. He still believed that solid analytical techniques could make stock investing consistently profitable for prudent investors.

A securities analyst using the Graham and Dodd approach would endeavor to calculate a stock's "intrinsic value" and then compare it to the actual market price of the stock. Graham and Dodd rejected the traditional definition of "intrinsic value"—the book value of a company's shares (assets per share minus liabilities per share). Their research showed that book value had no relationship to corporate profits or stock prices. Instead, Graham and Dodd argued that "intrinsic value" was "that value that was justified by the facts, e.g., the assets, earnings, dividends [and] definitive prospects" of a company.

To Graham and Dodd, "definitive profits" meant stable patterns of revenues and profits that could reasonably be used to predict earnings going forward, not the "capitalization of entirely conjectural future profits." They admitted that their approach was not suited for periods of rapid change or substantial uncertainty. It was "manifest . . . that future changes are largely unpredictable, and that security analysis must proceed on the assumption that the past record affords at least a rough guide to the future."

Graham and Dodd laid the groundwork for what is known today as "value investing." But the real significance of Graham and Dodd's work was that it set out a rigorous method of evaluating stock prices that went beyond simply looking at the current dividend rate. In a way, even though both Graham and Dodd disdained what they saw as the excesses of the New Era, their approach ratified one of the fundamental concepts underpinning the 1920s boom—that earnings, not dividends, ultimately drive stock prices.

Unfortunately, the international financial environment of the 1930s was not hospitable to new approaches to stock market investing. Instability and recurrent crises were the norm. By the later years of the decade, every major nation had been forced to abandon the gold standard. In its place, exchange controls were imposed; purchases and sales of foreign currency could only be made with government approval. The German control regime was the most comprehensive, with the central bank allocating foreign exchange only for imports of products that were deemed either "essential" or necessary "up to a certain extent." Importers of products that were designated "unnecessary" by the Reichsbank were denied access to foreign currency, effectively blocking imports of those goods. No foreign exchange was allocated for capital export.

In France the leftist Popular Front government threw out the regents governing the central bank, the Banque de France. The new governor, Ernest Labeyrie, believed that money markets and speculation should be rigorously controlled. Under his direction, the Banque began to "investigate" speculators who were alleged to be moving money abroad, thus undermining the franc. The government itself followed up with legislation imposing penalties on persons who did not disclose capital they had invested abroad, and on those who "attacked the state's credit" by organizing capital flight.[31]

John Maynard Keynes described, and endorsed, the new "nationalism" that was replacing the previous internationalism of finance in a 1933 essay entitled "National Self-Sufficiency." "I sympathize, therefore," Keynes wrote, "with those who would minimize, rather than with those who would maximize, economic entanglements between nations. Ideas, knowledge, art, hospitality, travel—these are the things which should of their nature be international. But let goods be homespun whenever it is reasonably and conveniently possible; and, above all, let finance be primarily national."

While the stock market was not the primary target of the new economic nationalism of the 1930s, the inevitable result was to drastically curtail the importance of world equity markets. Cross-border trading of stocks was largely eliminated, both by government restrictions and by uncertainties associated with rapidly fluctuating ex-

change rates. The brief revival of international investing that had occurred in the late 1920s was snuffed out.

Stock markets everywhere were far less important than they had
once been. The Berlin Stock Exchange was relegated to a minor role
in the Nazi-directed economy, while in the Soviet Union no markets
of any kind were permitted. In the United States the stock market
was severely discredited by the widespread belief that abuses and imprudent behavior had triggered the Crash of 1929 and the Great Depression. By 1939, average trading volume on the New York Stock
Exchange fell below one million shares per day for the first time
since the early 1920s; even the outbreak of war in Europe in September failed to spark a sustained increase in activity. In 1929, 125,000
people had been employed in the securities industry; by the end of
the 1930s the number had fallen below 40,000. In 1928, 17 percent
of all Harvard Business School graduates entered the investment
business; in 1940 only 4.4 percent did.[32] The *Christian Science Moni-
tor*, reflecting a widely held opinion, wrote, "A fair case can be made
for the thesis that stock exchanges in general are permanently
shrunken in economic performance in the last decade."

When World War II commenced in September 1939, it had little
immediate impact on world markets. The London Stock Exchange
closed for a mere six days before reopening, a far cry from the
lengthy suspension of trading that had occurred in 1914. The American stock market, unlike 1914, also showed little reaction. Foreign
investment was a much smaller factor in the markets of 1939 than it
had been in 1914, and the stock market was of much less importance
in an economy increasingly dominated by government.

In a way, the world stock market had come full circle. The trading
of securities had originated centuries earlier because of the growth of
government and government debt needed to finance wars. Over
time, as the laissez-faire ideas of Adam Smith triumphed over mercantilism, the importance of government in markets and the economy receded, replaced by free markets for private equity capital. But
in the first half of the twentieth century, pressures on free markets
arose from the urgent need to make war, a growing perception that
the new class of middle-class investors had often been maltreated by

market professionals, and, finally, the widely held belief that speculative capital flows undermined national economies. Under these pressures the heavy presence of government returned, at the expense of free, active equity markets. It can safely be said that as the world plunged into the dark abyss of World War II, stock markets had declined in importance to a point that they were almost irrelevant to the world economy.

BRETTON WOODS

JOHN MAYNARD KEYNES is generally regarded as the most influential economist of the twentieth century. His *General Theory of Employment, Output and Interest Rates*, published in 1936, challenged the basic assumptions of classical economics. Keynes provided a rationale for government intervention in the economy, through deficit spending and other measures, to mitigate the severity of economic downturns like the Great Depression of the 1930s. Keynes had more direct influence in the formulation of economic policy than any who had preceded him.

Lionel Robbins, himself an eminent economist, said of Keynes: "[He] must be one of the most remarkable men that have ever lived—the quick logic, the birdlike swoop of intuition, the vivid fancy, the wide vision, above all the incomparable sense of the fitness of words." Robbins said only a figure such as Churchill could be compared to Keynes, in that Keynes possessed the same "unique, unearthly quality of which one can only say is pure genius."[1]

Keynes was the dominant figure at the Bretton Woods Conference of 1944 held to establish a postwar international monetary system. Keynes hoped to create a radically different regime to replace the traditional gold standard. He felt that in the previous five hundred years, an international monetary system based on gold had worked tolerably well in only two fifty-year periods—the Elizabethan age in the late sixteenth century, when the world was awash in gold from Spanish America, and the Victorian age in the nineteenth century, when Britain, through a policy of free trade and overseas lending, kept the world supplied with gold and sterling. Keynes abhorred the chaotic mixture of floating exchange rates, competitive deflation, exchange rate depreciation, and restrictive trade legislation that had characterized the disastrous 1930s, as the gold standard broke down. The power of his intellect—and his ego—made it possible for him seriously to consider radically redesigning the world economic order.

What Keynes now proposed was to replace the gold standard with nothing less than a central bank for the world, performing a role not unlike that of the Bank of England or the Federal Reserve System. The bank would act as a lender of last resort to entire nations. Keynes went so far as to name a new international currency unit— the bancor—in which transactions between nations and the new world central bank would be denominated.

The U.S. delegation to the Bretton Woods Conference was led by the brash and often truculent Harry Dexter White, a close confidant of President Franklin Roosevelt. White's conception of the postwar economic order was very different from Keynes's. The Americans wanted, first and foremost, a stable system of exchange rates that would put a halt to the chaotic exchange rate fluctuations of the 1930s. Such a system, given the overwhelming preeminence of the American economy, would effectively make the American dollar the currency standard for the world and force other countries to adapt their economic policies to keep their currencies in line with the dollar. The Americans were very suspicious of Keynes's proposal for a world central bank. The United States was not about to fund any new international bank in a way that would allow other nations to draw upon it (and American resources) without very tight restraints.

Keynes and the British delegation struggled mightily to amend the American plan. They were concerned that the proposal would place a straitjacket on other nations, making them unable to respond to their own internal economic conditions. A world central bank, as Keynes proposed, would provide the liquidity necessary to allow greater freedom of action by individual nations. Lacking that, Keynes hoped to allow for more flexibility in the exchange rate mechanisms, so that the nations of the world would not be bound so tightly to the American dollar and thus to American economic policies.

Inevitably, friction developed. Keynes was never one to tolerate what he perceived to be a lack of intellectual rigor, and he did not make much effort to hide his contempt for some of the American proposals. Several members of the American delegation personally felt the sting of his acid remarks. One commented sarcastically that Keynes seemed to view himself as a "god-like" creature, preaching to mere mortals.

But no amount of intellectual brilliance on Keynes's part could compensate for the economic realities of 1944. The United States had by far the strongest economy in the world, while Britain was nearly broke. Grudgingly, the British delegation gave in. The eventual agreement created a monetary system in which currencies were to be fixed in relation to each other, within a small band of permissible fluctuation. The International Monetary Fund (a hollow version of the world central bank Keynes envisioned) was created to make temporary funds available to countries that had difficulty in sticking to the fixed exchange rates. But the fund was far smaller than Keynes wanted, and was burdened with restrictions that placed most of the onus of correcting exchange rate problems on the individual countries themselves. Nations with temporary balance of payments difficulties could draw on the fund, but they were expected to expeditiously take steps to eliminate their problems and repay the loan. Only those countries that faced a "fundamental" long-term disequalibrium in their balance of payments would be permitted to revalue their currencies. In effect, as Keynes feared, most nations in the world would have to conform their internal economic policies to those of the United States, or risk currency crises.

Keynes put on a brave face and worked diligently to sell the deal to a skeptical British government. As he admitted frankly during one point in the debate, "What alternative is open to us . . . ?"[2] Largely due to his efforts, the accord was ratified by a reluctant Parliament. Shortly thereafter, Keynes was forced to travel to Washington as a supplicant, seeking a loan to keep Britain afloat. It must have been a humbling experience. Having started his life as a member of the ruling class of a world empire, he was now reduced to the role of a beggar.[3]

Keynes soon fell ill with the sickness that would take his life less than one year later. He left as his legacy a radical new body of economic thought, eventually dubbed Keynesian economics, that allowed for much more proactive involvement by government in the private economy. The Bretton Woods system and Keynesian economics would dominate macroeconomic policy and international financial markets for years to come.

Largely overlooked at the time, the Bretton Woods accord also created a Bank for Reconstruction and Development (later to become the World Bank). The purpose was to make loans to developing countries. Included in the agreement was a provision encouraging the formation of private capital markets in developing nations, but this was generally ignored. Virtually no mention was made of a role for equity markets. In the eyes of policy makers, stock markets had diminished so much in importance that they were nearly irrelevant.

In fact, one area where Keynes had been in agreement with the New Deal Democrats setting policy in Washington was in his suspicion of unfettered international capital markets. He frequently compared financial markets to a casino. Keynes wrote, "Nothing is more certain than that the movement of capital funds must be regulated;—which in itself will involve far-reaching departures from laissez-faire arrangements."[4] The sentiment for capital controls drew heavily on what was seen as a definitive study by the economist Ragnar Nurkse, published at the time of the Bretton Woods negotiations. Nurkse examined the fate of the French franc after World War I:

> The post-war history of the French franc up to [restoration of the gold standard in] 1926 affords an instructive example of completely free and uncontrolled exchange rate variations . . . The dangers of . . . cumulative and self-aggravating movements under a regime of freely fluctuating exchanges are clearly demonstrated by the French experience . . . Self-aggravating movements, instead of promoting adjustment in the balance of payments, are apt to inten-

sify any initial disequalibrium to produce what may be termed "explosive" conditions of instability . . ."[5]

To contain this destructive instability, the Bretton Woods agreement *assumed* that controls would be maintained on capital flows between nations, even though the agreement required that signatory countries move to eliminate currency controls that affected foreign trade. This distinction was very important. There was a strong ideological commitment to the notion that free trade between nations was beneficial to the world economy. But there was an equally strong suspicion of speculative international capital flows, which were seen as unproductive and destabilizing.

Clearly the Bretton Woods accords did not contemplate global securities markets, including equity markets. In fact, while there was a smattering of tiny stock markets around the world in 1945, only two really mattered: those in the United States and Britain. And, as has been seen, the actual significance of even those markets was in doubt. Both markets had been discredited by scandal and by the protracted declines in stock prices during the early 1930s.

Corporations were turning away from the equity market as a source of financing. During the war, both the U.S. and British governments had exercised tight controls over new issues of securities, forbidding those that were not deemed critical to the war effort. (Only 1.5 percent of the money raised by new issues through the London Stock Exchange during the war was for private business.) But even after the war, major companies, flush with wartime profits, didn't really need new financing. Increasingly, big business was able to finance itself by means of internally generated funds.

In the immediate postwar period, the political climate was often overtly hostile to the very notion of free markets. Nowhere was this more evident than in Britain after the upset victory of Labour over Winston Churchill's Conservatives in July 1945. The *Financial Times* Index of London Stock Exchange Stocks immediately dropped 10 percent on the release of the election results. The incoming chancellor of the Exchequer, Hugh Dalton, had long been contemptuous of the stock market, seeing it as a speculative plaything of wealthy investors. He soon embarked upon a campaign to hold down dividends, arguing that "in the national interest, capital development must stand in front of higher dividends."[6]

Dalton initiated measures affecting the stock market that were clearly punitive, including an additional 7.5 percent tax on profits distributed as dividends and a doubling of the "stamp duty" on stock transactions from 1 to 2 percent. The Bank of England itself spelled out the new reality in 1946, concluding that "the [stock] market must resign itself to some general control over security movements for some time to come." Some Labour Party activists went even further. Robert Hall, an economic adviser to the cabinet, noted in his diary that "the Stock Exchange is mad anyway and I don't think we should take any notice of them."[7]

The socialists who dominated the Labour Party placed great faith in the ability of the government to manage the economy. Similar views were held by leading politicians on the Continent; in countries like France and Italy, the major opposition was the Communist Party, which routinely received one-third or more of the popular vote in national elections. In this decidedly leftist political environment, a stock market as a device to allocate capital was seen as little more than an anachronism.

Chancellor Dalton declared his intent to build a wall around the British economy, through a system of controls on capital and foreign exchange markets. The government also proceeded apace with its program for nationalizing key industries, including coal, electric utilities, and railroads. In Labour's view, government management of the economy had proven successful in the war, mobilizing the nation's resources to defeat Nazi Germany. Why not extend the same approach to peacetime? As Prime Minister Clement Attlee put it, "We have got to get something other than the profit motive. I cannot see why the motive of service to the community should not operate in peace as it did in war."[8]

Ironically, despite the overtly hostile attitude of the government toward market capitalism, the Labour program of nationalizing key industries initially had a positive impact on stock prices. The government planned to compensate stockholders in nationalized industries with government bonds; in theory, removing so many shares from circulation would create a "scarcity" value for other equities. When plans to nationalize the railroads were announced in 1946, the stock market jumped 3 percent in two days. A similar rise occurred when plans to nationalize the electric utilities were put forth two months later. It was presumed (correctly) that many former holders of these nationalized companies would not be satisfied with the low yields on the government bonds they received and would sell those bonds to reinvest the money in stocks that paid higher dividends.

Dividend yields remained the all-important measure of value. As one British analyst wrote, "Whether we like it or not, it is quite certain that it is dividend yields which govern security values."[9] A good example of this pervasive orthodoxy can be seen in a *Financial Times* commentary at the end of the war, which concluded that British stocks in general were overpriced. Comparing yields on industrial equities, which averaged 4.33 percent, to 3 percent consols, the *Financial Times* concluded: "It cannot be said that a 1.33% gross is sufficient margin for the difference in risk between gilt-edged stocks and a commercial venture."[10] No allowance was made for any growth in earnings that might occur.

The inevitable result was stock prices that appear to be quite cheap by today's standards, and (conversely) dividend yields that appear quite high. After wartime controls were relaxed in the late 1940s, the P/E ratios of stocks listed on the London and New York exchanges were routinely less than 10 to 1. For example, in 1949 representative P/Es for industrial stocks in the United Kingdom averaged 7.75 to 1, while in the United States they worked out to a mere 6.17 to 1, one of the lowest figures of the twentieth century.

Understandably, equity financing was not an attractive alternative for companies facing the prospect of selling their stock at such cheap prices. This particularly hurt firms in industries defined by radical new technologies, which needed access to attractively priced equity capital to finance their rapid growth rates. The fates of companies in two important postwar American "growth" industries—television and computers—are illustrative of the problem.

As demand for television sets exploded, the stocks of companies that produced the sets (such as Motorola, Zenith, Admiral, Emerson, and RCA) took off. The sharp share price rises, however, caused dividend rates to fall to between 3 and 4 percent, well below what was available elsewhere in the market. *Business Week* took note of the problem, warning that future dividend increases in the group would not keep pace with the jump in stock prices. "When you are growing as fast as TV," *Business Week* cautioned, "you have to conserve cash to take care of expansion costs and needs for new working capital. It is doubtful if the industry will be able to pay out in dividends more than a small part of earnings for a long time." Perversely (at least by today's standards), rapid growth financed by retained earnings was seen as a mixed blessing, because it consumed money that could otherwise be paid out in dividends. As a result, most of the television manufacturers were forced to increase their dividends, in spite of the need for capital to finance growth, in an effort to satisfy investors. The need to conform to Wall Street's time-honored standards could not be ignored.

These conservative standards also crimped growing companies in the nascent computer industry. A good example was Eckert-Mauchly Computer Corporation, one of the few manufacturers of computers in the immediate postwar period. The company seemingly had a promising future, but heavy start-up costs meant that earnings would be skimpy in the early years and dividends would be nonexistent. Because of this, the equity capital markets were closed to Eckert-Mauchly; investment bankers would not underwrite shares in such a "speculative" company, and the public would not buy. Commercial bank financing was likewise unavailable. Like many small, fast-growing companies, Eckert-Mauchly was finally forced into a merger with Remington Rand to form Univac. At the time, a merger with a larger, deep-pocketed firm was often the only way for a promising small company to secure the financing necessary to expand.[11]

In Britain the effect of orthodox valuation standards was even more acute. Because of pressure from the Labour government to hold down dividends, payouts to shareholders had not been growing as fast as earnings. The market, focusing on the low dividends, virtually ignored growth in profits. Good examples can be seen in the case of two blue-chip British companies, Glaxo Labs and Joseph Luca, Ltd. Glaxo was growing rapidly, and was solidly profitable, but the company reinvested earnings in expansion rather than paying out those earnings to shareholders. Its dividend yield was only 3.85 percent. As a result, Glaxo stock, in spite of the company's record of impressive growth, traded at the stunningly low P/E ratio of 2.2 to 1. Joseph Luca, with an equally impressive record of earnings but also a small dividend, was valued by the market at a P/E of a mere 2.6 to 1. The P/E ratio for the overall market was not calculated at the time, but the best estimate is that it was no higher than 5 to 1.

At midcentury the stock markets of the world (largely confined to Britain and the United States) were straitjacketed by conservative standards of valuation, and either ignored or treated with disdain by governments and the public. But hidden within this generally gloomy picture, inklings of change could be found. One new force that would ultimately drive stock prices higher—and eventually make stock markets far more important—was a growing fear of inflation. During the 1930s deflation had been the norm throughout the developed world; falling consumer prices had been bad for stocks but good for high-quality fixed-income investments like bonds. But the burst of pent-up consumer price inflation that occurred in the United States after wartime controls were eliminated, and the seemingly inevitable inflation projected to accompany the easy-money, socialist policies of the Labour government in Britain, caused inflation to be a very real concern for investors. An editorial in *Barron's* in 1949 made the case succinctly. "The State," opined *Barron's*, "is growing omnipotent, and it is doing so through the use of the money power. The policies of the welfare state create inflation, feed on inflation, and necessitate inflation."

In an inflationary environment, bonds, which paid only a fixed amount of interest and a fixed amount of principal at maturity, were unattractive. Stocks, on the other hand, which represented a claim on the real earnings power of growing corporations, were much more interesting, as a hedge against the expected rise in consumer prices. The strong bull market that developed in the United States in the late 1940s was driven by expectations of an economy intrinsically beset by inflation. As one respected analyst put it in 1949, "The stock market is sounding the warning bell on inflation."[12]

But what of the nations that, outside of Britain and the United States, had been the largest industrialized countries prior to the war: Germany and Japan? Both nations were occupied by the victorious

Allied powers. The occupying authorities seized the opportunity to restructure the German and Japanese financial systems, largely along American lines.

In Germany, the Allies moved to dismantle the big three banks that had dominated the prewar German economy: Deutsche Bank, Dresdner Bank, and Commerzbank. The banks were condemned for their close cooperation with the Nazi government and were broken up into smaller regional banks. The German equity market itself was prostrate and essentially nonfunctioning in the immediate postwar period. Most of the public had lost its savings during the war, and companies were unable to raise external funds; self-finance was the only option if they sought to expand. After currency reform in 1948 reestablished a stable value for the German mark, an embryonic stock market came into being, but it was of very little practical significance.

Once the occupying authorities left Germany, the big banks were allowed to reconstitute themselves. The German stock market had never developed to the point where it could provide the necessary financing for German business, even before the war. The quick revival of the system of universal banking after the occupying powers departed is indicative of how deeply ingrained the tradition of universal banking was in Germany. The stunted German stock market would continue to be of only peripheral importance to the German economy.

In Japan, the occupying authorities under General Douglas MacArthur essentially imposed the 1930s New Deal regulatory regime on the Japanese stock market. The American securities acts of 1933 and 1934 were adopted, often almost verbatim, as a model for the new Japanese system. The constitution imposed after World War II forced dissolution of the largest *zaibatsu*—the ten family-dominated conglomerates that controlled fully three-fourths of the Japanese economy. The postwar Japanese government also sold its portfolio of stockholdings in major institutions, including the Bank of Tokyo and the Industrial Bank of Japan. The objective was nothing less than to create a Japanese middle class, with widely distributed shareholding. Gone would be the days when giant conglomerations of wealth like the fabled House of Mitsui would employ over three million workers—more than any other business organization in history.[13]

The equities market had previously been the realm of large banks controlled by the *zaibatsu*. But the new "Americanized" rules gave the role of stock trading and distribution to nonbank securities firms, breaking the power of the banks. (Banks were permitted to own no more than 5 percent of brokerage firms.) By the early 1950s, with the dissolution of the *zaibatsu*, nearly 70 percent of Japanese stocks were owned by the general public, served by a new network of brokerage firms very similar to that in the United States. It was a revolutionary development, which would set the stage for a modern Japanese stock market that would prove to be far more dynamic and important than that of Germany.

Regardless of country-by-country differences, however, in the immediate postwar period all the world's stock exchanges operated in a climate that was generally quite hostile to the notion of free, open markets. The legacy of the 1930s (as reflected in the Bretton Woods accords) was one of deep-seated suspicion of the workings of unfettered capital markets. But intellectual opinion is rarely unanimous for long periods; occasional voices did speak out, questioning the prevailing orthodoxy.

In 1944, the year in which the Americans and British sought at Bretton Woods to establish rules for the postwar economic order, an iconoclastic Austrian economist named Friedrich von Hayek published *The Road to Serfdom*, a broadside against the advance of collectivism and central planning. Had it not been for the paper rationing in Britain during the war, Hayek's work, written for an audience of laymen, not professional economists, might have become a best-seller. It did attain a much wider readership when it was published in the United States by the University of Chicago Press and later, in a condensed version, by *Reader's Digest*. But despite this encouraging popular response, the reaction among academic economists was decidedly chilly. Hayek himself later admitted that writing the book in a style suited for mass consumption discredited him with serious economists. If anything, the response from government officials was even less receptive. At the request of the Soviet Union, the Allied occupation authorities banned the book in Germany after the war.

Hayek was a vocal critic of Keynes's ideas, although the two men maintained a friendship as long as Keynes was alive. Hayek did not believe that Keynes's so-called middle course—between laissez-faire capitalism and state socialism—was feasible. In Hayek's view, modern economies were too complex to be administered effectively by any central authority. Instead, the role of government should be limited to creating a system of law and the institutions necessary to maintain it. Hayek was well aware that he faced a long struggle to overcome what was becoming "Keynesian orthodoxy." But he did gradually gain converts. Perhaps the most influential disciple would turn out to be a young Oxford undergraduate who eagerly read *The Road to Serfdom* shortly after it was published. Her name was Margaret Roberts, later to become Margaret Thatcher.

In the United States, the most persistent dissident viewpoint was voiced by a young economist named Milton Friedman. A smallish man with large ears that gave him the appearance of an elf, Friedman was the son of poor Jewish immigrants in Brooklyn. At one point, his parents had been forced to work in sweatshops sewing clothes to make ends meet. Friedman graduated from Rutgers College in 1932, having displayed a penchant for economics and mathematics, then commenced graduate studies in economics at the University of Chicago but was forced to withdraw for financial reasons. Fortunately, he was able to secure a generous grant from Columbia University, where he quickly established a reputation as a scholar with a "stick it in your ear" attitude, willing to be abrasive and challenge conventional wisdom. His quick temper and bluntly expressed opinions did not often win him friends.

One of Friedman's early works argued that restrictions on entry into the professions (such as medicine) favored by professional societies limited the number of these professionals. He concluded that the restrictions created an unnecessary shortage that only benefited other members of the profession. Needless to say, this conclusion was not popular with professionals and many intellectuals, who fancied themselves as being above such mundane considerations.

In 1946 Friedman published a stinging critique of rent regulations in the housing market. Unlike most academic articles, which were written in the turgid prose typical of published scholarly research, Friedman employed catchy phrases and a breezy style directed more to a mass audience. This raised eyebrows among fellow academicians, who thought the approach bordered on pandering and found it demeaning. But it also made Friedman's arguments accessible to many people outside of academia. Once he returned to a professorship at the University of Chicago, his newfound fame helped launch his career as one of the most influential economists of the century.

Friedman did not at first fully embrace a comprehensive free-market philosophy; as late as 1951 he wrote an article suggesting that a Keynesian policy of government manipulation of interest rates could succeed. But as the 1950s progressed, his views hardened. He became an outspoken critic of the portions of the Bretton Woods accords that condoned international capital controls. Specifically, Friedman attacked the landmark study of the French franc by Ragnar Nurkse that had provided an intellectual justification for controls on capital movements. "The evidence given by Nurkse," Friedman scoffed, "does not justify any firm conclusion. Indeed, so far as it goes, it seems to me clearly less favorable to the conclusion Nurkse draws, that speculation was destabilizing, than the opposite conclusion, that speculation was stabilizing."[14] Friedman set himself fast against the idea that governments, through the use of judicious tax policy and economic controls, could hope to properly direct a complex modern economy. The first crack in the façade of intellectual support for "statist" interventions in markets had opened.

By coincidence, just as Friedman was beginning to establish what would eventually come to be known as the Chicago school of economics, a young Ph.D. candidate at the University of Chicago hit upon an idea that would eventually win him a Nobel Prize and revolutionize the way money was invested in the stock market. Prior to the 1950s the stock market had not been considered a fertile ground for academic research. What little scholarly work had been done on the subject invariably involved techniques to value individual stocks. In 1952 a lanky, sandy-haired young man named Harry Markowitz was to change that.

Markowitz admitted that as a boy he could have been classified as a nerd. In high school he never tried out for sports, instead reading voraciously, playing chess and the violin, and joining a national club for amateur cryptographers. The summer he turned fourteen he read Darwin's *Origin of Species* and was greatly impressed. Markowitz's hero was the Scottish philosopher David Hume, who died in 1776. When he applied for admission to the University of Chicago, Markowitz was able to overcome concerns about his mediocre high school grades by impressing the admissions officers with what he had learned from his own reading.[15]

The undergraduate decided to major in economics because it was the only social science with a mathematical bent. Once, while waiting to consult with his academic adviser, he happened to meet a stockbroker who urged him to apply techniques of economic analysis to the stock market. The idea intrigued both Markowitz and his adviser, but neither was knowledgeable enough about the market to know where to start. Markowitz was forced to go to the dean of the Business School for suggestions.

The dean referred him to what was then the authoritative work on the valuation of financial assets, a thesis written by a Harvard Ph.D. student in 1937 entitled *The Theory of Investment Value*. The author, John Burr Williams, had developed a three-step model for valuing individual stocks. First, a long-term projection of the company's future dividends payments would be made. Next, an estimation of the accuracy of the dividend estimates would be attached; for example, forecasts for an industrial stock whose earnings varied substantially over time would be less accurate than forecasts for a utility that had a much more stable pattern of earnings. Finally, projected future dividends would be "discounted" back to the present to determine the "present value"* of the dividend stream. Williams called his creation

---

*The concept of "present value" provides a means of comparing dollars to be received in the future with dollars received in the present. Since it is assumed that a dollar received now can be invested to generate income, a dollar received in the present is worth more than a dollar to be received in the future by the amount the "present" dollar would earn until the "future" dollar is received. Put another way, the value of the dollar to be received in the future is "discounted" back to the present using an interest rate that reflects what the present dollar could earn over that time.

the *dividend discount model* and used it to estimate what he called the "intrinsic value" of a stock.

One implication of Williams's work bothered Markowitz. Williams seemed to be saying that an investor should select the single stock that had the highest expected return and invest everything in that one stock. But this appeared to Markowitz to represent a very risky strategy; unfortunately, there was nothing in Williams's paper to account for risk. As Markowitz put it, "that afternoon in the library, I was struck with the notion that you should be interested in risk as well as return."[16]

Markowitz had stumbled on a question that had been largely neglected: the tension between risk and return in investments. Investors in stocks had typically focused purely on the maximization of return. Markowitz's 1952 paper developed the notion of a trade-off between risk and return that seems intuitively obvious today. He then went on to develop the concept of a "portfolio" of securities, which represented a radical departure from the way stock market professionals traditionally selected investments. Markowitz's insight was that the risk inherent in a portfolio of securities depended on the covariance of the securities in the portfolio (in other words, the degree to which the prices of those securities moved together), rather than the riskiness of each individual security. Thus it was possible to construct a portfolio of relatively risky securities that would itself not be unacceptably risky, if the securities making up the portfolio had low covariances (did not tend to move together). Diversification was the means to minimize risk and maximize return, but it had to be the right kind of diversification. The securities selected should be in different industries and consist of different types of companies. As Markowitz put it, "It is necessary to avoid investing in securities with high covariances among themselves."[17]

The notion of assembling a diversified portfolio of stocks as a means of controlling risk is commonly accepted today. But before Markowitz, diversification was often frowned upon. Keynes himself had disdained diversification:

> I get more and more convinced that the right method of investment
> is to put fairly large sums into enterprises which one thinks one

knows something about and in the management of which one thoroughly believes. It is a mistake to think that one spreads one's risk by spreading too much between enterprises about which one knows little and has no reason for special confidence . . . there are seldom more than two or three enterprises at any time in which I personally feel myself entitled to put full confidence . . . To carry one's eggs in a great number of baskets, without having time to discover how many have holes in the bottom, is the surest way to increasing risk and loss.[18]

Milton Friedman was one of the members of the panel at the University of Chicago that reviewed Markowitz's Ph.D. thesis. During the candidate's presentation, Friedman had a bit of fun at Markowitz's expense, complaining that the thesis, dealing with subject matter highly unusual for academia, was neither "economics, nor math, nor even business administration." For a moment, Markowitz feared that all was lost and that his thesis would be rejected. But Friedman and the other economists on the panel immediately recognized the significance of Markowitz's conclusions. Once Markowitz left the examination room, they awarded him his doctorate after a mere five minutes of deliberation.

Markowitz's ideas, when they finally received the attention they deserved, dramatically changed the way investments were managed. Previously, investors (like Keynes) had focused almost exclusively on analyzing the prospects for individual stocks, not an entire portfolio of stocks. This tended to make them more conservative, shunning "speculative" stocks (with little or no history of consistent earnings and dividends) in favor of less risky choices. But, as Markowitz showed, a properly diversified portfolio could include stocks that were more risky individually without creating an excessively risky portfolio.

It would take years for Markowitz's ideas to become widely accepted. The most obvious consequence of what would come to be known as *modern portfolio theory* was a newfound enthusiasm for stocks among institutional money managers, including rapidly growing pension funds. It was now possible for managers with fiduciary responsibility to buy "riskier" stocks, as opposed to "safer" bonds, if the stocks were purchased as part of a well-diversified portfolio. The massive influx of pension and retirement money that would drive stock markets in the later decades of the twentieth century would not have been possible without the diversification theory first put forth by Markowitz.

Markowitz's idea would eventually lead to another very important, but less immediately obvious, result. Throughout the history of stock markets, overseas investment in equities had always been perceived as risky. High-profile losses suffered by European investors in various Latin American and U.S. "busts" over the nineteenth century had provided repeated (and often quite painful) evidence of this risk. But what if the various emerging stock markets around the world could be shown to be largely independent of one another? If, for example, the Argentine market was falling at a given point in time, might perhaps markets in Australia, South Africa, or Canada be simultaneously rising? If so, might an investor buy a portfolio of stocks that was diversified across different national markets, and in this manner be able to offset the risks inherent in overseas investing? There is no evidence that Markowitz considered the question of international markets as he developed his theory of portfolio diversification, and it would take decades for the implications of his work for cross-border investing to become clear. But the young self-described "nerd," doing research at an American university, had stumbled onto something. Markowitz had reopened the door—albeit tentatively at first—that would ultimately lead to the rebirth of global investing.

As the 1950s progressed, the stock markets of the United Kingdom and the United States (comprising more than 90 percent of the total world capitalization of publicly traded companies) gradually adjusted to new ideas—such as Markowitz's theory of diversification—and to the inflationary bias that had been introduced into the economy. One of the first people in Britain to recognize what was happening was investment manager and former stockbroker Lewis Whyte, who published a textbook in 1951 entitled *The Principles of Finance and Investment.* At the time it was the only book of its kind available. Whyte argued passionately that standards by which stocks were valued must change, to reflect the new market realities. He went so far as to say that stock dividend yields should be below bond

yields, to take into account both future growth in earnings and anticipated inflation.

Rising stock valuations characterized much of the ensuing decade.
While stock prices would have appreciated anyway, as the economies
and corporate profits in the United States and Britain grew, the upward trend in valuations (P/E ratios) meant that the rate of stock
price increases exceeded the rate of economic growth. In Britain,
where valuations had lagged behind those of the United States,
the advent of new standards was brought into abrupt focus by a single improbable event, orchestrated by a colorful character named
Charles Clore.

Clore had the audacity to do something that was virtually unheard
of among the gentlemen brokers and jobbers who did business in the
City of London: he launched a "hostile" takeover bid. Clore's target
was a rather ordinary shoe store chain named J. Sears & Company.
Despite a consistent pattern of profitability, the stock of J. Sears
traded at a P/E ratio of barely 3 to 1. To Clore, this was grossly undervalued, and was the result of what he felt was a hidebound con-
servatism on the part of a management that had consistently failed to
maximize what would today be called "shareholder value." Clore,
never one to be bashful, announced that the J. Sears stock (and, by
implication, that of many other British firms) was too cheap, and that
poor management was largely to blame.

When Clore succeeded in buying control of J. Sears (ultimately
paying nearly double the previous market price for the shares), a
storm of controversy broke loose. For a brief moment, Clore succeeded in uniting normally conservative business leaders with
Labour Party politicians. Corporate directors suddenly feared for
their jobs, thinking that their firms might too become the target of
raiders like Clore if they failed to take steps to raise stock prices.
Labour leaders viewed Clore with suspicion because they saw him as
an old-fashioned buccaneer capitalist, and because Clore's ideas
seemed to imply higher dividends for shareholders, always anathema
to class-conscious Labour politicians.

Undeterred, Clore went on to lead additional hostile takeover efforts, and actually succeeded in creating something of a takeover
frenzy, as others copied his idea. Clore vigorously disputed the

charge that his activities would lead to "ruin and destruction." Such "ruin and destruction," Clore countered, would instead come "where the rigid preservation of the status quo is the order of the day, where enterprise is regarded as speculation and the full use of resources as dissipation . . ."[19]

The hostile takeover, which Clore forced upon Britain, would go on to take an increasingly important and controversial role. The ownership base of publicly traded companies in the United States and the United Kingdom was becoming more widely dispersed as middle-class investors, and institutions, increased their participation in the market. With ownership now diffused among a large number of stockholders, corporate managements were no longer dealing with a few major shareholders who exercised close control; managements found themselves much less constrained by shareholder concerns. The hostile takeover became the mechanism through which share-holders could redress the new imbalance of power and discipline recalcitrant managements. If the people running a firm did not pursue policies that enhanced "shareholder interests" and caused the stock to rise, some outside group could step in, buy up the shares at low prices, and oust management. In an era where professional managers were increasingly divorced from shareholders, the hostile takeover became a blunt force instrument by which shareholder interests could be enforced.

Clore succeeded in roiling the political and financial waters in Britain because his timing was right. Stocks were undervalued, and managements often saw little reason to be concerned about such undervaluations. A defining event like the J. Sears takeover fight accentuated the dramatic upward adjustment in valuations during the 1950s. By 1959 British stock prices had tripled, while the bond market (due to inflation and the resultant higher interest rates) had fallen by one-third. Over the same period in the United States, the P/E ratio for New York Stock Exchange stocks jumped from approximately 7 to 1 to 17 to 1. American stock prices advanced roughly 250 percent faster than earnings, while the rate of increase of British stock prices more than doubled the concomitant increases in corporate earnings. These gains did not come simply because of the threat of hostile takeovers, which were actually relatively rare. Rather, the hostile takeover itself was a product of a changing climate of opinion on how managements of publicly traded firms should behave, how shareholder value should be enhanced, and, most fundamentally, how stocks should be valued.

A stark indication of how much things had changed took place in 1958–59, when stock dividend yields, for the first time in history, fell below interest rates on government bonds in the United States and Britain. Orthodox investment theory required stock yields that exceeded bond yields to compensate holders of stocks for the fact that equities were more risky than bonds. But fear of inflation, and a growing willingness to consider potential future earnings growth when valuing stocks, resulted in a fundamental readjustment of traditional standards.

It is surprising how abrupt and how permanent this change was. Once dividend yields on American stocks fell below bond rates in 1958, they would never again exceed them. Exactly the same thing happened in Britain in 1959, as dividend rates fell permanently below bond rates. A relationship between bond and stock yields that had existed since the beginning of organized markets was reversed. Never again would stocks in either Britain or the United States yield more than domestic government bonds for any significant period of time.

The March 1959 issue of *Fortune* attempted to provide a comprehensive explanation of what was happening. The article quoted unnamed financial columnists who saw the market's rise as a sign of "quiet desperation" about the "coming inflation." But *Fortune* also found other reasons for the market's strong performance. One obvious source of buying came from rapidly growing institutional participation in the market. *Fortune* reported that in 1957 American mutual funds accounted for $2.3 billion, or 62 percent of the net buying of stocks, with pension funds responsible for $1 billion more, or 27 percent of total net buying. Together these institutional purchases represented 89 percent of all net buying. As of January 1, 1959, *Fortune* estimated that mutual funds had assets of $13 billion, up $4.5 billion from the previous year. Likewise, the magazine estimated that by 1959 pension funds had 30 percent of their assets invested in stocks, up from 10 percent in 1950. Although mutual funds and pension funds still held only about 10 percent of all stocks, their share of the market was rising rapidly, driving share prices higher in the process.

A similar trend toward vastly expanded institutional involvement in equities was under way in Britain. One of the leading advocates of increased equity market participation by pension funds was Ross Goobey, the investment manager for the Imperial Tobacco Pension Fund. Goobey was an avid golfer; he was once introduced at an investment conference as "the only pension fund manager with a golf handicap lower than the yield on his fund."[20] Goobey had been investing 80 percent of his funds in equities for some time, a strategy considered quite radical in the late 1950s. Goobey rejected criticism that he was taking too much risk. Quite the contrary, he argued, those more conservative fund managers who disdained equities were the ones who were engaged in a risky investment scheme, in that they were failing to protect themselves from the ravages of inflation.

Goobey turned out to be a prophet of things to come. The investment of pension fund proceeds in stocks would be one of the primary engines driving the British and American stock markets in coming decades. And it would be the absence of such investment that would hold back stock markets in other developed nations. In France and Italy, for example, private pension funds, when they existed, were typically funded by corporate employers on a pay-as-you-go basis. As a result, there were no accumulating pools of monies to be invested in the financial markets. In Germany the development of generous state-sponsored pension plans largely preempted any need for private retirement funds. Thus the American and British equity markets, which were already far ahead of European markets in terms of depth and sophistication, received another boost, this time from private pension money, which would further solidify their preeminent position.

British equity markets, however, although mirroring the reversal in the bond-stock yield relationship that had occurred in the United States, continued to lag behind the American market in a number of other areas. One of the most important was *transparency*—the degree to which accurate information on publicly traded companies was readily available. The burst of reform in the United States in the

1930s had produced a comprehensive set of requirements that made the American stock market the most regulated in the world, a status it holds to this day. Increased transparency was one of the primary objectives of the reforms. New rules in Britain requiring more transparency, however, had only come piecemeal over time, usually as a result of individual scandals. Managements of public companies were traditionally reluctant to make information available, ostensibly for competitive reasons. This placed quite a handicap on investors seeking to make informed judgments.

In 1955 seven stockbrokers and investment managers banded together in London to form the Society of Investment Analysts, which had as its objective the publication of basic research on British firms. They met a great deal of resistance; hard data on British companies was devilishly difficult to obtain. For example, an analyst attempting to ascertain the true profitability of a British automobile company would be forced to deduce from a press release how many cars the company had sold, a figure normally cloaked in secrecy. Then he would try to construct estimates of the profit margin the company might earn per car, pieced together from different sources. From this he would then reach a very tentative conclusion as to the firm's overall earnings. Needless to say, this cumbersome process consumed much time and was prone to error.

The fact that many British firms did business in the United States and were thus forced to comply with the much stricter American disclosure standards sometimes provided the best means by which British analysts and investors could get needed information. For example, some U.S. states required British insurance companies operating there to make available quarterly operating figures for public inspection well before the customary semiannual and yearly results were published in London. Other major British companies operating across the Atlantic faced similar requirements. More often than not, the stiffer American disclosure regime was regarded by British firms as an unpleasant cost of doing business.

By the 1960s, demands for improved transparency were pressuring British companies to make more information public, even in their home markets. In 1962 the *Financial Times* described the irritation felt by managements toward the new breed of analysts and financial journalists clamoring for what had traditionally been proprietary information: "It is not just that analysts everywhere—and financial journalists—are regarded by some industrialists as direct descendents of Oliver Twist and Mrs. Nosey-Parker; . . . there is understandable resentment at this dangerous importation from the New World."

Understandable or not, the resentment British managements felt was pushed aside. Most companies reluctantly moved toward the improved transparency already well established in the American market. For those that continued to drag their feet, the British Parliament stepped in. A new Company Bill in 1964 mandated full disclosure of all major assets and the publication of detailed sales figures. No longer would it be possible for large publicly held corporations to hide behind hazy reporting standards and obtuse accounting methodologies. Publicly, managements feared that such disclosure would aid competitors, who could now glean useful proprietary information from published reports. Privately, they worried that their own performance would now be subject to closer scrutiny by shareholders. But the benefits to the entire market—and the overall economy—that came from better, timelier information would prove to be well worth the price.

Increased institutional participation in the market, in the form of professionally managed pension and mutual funds, further increased the demand for accurate, timely corporate earnings data. In the early 1950s nearly 80 percent of stocks had been owned directly by individuals, in both Britain and the United States. By the late 1960s half of all shares in the American stock market were controlled by institutions. Analyst and consultant services sprang up to evaluate the performance of the newly important professional portfolio managers. Firms such as Arthur Lipper & Company provided an independent means of comparing fund results. This existence of comparative data created an environment where great emphasis was placed on short-term "performance." New money flooded into funds that had done well, but quickly dried up for funds that lagged behind. The great performance race was on.

Nimble, fast-trading "go-go" funds were very much in vogue. Some new portfolio managers bought and sold stocks so quickly that the turnover* in their funds exceeded 100 percent annually, an unheard-of figure. New York Stock Exchange president G. Keith Funston declared that the emphasis on performance "is the most significant change in the marketplace today."[21] Most of the performance fund managers were relatively young—usually in their thirties. It was almost as if anyone older was presumed to be too tainted by past experience to adjust to the new market realities.

The quest by portfolio managers for short-term performance was largely an American phenomenon, with some imitators in Britain. The American stock market in the 1950s and 1960s was insulated from the rest of the world by foreign restrictions on capital flows. The effect of capital controls on financial markets was demonstrated by several studies. One analysis focusing on the bond market found that "covered interest rate differentials" were as much as 2 percent in the United Kingdom and 1 percent in Germany.[22] (In other words, although better bond-market investment opportunities might exist across national borders, investors were prevented from transferring money abroad to take advantage of those opportunities, allowing the disparities to persist.) The author of another study concluded that controls "clearly . . . had a very substantial effect" on preventing the free flow of capital necessary to eliminate price discrepancies between different national markets.[23]

George Soros, shortly after graduating from the London School of Economics, recognized that if he could get around capital controls, he could exploit international discrepancies in stock prices. Having lived in New York since 1956, Soros was one of the few investors in America to follow European securities. As he put it, "Nobody knew anything about [European securities] in the 1960s. So I could impute any earnings I wanted to the European companies I followed. It was strictly a case of the blind leading the blind."[24]

---

*Turnover is the rate at which a portfolio manager buys and sells securities. It is calculated by dividing the total number of shares traded in a given year by the total number of shares in a portfolio. A ratio of 1.0, for example, would mean that the turnover was 100 percent.

While working at Wertheim & Co., one of the few firms that engaged in overseas trading, Soros discovered that the stock of the German insurance giant Allianz was selling at a substantial discount from its asset value. The company held a large portfolio of stock and real estate that was valued on the books at cost, rather than at its (much higher) current market value. Soros published his findings and was proven correct when Allianz stock rose substantially. It was the first of many shrewd market calls that were to make his reputation.

Foreign stocks were attractive by American standards. The growing acceptance in the United States of the new methodology of valuing stocks, based on future growth potential rather than current dividends, meant that American stocks generally traded at higher valuations (P/E ratios) than non-American stocks. Soros believed that valuations overseas were sufficiently cheap to justify putting up with burdensome foreign capital controls that often prevented American investors from quickly repatriating monies they invested overseas.

Unfortunately, Soros was prevented from implementing this strategy. In 1963 the United States joined most other countries in enacting restrictions on capital outflows. The specific vehicle was President Kennedy's Interest Equalization Tax, which was designed to prevent American investment money from flowing to other developed countries. The mighty U.S. dollar, so dominant immediately following World War II, had been progressively weakened by years of persistent outflows to finance large overseas military spending and foreign aid as well as foreign expansion by U.S. multinationals. For Kennedy, a devaluation of the dollar would have been unthinkable; the fixed-rate regime imposed by Bretton Woods was still the bedrock of American international economic policy. The only alternative was to do what most foreign countries already did: impose controls on investment money moving out of the country.

The new "tax" was levied up-front on investments made in certain (primarily European) developed countries by American citizens. Canada and developing countries were exempted. A sliding scale was established, with the tax varying from 1.05 percent on very short-term foreign bonds to 15 percent on long-term bonds and all stocks. Needless to say, this rate was prohibitive for equity investors. It effectively put a stop to any American purchases of stock in the affected countries, which included most of the industrialized world.

Capital controls, such as the Interest Equalization Tax, sealed off national stock markets from one another. The domestic British and American stock markets were booming; at its peak on January 31, 1969, the *Financial Times* All Share Index (500 industrials) had a P/E of 23 to 1 (compared with P/Es that had routinely averaged below 10 to 1 immediately after World War II), while P/Es of large-capitalization growth companies in the United States frequently hit 40 or 50 to 1. But there was no mechanism for this strength to spill over into other equity markets, to take advantage of cheaper valuations that existed elsewhere, because capital controls prohibited Americans and Britons from investing overseas. Most equity issuance, and trading, remained concentrated in Britain and the United States.

As a measure of just how unbalanced world equity markets were in the 1960s, the New York Stock Exchange market capitalization of one large American company—International Business Machines (IBM)—was greater than the capitalization of the *entire* German stock market, as measured by the Frankfurt Stock Exchange. Nearly 15 percent of American households owned stock, either directly or indirectly through mutual funds; in only three other countries (the United Kingdom, Holland, and Japan) was the percentage even over 5 percent. In India, the largest non-Communist country in the world, less than one-tenth of 1 percent of the population owned stocks. Only one Indian company—Tata Steel—had a number of stockholders that, adjusted for the size of the country, was more than the *average* number of shareholders of the 1,500-plus companies listed on the New York Stock Exchange. Vibrant equity markets remained almost exclusively an Anglo-American phenomenon.

By 1970 substantial cracks were beginning to appear in the Bretton Woods regime. Persistent critics of statist policies restricting capital flows (such as Milton Friedman) were gaining influence. The dollar—the cornerstone of the Bretton Woods accords—had weakened to the point that it had to be propped up by foreign exchange controls through the Interest Equalization Tax. The breaking point would soon come, when the entire postwar economic order so meticulously pieced together in 1944 would break down. The resulting turmoil would send stock markets in Britain and the United States on a scary ride, with greatly increased volatility. But ironically, it would also tear free the restraints that prevented the development of equity markets elsewhere in the world.

CHAOS

PRESIDENT RICHARD NIXON believed that a strong leader must be "bold." Boldness, to Nixon, included a willingness to change course quickly when events demanded it, to abruptly discard past policy and the ideological baggage that accompanied it. Critics called it opportunism, and questioned whether Nixon possessed any firm beliefs not subject to the whim of the moment. But Nixon was quite willing to countenance radical shifts in policy if necessary to give the United States the strong leadership he believed it required, and which he so desperately wanted to provide.

Still, the events of August 15, 1971, came as a profound shock even to many Nixon intimates. In a hastily scheduled television address on a Sunday evening, Nixon announced what he called a "new economic policy." The policy certainly was new; it completely reversed most of his previous economic program, to which Administration officials had tenaciously clung in the face of mounting criticism. Nixon imposed a ninety-day wage-price freeze, announced a 10 percent surcharge on imports, and took the United States off the gold standard, effectively devaluing the dollar. Treasury Secretary John Connolly half-jokingly said that the plan would "shake 'em up" overseas. He was correct. The immediate reaction of world financial markets was consternation; foreign stocks dropped sharply and currency markets were thrown into such turmoil that many were forced to shut down temporarily.

It can be said with hindsight that the imposition of wage and price controls, by which the federal government attempted to comprehensively regulate all economic activity, marked the high-water mark of the postwar tendency of governments to control the economy. The Conservative Party government of Edward Heath in Britain soon announced similar measures in an equally desperate attempt to rein in inflation. Such actions would be inconceivable today in any major industrial nation, even with left-of-center governments. But in the early 1970s it was administrations run by the "conservative" parties in both the United States and Britain that chose to resort to massive government controls. Never had belief in the power of government been so great, or faith in private markets so limited.

There were important conservative critics of Nixon's move. Alan Greenspan, then a private-sector economic consultant, said the suspension of dollar-gold convertibility revealed "the shabby secret" of the welfare state. "Deficit spending," Greenspan charged, "is simply a scheme for the hidden confiscation of wealth. Gold stands in the way of this insidious process. It stands as a protector of property rights."[1]

Ironically, although it was not obvious at the time, the move Greenspan decried—taking the dollar off gold—actually marked the beginning of a turn away from government controls, albeit one forced by circumstances. For three years after August 1971, international monetary officials scurried about in a frenetic effort to repair the rickety Bretton Woods regime; at one point an agreement was actually pasted together that Nixon declared to be "the most significant monetary accord in the history of the world." The arrangement lasted barely seven months, then disintegrated in chaos. A new unplanned and uncontrolled "nonsystem" came into being by default. Major currencies would now float at levels set by market forces, not at rates fixed by governments.

The Nixon wage-price controls would ultimately prove disastrous, and would be abandoned in 1974, releasing another sharp burst of the very inflation they were designed to prevent. But the decision to "float" the dollar, and the dramatic collapse of the system of fixed exchange rates in the 1970s, had profound reverberations beyond the currency markets. The climate of intellectual opinion on the subject of markets and controls had already begun to shift; outsiders like Friedrich von Hayek and Milton Friedman were now (grudgingly) beginning to be accorded a respectability they had previously lacked. (Hayek received the Nobel Prize for economics in 1974, although the award outraged many "mainstream" economists who still saw Hayek as a right-wing crank.)

More and more, control regimes, such as the Interest Equalization Tax that had stymied farsighted international investors like George Soros, were condemned as failures. All the Interest Equalization Tax had accomplished, it seemed, was to create undesirable distortions in the capital markets, forcing overseas investments to be rerouted through exempt countries like Canada and to take different forms. (For example, the fact that the tax applied to American purchases of foreign stocks and bonds, but not to loans by American banks to foreign entities, caused overseas bank loans to nearly triple after the tax went into effect.) The tax also had the very undesirable effect of strengthening foreign capital markets, particularly London, at the expense of American financial centers, as foreign stock and bond transactions were diverted away from the United States.

Friedrich von Hayek and Milton Friedman, of course, had been crusading against government economic controls for nearly two decades; the failure of mechanisms like the Interest Equalization Tax and wage-price controls did not surprise them. Hayek and Friedman opposed government controls because they felt the controls would inevitably be hopelessly misdirected, in that governments could not possibly understand the complex workings of modern economies well enough to design effective systems to manage capital movements. Unfortunately, their critics argued, this reasoning ignored the risks inherent in the noninterventionist policies Hayek and Friedman advocated. Market disturbances (such as the panicky flights of capital across borders that had torn apart the gold-based monetary system in the 1930s) could do great harm if allowed to take their course unimpeded. As long as unrestrained markets were seen to be dangerously fickle and unstable, efforts by governments to rein in market excesses would seem to have some benefit, Hayek's and Friedman's reservations notwithstanding.

By the 1970s, however, a significant body of academic evidence had begun to raise questions about this view of markets. One of the most prominent revisionists was Eugene Fama, a third-generation Italian-American born in Boston in 1939. One of Fama's college professors wrote a stock market investment letter that used an approach which today would be called "momentum" investing, seeking out rising stocks that would presumably continue to rise. The professor wanted to perfect his system for picking stocks, and hired Fama part-time to assist him.

Unfortunately, the two men were unable to devise methodologies that consistently predicted market movements. But Fama's curiosity was piqued. He decided to pursue his postgraduate studies at the University of Chicago business school, which had become the leading institution conducting academic research on the stock market.[2]

Fama published his Ph.D. in 1965, in the *Journal of Business*. In it, he coined the term "efficient capital market," a concept that would dominate academic research on the market for decades to come. Following up on Louis Bachelier's work at the Sorbonne in 1900, Fama argued that in an efficient market, stock prices would instantaneously adjust to any new information that became available. Thus it would be impossible to beat the market by anticipating future price movements, since the current market price already incorporated all relevant information.

Less than a year after his article appeared in the *Journal of Business*, Fama published a less quantitative piece intended for a wider audience in the *Financial Analysts Journal*. The title was "Random Walks in Stock Market Prices." The term "random walk" had been used before, but Fama popularized it, comparing stock price movements to the random walk of a drunk stumbling from point to point. Since the market efficiently represented the best valuation of any given stock at any given time, future movements of that stock's price could only be driven by unpredictable new information, and thus must be viewed as random.

Fama's ideas attracted surprising attention from the general public, as well as from academics. He was featured on television talk shows and was profiled in *Forbes, Fortune,* and the *Wall Street Journal.* He joked that "insofar as you can become famous from writing an article in an academic journal, I became famous."[3] The significance of what he was saying could not be ignored. If the stock market was efficient and stock price movements truly random, it would be impossible for any investor to consistently outperform the market. And if no one could beat the market, there was no reason for most professional portfolio managers and stock analysts (many of whom were very highly paid) to exist.

While Fama's efficient market theory specifically dealt with stocks, the implications for other markets—and international capital flows—were clear. If markets are efficient, providing the best possible economic forecast at any given time, justifications for government intervention in those markets become weaker. Friedman maintained that it was not really possible for governments to control markets effectively. The implication of Fama's work was that it would be undesirable to do so, even if it was possible. Combined, the two arguments were extremely compelling.

At the same time that Fama was researching his dissertation, two University of Chicago professors, James Lorie and Lawrence Fischer, dropped another academic bombshell. Making good use of the vastly increased power of computers, they analyzed stock market returns from 1926 to 1960 and discovered that an investor who had bought into the market in 1926 and had reinvested all his dividends would have earned a 9 percent annualized return over the period. This result was quite surprising, given that the years in question included the 1929 crash and the Great Depression.

A 9 percent rate of return was much larger than that received by bond investors over the same period. This seemed to confirm the conclusions reached by Edgar Lawrence Smith in 1924, which had helped provide an intellectual basis for the New Era boom of the 1920s, but had been discredited after the crash. The Fischer-Lorie study demonstrated that very good long-term results could be achieved simply by buying and holding a portfolio of stocks representative of the overall market.

The stock market had finally become a respectable subject for scholarly inquiry. The sharp declines experienced by most markets in the early 1970s sparked further interest in the new academic theories. Most of the "performance" managers of the late 1960s had crashed and burned; it became obvious that these go-go operators had been taking a great deal of risk to achieve their impressive returns, risk that could prove disastrous in a bear market. Suddenly Harry Markowitz's insight from the 1950s—that a trade-off existed between risk and return, and that risk could best be managed by diligent diversification—seemed quite relevant.

What has become known as modern portfolio theory finally took root in the 1970s. The ideas of Harry Markowitz and others were incorporated into the theory, through a model developed by William Sharpe, a self-described "computer nerd."[4] In the course of acquiring his doctorate in economics at UCLA, Sharpe had bumped into Markowitz, then in the process of completing his work on risk-reward relationships in portfolio theory. Sharpe, under Markowitz's guidance, zeroed in on a vexing problem inherent in the Markowitz approach to selecting the most risk-efficient portfolio: how to ensure proper diversification by calculating the extent to which the securities included in the portfolio moved together (covariance).

Under the Markowitz regime, the covariance of returns of each selected stock with every other possible stock had to be calculated individually. This was a daunting task. But Sharpe had an insight, which would ultimately help win him a Nobel Prize. Instead of laboriously attempting to calculate how different stocks moved relative to one another, he would try to identify a "basic underlying factor" that influenced the movement of all stocks, and compare each stock to that single factor.

Sharpe quickly determined that the basic underlying factor influencing the returns of individual stocks was the overall market itself. Markowitz himself had observed, "The returns on most securities are correlated. If the Standard & Poor's Index rose substantially, we would expect United States Steel to rise. If the S&P rose substantially, we would also expect Sweets Company of America to rise. For this reason, it is more likely that U.S. Steel will do well when Sweets Company does well."[5] In other words, the movements of U.S. Steel stock and Sweets Company stock were related by virtue of the fact that they were both influenced by the entire market.

Like many great insights, this observation seems intuitively obvious. But it had very significant implications. According to Sharpe, an analyst seeking the most risk-efficient portfolio need now only calculate the relationship of each stock with the overall market; if a stock is more volatile (risky) than the market, its addition to a portfolio will make the portfolio more volatile (risky), and vice versa. Sharpe found that about one-third of the movement of an average stock was a reflection of the movement of the overall market, while the rest was explained by the stock's relationship to other stocks in similar industries or by the unique characteristics of the stock itself. Significantly, however, he determined that in a properly diversified portfolio the non-market-related factors canceled one another out, leaving the influence of the market as the primary factor affecting the value of the portfolio.

In Sharpe's *capital asset pricing model*, the expected return earned by a stock consisted of the sum of the "risk-free" rate of return (defined as the interest rate paid on a riskless asset like a U.S. government bond) and a *risk premium* (representing the additional return over the risk-free rate that an investor must expect to receive as compensation for taking the extra risk involved in purchasing the risky asset). The risk premium in turn was determined by two factors: an *alpha factor*, which represented the specific return due to the unique characteristics of the stock itself; and a *beta factor*, which represented the influence of the overall market's return on the individual stock. (The so-called beta coefficient simply represented the degree to which an individual stock moved with the market; for example, a beta of 0.75 meant that the stock was expected to move up or down about 75 percent as fast as the overall market moved, while a beta of 1.5 meant that the stock was expected to move one and one-half times as fast as the market.) Since in a diversified portfolio the alphas of the different stocks tended to cancel out, the beta factor became predominant and was termed the "systematic" (or market-related) risk. The risk premium of a given stock was thus a function of this beta risk.

Just as market participants were digesting these radical new theories, the stock markets of the world were hit by shocks that threatened to overturn conventional wisdom on another subject: inflation. Since the late 1940s, interest in stocks, particularly in the two dominant markets in the United States and Britain, had been enhanced by fears of inflation and by the widely held belief that stocks represented a good hedge against that inflation. But that comfortable notion was to be shattered in the turbulent 1970s, when the rates of inflation in many industrialized countries surged to levels unprecedented in peacetime. Stocks, far from performing well, stumbled badly.

American shares, as measured by the Dow Jones Industrials, dropped 35 percent in 1969–70, while the *Financial Times* index of British shares fell 25 percent. Worse was to come. After a recovery in 1971–72, both markets plummeted again, with U.S. stocks dropping 45 percent in 1973–74 and British stocks plunging a terrifying 73 percent.

What went wrong with the conventional wisdom that stocks were a good hedge against inflation? In one sense, the damage done to stocks in 1970 was a logical response to higher interest rates. The noted economist Henry Wallich observed that rates had risen "more drastically in recent years than in any comparable prior period," and observed that long-term corporate bond rates of 10 percent (and more) were "outside the realm of civilized financial experience."[6] (By comparison, corporate bond interest rates had averaged 2.5 percent in the United States in 1950 and around 4 percent in the United Kingdom at that time.) The high rates of the 1970s sharply depressed the present value of the growth stocks' future earnings stream. Unless expectations of future growth increased to offset the effect of higher rates, the prices of growth stocks must decline.

Future earnings growth was crucial. In theory, the present value of future earnings should not be adversely impacted by inflation, because the nominal amount of future earnings will be increased by inflation, and these higher nominal earnings should offset the effect of higher interest rates in making the present value calculations. Over the long run stocks should still be a good hedge against inflation.

But, as John Maynard Keynes once remarked, "in the long run, we're all dead." In the short term in the early 1970s, stocks did not prove to be a good inflation hedge at all.

There are several possible reasons why stocks might perform poorly over the short run in periods of inflation. One is that in "cost-push" inflation, where prices are forced higher by rising raw materials or labor costs, businesses may be unable to pass on all those costs to the consumer, resulting in a profit squeeze. (The large increases in OPEC oil prices in the early 1970s created cost-push inflation.) Another reason is that corporate taxes do not properly adjust for inflation. In effect, corporations pay tax on illusory profits, reducing real after-tax earnings. (Depreciation, inventories, and capital gains are all calculated for tax purposes in terms of "nominal," not "real," dollars, resulting in an "inflation tax.") And finally (probably most importantly), fears that central banks will act to restrain inflation by attempting to slow the economy can hurt the stock market.

This unpleasant reality created a paradox for the owners of growth stocks. Fear of inflation had originally been the driving force behind "growth" investing. But, at least in the short run, the experience of the 1970s showed that inflation could prove quite bad for stocks, because of inflation-induced interest rate increases, dislocations in earnings, and fears of central bank action.

An article in *Barron's* in June 1970 starkly defined the new environment. Entitled "Equity Backlash," the article quoted bond market authority Sidney Homer, who argued that inflation and the resulting rise in interest rates had fundamentally distorted the capital markets. Irreversible changes had occurred in the relationship between the debt (bond) and equity (stock) markets. Bond interest yields had risen decisively above stock dividend rates in the late 1950s and had remained permanently above dividend rates thereafter. The relationship between interest rates and dividends that had held since the dawn of organized markets had been reversed. Now, Homer said, another assumption of market traditionalists—that the stock and bond markets usually move in opposite directions—was most likely no longer valid. Historically a booming economy had caused stocks to rise but bonds to fall, as increased corporate profits spurred stocks higher while increased corporate demand for funds forced interest rates up (and thus bond prices down). In the new environment, the same inflation that drove down bond prices would also hurt stocks. Homer anticipated that in the future the bond and stock markets would move down together under the stress of inflation.

Homer could not have been more prescient. He described in a nutshell precisely what would happen in the 1970s, when the stock market's love affair with inflation was shattered. Several empirical studies performed over the decade would corroborate what a casual observer could readily see—that, contrary to all accepted wisdom, stock prices fell in the face of anticipated (and unanticipated) inflation.[7]

The precipitous decline of the British stock market in 1974–75 also signaled the end of the long ascendancy of "Anglo" stock markets. The London market, which had been the preeminent marketplace for stocks prior to World War I, and second only to New York after the war, was now eclipsed by a new player half a world away. In 1975, for the first time ever, the market capitalization of the Japanese stock market surpassed that of Britain.

The Japanese market had come a long way from its nearly prostrate position after World War II. Ironically, in spite of the obviously immense cultural differences between the West and Japan, in one important way the Japanese market was more "modern"—more like the successful Anglo-Saxon model—than many European bourses. General MacArthur, as head of the occupying authority in postwar Japan, had imposed a regulatory system almost identical to the extensive New Deal reforms implemented in the United States in the 1930s. Companies listed on Japanese stock exchanges were required to submit audited financial statements, and manipulative (fraudulent) practices that had been prevalent before were prohibited. The breaking up of the *zaibatsu* and the sale of the government's large shareholdings to the public had created a large pool of individual shareholders, unrivaled outside the United States and Britain. A requirement much like the Glass-Steagal law in the United States banned banks from operating brokerage firms, largely eliminating (unlike in Germany) the large banks that had in previous years dominated the Japanese equity market. Nonbank Japanese brokerage firms scrambled to open branch offices in the 1950s and developed strategies to attract the burgeoning savings of the new Japanese middle class.

The "big four" Japanese brokerage firms—Nomura, Daiwa, Nikko, and Yamaichi—dominated the new retail market. Recognizing that women controlled the purse strings of Japanese families, the firms set up kiosks in department stores that dispensed investment advice and sought to inform people about the stock market. Perhaps the most brilliant piece of marketing was conceived by Nomura, which launched the "Million Ryo Savings Chest" campaign in 1953. The ryo was an ancient unit of Japanese currency; in the popular lexicon, a Japanese wishing for riches would sigh, "I wish I had a million ryo."[8] Nomura constructed thousands of wooden strongboxes, which its salesmen peddled throughout the country. Individual citizens would "save" by placing coins in the lockboxes. Once the chest was full, the saver would call a Nomura salesman for the key. The proceeds of the box would then be invested in the stock market through a Nomura investment trust.

Driven by a strong Japanese economy and extremely high savings rates on the part of Japanese investors, the Japanese stock market boomed. The "golden years" of the late 1950s and early 1960s saw double-digit economic growth; the stock market tripled in the five years from 1957 through 1961. Brokerage firms seized upon the Wall Street concept of growth stocks to push shares of companies like Matsushita Electric Industrial Company, which would become the world's largest producer of consumer electronics in the late 1970s. When Sony began assembling radios, its stock price skyrocketed like a modern-day Internet venture.

High-pressure sales tactics of the Japanese brokerage firms succeeded in wringing large sums for stock investments from thrifty Japanese. Legions of *kubuya* (stock salesmen) would fan out in door-to-door selling campaigns, often under strict instructions from their sales manager not to come back until they had an order. Young *kubuya* quickly learned always to pack an extra shirt in their briefcase, drink whiskey and beer with clients until early morning hours, and sleep in cheap "capsule" hotels (in coffinlike drawers that slid into the wall). It was said that visitors at brokerage offices in the

morning could hear the continual hum of electric razors from salesmen who had not been home the night before.

The pressure on the stockbrokers was intense. It was not uncommon for managers to dress down struggling salesmen in front of their
peers. In one instance, a branch manager openly berated a young
broker who had not met his quota. "You have failed," the manager
shouted. "Do not come into my sight again until you have sold all
your shares."⁹ The young man was later hospitalized with a stress-
related illness.

The Nomura Securities training program instructed trainees to
avoid selling to old ladies and celebrities. Old ladies, it was assumed,
were lonely and would tie up salesmen on lengthy, unproductive telephone calls. Famous clients, on the other hand, would be likely to
use their celebrity status to draw press attention in case a dispute developed; what Japanese brokers wanted least of all was bad publicity.
But dissatisfied clients were inevitable, given the often outlandish
claims made by ambitious brokers seeking orders.

The firms exposed themselves to potential conflicts by often
"guaranteeing" investment results; for example, it was not uncommon for salesmen to promise prospective investors that they would
make at least a 10 percent annualized return. Needless to say, if the
market failed to deliver the expected gains, customers became dissatisfied. Small investors had little recourse but to accept their fate,
whereas it was not uncommon for brokerage firms to at least partially
reimburse large customers for losses, a practice that could (and
would) create serious problems in a prolonged downturn. According
to popular belief, an investor who had only one million yen to invest
would almost certainly suffer losses, but an investor with one hundred million yen in the market would not be allowed to lose.

Despite the fact that Japanese markets operated under American-
imposed rules, there were profound differences between the stock
markets of the two countries. Price-earnings ratios, which had by the
1950s become the basic standard of valuation in the United States
and Britain, were largely ignored in Japan. Instead, investors simplis-
tically looked at the absolute price per share of a stock, and, curi-
ously, assumed that the higher the stock price, the better the

company. Matsushita, for example, trading at 350 yen per share, was seen as superior to Hitachi, trading at only 150 yen, regardless of the relative earnings of the two companies.[10] Tremendous pressure was placed on brokerage firms to maintain high stock prices, to keep both their corporate underwriting and individual customers happy. As one broker put it, "There was a social prestige within each industrial grouping on the stock exchange and if you could not keep up the stock price of your client, then the underwriting deals went to someone else."[11] The manipulation required to maintain "acceptable" prices was clearly illegal under the rules established during the American occupation. Tellingly, the rules were not enforced.

Yamaichi Securities was the leading Japanese underwriter in the early 1960s. To maintain its dominant position, it became more and more active in buying client company stocks in the mid-1960s to support prices, as the stock market staggered under the weight of heavy new supply. By 1965 there were 1,700 stocks traded on the Tokyo Stock Exchange, compared with 790 four years earlier. In spite of heroic efforts to prop up the market, stock prices slid steadily lower.

Akira Miyazawa, the chief of the securities bureau at the Bank of Japan, became concerned about the state of the brokerage industry. Before Miyazawa assumed his post in 1963, the low social status of stockbrokers had meant that even top officials of firms like Nomura and Yamaichi were never invited to meet with Bank of Japan officials. Miyazawa's own father had described stockbrokers as parasites who "use other people's money and give nothing back to society."[12] Miyazawa broke with past bank practice, arranging meetings with major brokerage firms to ascertain their financial health. He was stunned by what he found.

Yamaichi actually had a negative net worth measured in billions of yen. The firm was buried under the weight of massive stock purchases it had made to shore up the market prices of its clients' shares. Of the big four brokers, only Nomura appeared healthy enough to survive on its own. Miyazawa went to the board of directors of the Bank of Japan, arguing that if immediate assistance was not provided by the central bank, an awful collapse was in the offing. He was turned down by his superiors. The bank was legally prohibited from lending directly to securities firms, and senior officials were not eager to bend the rules.

Miyazawa then took an action unprecedented in the annals of central banking. He personally authorized large loans to the big four brokers, strictly on his own authority and without informing the board of directors. In order to preserve secrecy, he kept the amounts of the loans in his head; they ranged from 13.5 billion yen to Nikko to 5.2 billion yen for Nomura. Unfortunately, it soon became evident that even these amounts would be grossly inadequate. Customers of Yamaichi, unsettled by ominous rumors, were hastily withdrawing their funds from the firm. Miyazawa could see catastrophe looming.

By May 1965, leading newspapers were aware of Yamaichi's difficulties, as were reporters for NHK, the government-run television network. Officials of the opposition Socialist Party also caught wind of the impending crisis. In the United States or Britain, such a story could not possibly have been contained. But in Japan reporters and even opposition politicians felt they had a patriotic obligation to the country that superseded their own eagerness to break a major story. When asked by Ministry of Finance officials to suppress the story, they did so.

But the powerful bureaucrats in the ministry overlooked an obscure reporter named Tsutomu Matsuo employed by the regional daily *Nish-Nippon Shimbun*. Matsuo was given the story by an unidentified Yamaichi employee. Since Matsuo had not been asked to hold back, he broke the news with the understated headline "Yamaichi Ready for Reconstruction."

A full-scale panic broke loose. More than ten billion yen were withdrawn by fearful Yamaichi customers, and stocks associated with Yamaichi plummeted. "Please lend us some money," pleaded a Yamaichi officer to a Ministry of Finance official. "Nobody will lend us even a million yen." Reportedly, the government bureaucrat heard crying at the other end of the phone.[13] After the market closed on May 28, an emergency meeting of Bank of Japan and Ministry of Finance officials was convened, with heads of major banks in attendance. By this time, Kakuei Tanaka, the finance minister, had seen enough. He recognized that the panic had to be stopped.

Tanaka was not well liked by the bankers at the meeting; he was seen as arrogant and contemptuous of those who disagreed with him. He quickly lived up to his reputation. In insulting tones he derided the bankers at the meeting who wished to proceed with caution. Within an hour he had bludgeoned them into accepting his ideas. Although Tanaka technically did not have the authority to compel action, the "unofficial" status of the Ministry of Finance as the preeminent authority in the Japanese economy was such that no one could question him, including the officials from the Bank of Japan itself. A statement was released to the press stating that the government and the major banks were prepared to lend an unlimited amount to Yamaichi and the Japanese securities industry.

The director of a smaller brokerage firm, Fujio Kodama, said later that the entire securities industry in Japan would have disintegrated had not a prestigious member of the big four been the first firm to nearly collapse. Only the threatened collapse of a major firm could have forced the government to step in. According to Kodama, "the Japanese Financial World would have been a lot different if Tanaka had not forced the Bank of Japan to lend money."[14]

Yamaichi and other recipients of forced loans did not escape unscathed. The top officials of all the big firms other than Nomura were forced to resign, and the stigma attached to stockbrokers was accentuated. (Yamaichi employees refused to put the customary firm stickers on their cars for fear they would be abused or beaten up.) The bailout also established an important, and dangerous, precedent. In bailing out firms that had sought to artificially support stock prices, the government implicitly condoned the manipulation of stock prices to maintain values.

The authorities soon went even further. To support sagging stock prices in 1965, the government itself created two separate funds that purchased stocks totaling 2.5 percent and 3 percent, respectively, of the market's capitalization. The Japanese bureaucracy would not allow the market, and its support network, to collapse, even if this meant that direct intervention to support prices would be required.

As in the United States and Britain, scandals in the Japanese stock market did lead to some substantive reforms. A key instance resulted from the shocking declaration of insolvency by Sanyo Special Steel on March 3, 1965. It was later discovered that since 1959 the company had been posting fraudulent earnings and had been paying dividends of between 10 and 12 percent from these overstated earnings. The company had also paid its directors three times the amount disclosed; apparently the firm's auditor had known of the fraud but ignored it. The scandal caused the Ministry of Finance to rewrite the laws regulating accounting practices of public companies and to strengthen its own Securities Bureau for enforcement. The Sanyo Special Steel Case eventually led to a wholesale reevaluation of the commercial code, with increased power given to statutory examiners, and a requirement that all firms having capitalizations of more than one billion yen be made subject to independent audits.

The year 1965 marked a decisive turning point for the Japanese market. The all-powerful Ministry of Finance established the principle that the performance of the stock market would be closely monitored by policy makers and that the government would not hesitate to intervene, both to police irregularities and to actually manipulate the direction of the market when required. Going forward, the Japanese stock exchanges, far from being the independent institutions envisioned by the American-mandated rules of the postwar period, would instead become ever more inextricably enmeshed in an informal web of alliances among brokers, banks, and government.

Then, in 1969, Japanese authorities took a step that would significantly increase the role the stock market played in the Japanese economy by eliminating a traditional restriction on the way stock issues by public companies were priced. Previously, public Japanese companies had been required to offer any new stock they wished to sell at par value (usually the price at which the companies had originally gone public), even if their stock prices had since risen substantially above that level. Under this antiquated procedure, rights to purchase stock would be issued to existing shareholders at the time of a stock offering, entitling them to buy one additional share at par for each share they already owned. Obviously these rights could be very valuable, depending on how much above par the stock was trading at the time of the new issue. In this way, the benefit of a higher stock price had accrued to existing stockholders, not the company itself.

The effect of this system had been to discourage publicly traded firms from financing themselves with equity. As a result, Japanese firms had traditionally relied much more heavily on debt finance (particularly bank loans) than most American and British firms. By the late 1960s, most major companies listed on the Tokyo Stock Exchange had net worth (equity) that was less than 20 percent of total capital, far lower than comparable firms in Britain and the United States.

Starting in 1969, the requirement that stock offerings by public companies be sold at par was eliminated. The first company to take advantage of the new system was Nippon Gakki (now Yamaha, the maker of musical instruments). A flood of new equity offerings followed. In the period 1960–69, companies listed on the Tokyo Stock Exchange had raised a total of only 4 trillion yen through new stock offerings. In the following decade, despite difficult market conditions stemming from oil price shocks and recession, exchange-listed firms issued 11.6 trillion yen of additional equity.[15] Suddenly, the stock market was a potent force in Japanese corporate finance.

Companies now had a very important stake in their stock price, if they had any intention of raising more equity capital in the future. This should have made managements more responsive to individual shareholders and to the brokerage community, as had occurred in the United States and the United Kingdom, where managements sought to ensure that the marketplace viewed their firms favorably. But significantly, such an evolution in attitudes did not occur. Instead, a uniquely Japanese form of shareholder capitalism evolved.

The *keiretsu* system, as it came to be called, was actually a throwback to the old prewar *zaibatsu* arrangements. *Keiretsu*, literally "grouped in order," refers to the practice whereby companies with business relationships (customers, suppliers, etc.) buy stock in one another, with the intent of fortifying those relationships *and* supporting stock prices. For example, a company supplying parts to a manufacturer would be expected to buy shares in the manufacturer in order to obtain and maintain the supply contract. Or a trust bank, seeking to manage a company's pension fund, would be expected to buy stock in that company. The advantage of this system is that it creates a bulwark of stable shareholders who will not be very demanding of management and who will be disinclined to sell their shares as long as the business relationship exists. If these *keiretsu* holders comprise a significant portion of a company's shareholding base, management will be freed of the burdensome problem of placating more independent shareholders who might press bothersome demands such as improved short-term profitability or higher dividends. And such stable shareholdings will render the greatest fear of many managements—a hostile takeover designed to replace the existing management team—a hollow threat.

The all-powerful Ministry of Finance encouraged this process as a means to make equity capital cheaper for Japanese business and to increase stability in the market, so as to avoid a repetition of the unpleasant events of 1965. Because of *keiretsu* buying, the percentage of shares owned by corporations rose steadily, while the percentage held by individuals fell. Over the next decade, even though the overall Japanese economy grew quite rapidly, the number of shares available for trading in the stock market (the "free float") actually declined, as more and more stock was locked away in the *keiretsu* system of intertwined corporate investments.

As the Japanese government began to liberalize external capital controls in the 1970s, *keiretsu* cross-holdings made it very difficult for foreign investors, now allowed broad access to the Japanese market, to acquire controlling interests in Japanese companies. Too many shares were closely held by *keiretsu* interests friendly to existing managements. The buildup of cross-holdings also had the effect of pushing up stock valuations to higher levels, meaning that the stock market now provided capital at extremely low cost to companies seeking financing. And finally, the stability of *keiretsu* holdings also enabled linked companies to have long time horizons. Managements did not need to be overly worried about short-term earnings performance if major stockholders were locked into long-term relationships. This allowed Japanese firms to concentrate on expanding market share rather than generating current profits, a characteristic of Japanese managements that persists to this day.

By the mid-1970s the Japanese stock market had become an integral part of the Japanese economy. It is interesting to compare this state of affairs with that of Germany, because there seemed on the surface to be important similarities between Germany and Japan.

Both countries had highly concentrated banking systems and heavily industrialized economies that had traditionally been dominated by large business organizations.

The German stock market in the 1970s, however, was tiny compared to the Japanese. German companies made very sparing use of equity financing. As explained by one economist, before the 1980s new equity issues by German companies were a "completely insignificant" method of financing.[16] Equity made up a smaller percentage of new capital for large German companies, and German firms financed a much smaller proportion of their capital needs by new share offerings than did comparable Japanese firms.

Why the dramatic difference? The answer lies in the nature of the reforms imposed on Japan after World War II. The large *zaibatsu* industrial combinations in Japan were broken up and sold off to individuals, creating an army of small shareholders. Banks were forbidden to underwrite or deal in corporate securities, meaning that large banks, while still very important to the overall Japanese economy, would not be able to co-opt the nation's equity markets.

In Germany, on the other hand, the biggest German banks, which had been temporarily broken up after the war, were quickly allowed to reconstitute themselves. No effort was made to separate the stock brokerage and underwriting business from commercial banking operations. The "universal bank," as the principal financing mechanism of the German economy, remained intact. German new equity issuance was almost nonexistent; in 1972, for example, only one German company went public, compared to hundreds in the United Kingdom and the United States. German stock markets, to the extent they were significant at all, were clearly subordinate to the banking system.

Elsewhere in Europe, stock markets were generally of trivial importance in the 1970s. The *Financial Times* wrote, "As a source of capital, Italy's Stock Exchange is hardly a serious institution." Few Italian companies raised significant amounts of capital from the public sale of stock, and the market itself was illiquid, volatile, and of little interest to the public. The Belgian market, in spite of fairly liberal rules that encouraged foreign investment, was described as a "sad, rather deserted place."[17] In France, the market languished throughout most of the 1970s on relatively low trading volume and little new-issue activity. Even after the sharp drop in British stock prices in the mid-1970s, the U.K. market was still by far the largest in Europe. Over 4,000 companies had shares quoted on British exchanges in the late 1970s, compared to 1,000 in France and a mere 500 in Germany, although both the French and German economies were larger than that of Britain.

Profound cultural differences reinforced economic factors (such as universal banking) in stunting the growth of stock markets in non-Anglo countries. For an American or British entrepreneur, taking one's company public was a crowning achievement. The entrepreneur was willing to relinquish complete control in exchange for a quick infusion of capital, enhanced personal wealth measured by a public stock price, and the prestige associated with being part of a much more visible entity. The act of selling stock advertised that the business was successful and that it possessed great future potential. And of course the generally high valuations prevalent in the U.S. and U.K. markets made it quite attractive financially for the entrepreneur to sell shares.

Businessmen in other nations (outside Japan) tended to look at new stock sales very differently. Most firms were closely held by one family, with the objective of passing on ownership to succeeding generations. Selling stock to outsiders was seen as a sign of weakness, almost as humiliating as mortgaging the family homestead. Going "public" invited unwanted and potentially bothersome scrutiny from outside investors. Finally, the low valuations attached to stocks in many markets made new issues of stock unappealing to growing companies; selling equity was a very expensive means of financing.

In Europe and most of non-Japan Asia in the 1970s, privately controlled companies were the norm. The relatively few companies that did issue shares to investors frequently sold special nonvoting classes of stock, while the voting shares remained closely held. These nonvoting shares, sometimes called "savings shares," were quite respectable, often offered by large, established firms and underwritten by reputable banks or brokerage houses. But the use of nonvoting shares inevitably meant that public investors had little or no influence over corporate decision making. Corporate managements were much less concerned about what was happening in the stock market, and to their minority investors, than were managements in the United States or Britain.

In Germany, most large companies had at least one person or institution controlling enough shares to strongly influence management. In many instances this shareholder was a bank. (Sixty percent of all German shares were either owned directly by banks or controlled by banks that held them on deposit for individuals.) In the United States and Britain, on the other hand, most large companies had widely dispersed ownership, with no controlling shareholder. Advocates of the "German system" argued in the late 1970s that Germany's superior record of investment (investing more as a percentage of GNP in the postwar period) made the German approach better than the U.S.-U.K. model. It was said that businesses controlled by a large shareholder were less concerned with "short-termism," defined as the tendency of managements in the United States and Britain to place too much emphasis on managing short-term earnings to keep stock prices high, presumably causing firms to lurch from one shortsighted strategy to another at the expense of long-range planning.

Supporters of the universal banking system in Germany saw it as an important reason for the country's postwar success. As one historian wrote, "The banks helped rebuild German industry . . . after WWII. Firms rely extensively on loan, as against equity, finance, and the banks exercise an important monitoring role through their representatives on the Supervisory Board [of client companies] . . . the role of the banks tends to counter short-termism, and provides a mechanism for reorganizing management in good time, when a company starts running into trouble."[18] Because of their close involvement with their clients' business, German bankers were more willing to make long-term loans than their American or British counterparts. If a company was worth lending to, it was probably worth lending to long-term. And if it was worth lending to long-term, then it would probably be worth lending more to in the future.

The fact that the large banks had close contact with corporate management, often being substantial shareholders themselves and/or representing depositors who were shareholders, meant that the banks would be good monitors of company performance. In the United States and Britain, small shareholders, and institutions managing money for individual investors and pensioners, usually did not get involved in management. If they disliked the course of action chosen by a company's managers, the usual recourse was simply to sell the shares and invest elsewhere. In the British and American markets, the only real means of disciplining poor managements came from the threat of a hostile takeover, a messy and cumbersome process.

One important consequence, however, of the Anglo-American managerial focus on short-term stock price movements was that minority shareholders have generally been treated with much more consideration than in other countries. Because the daily trading volume of most stocks is small relative to the total number of shares outstanding, marginal buyers or sellers can have a significant price impact. Managements in the United States and Britain, very concerned about their stock price, thus do everything possible to woo current shareholders and potential investors, to keep them buying (or at least not selling) the company shares.

In contrast, in most other countries minority shareholders have been ignored, if not actually treated as a nuisance. Managements, responsive to the controlling shareholder(s), see little reason to coddle smaller investors in order to raise the stock price. Hard information on the company is difficult for outsiders to obtain, and corporate decisions are often made without considering the interests of minority holders. Family firms frequently prefer debt rather than equity financing in order to maintain tight control, resulting in much higher levels of debt financing (usually bank loans) than in U.S.-U.K. markets. Clearly these practices do not make for a broad, liquid stock market; in fact they discourage mass participation. Active, broad-based stock markets cannot exist where corporate managements view minority shareholders as adversaries rather than allies, and where most investors doubt that managements really seek to act in their interests.

Despite these drawbacks, the strong relative performance of the Japanese and German economies in the 1970s inevitably focused attention on the economic models employed in those countries. The neatly ordered, American-dominated postwar world, after the collapse of the Bretton Woods system and the devaluation of the dollar, no longer existed. Inflation, in theory beneficial to stocks, proved instead to have a devastating impact; the U.S. stock market, adjusted for inflation, fell by nearly two-thirds over the course of the decade. Radical new academic theories of portfolio management and market efficiency undermined traditional views of the market. As a percentage of world gross national product, total equity market capitalization in 1980 was *smaller* than it had been in 1913.

RETURN OF THE BULL

ON THE MORNING of May 3, 1979, the following call to arms appeared in the *Financial Times* of London: "The time to arrest the trends of the decades of post-war history is now. No one can be certain that the Tories will succeed. But they must be given a chance to try."

May 3 was the date of a long-awaited British general election. The Conservative Party, led by Margaret Thatcher, proposed nothing less than to throw off the statist doctrines that had for years dominated both the Labour and Conservative agendas. If the Tories won, henceforth market forces, not government planners, would direct the British economy. The brokers and jobbers of the City of London, like the editors of the *Financial Times*, overwhelmingly supported the Conservatives. Anticipating a Tory victory, the London stock market surged to an all-time high on election day.

The Conservative Manifesto specifically promised trade union reform, lower taxes, a reduction in government borrowing, and denationalization of aerospace and shipbuilding. Some observers questioned whether a Thatcher government could really reverse the seemingly inexorable trend toward expanded government intervention in the economy. The electorate, soured by years of inflation, stagnant growth, and labor unrest, gave the Tories a working majority in Parliament, but the result fell far short of a landslide. Arguably the election result was as much a vote against Labour as a vote for the Conservative agenda.

Ignoring the skeptics, Prime Minister Thatcher soon made it clear she intended to radically reshape the British economy. The Queen's speech on May 15 left little doubt that the Tories proposed to sink or swim with a free market. The Price Commission was abolished, ending an era in which the government routinely attempted to set prices for major products. A thorough review of all nationalized industries was initiated, with the intent of selling off those companies that were economically viable. Within weeks, controls on dividends were eliminated and a phase-out of foreign exchange controls was announced.

It is hard to appreciate today, when free-market policies are the norm rather than the exception, how dramatic these policy changes were. Followed a year and a half later by the election of the like-minded Reagan Administration in Washington, the new direction announced in London in 1979 marked a decisive turning point in both economic policy and intellectual opinion. The free-market critique of dissenters like Milton Friedman and Friedrich von Hayek had won out. The role of markets—including stock markets—would henceforth be far greater than before.

The immediate fate of the British stock market, however, was disappointing. After peaking at the time of the Conservative election victory, the market slid a distressing 30 percent over the remainder of the year. The open embrace of free markets did not resolve the problem posed by double-digit inflation, which the Thatcher regime proposed to strangle with a harsh monetary policy that would, in the short run, hinder economic growth and hit corporate profits hard. Just as the British economy was to be set free of regulation, it was to be straitjacketed by tight money.

By mid-November the Bank of England's lending rate had been pushed up to a record 17 percent. The monetary screws bit deep into the economy, with the general corporate distress unmitigated by the government's stated policy of allowing noncompetitive businesses to go under, without hope of bailouts. Even so, the City and the British business community remained supportive of Thatcher, anticipating better days ahead. Indicative of sentiment was a forecast issued by the investment firm Rowe and Pittman. Looking beyond the short-term pain inflicted by monetary stringency, the Rowe and Pittman analysts saw a new day of prosperous, deregulated markets that would follow. "In explorer's language," the report opined, "the valley threatens to be much deeper than expected, but the light across it is that much brighter."

The London stock market bottomed in mid-November 1979, just as the burden of tight money seemed to be crushing the life out of the economy. A few farsighted investors recognized that stocks, at then-current depressed levels, would prove to be good investments whether the Thatcher anti-inflation policy succeeded or failed. If the policy did not achieve its aims, so the reasoning went, stocks would at least protect investors from resurgent inflation in the future. But if the tight money policy did squelch inflation, the monetary easing that would eventually follow would create an environment in which business would prosper, allowing for increased profits and hence higher stock prices.

The belief that stocks would be a good hedge against inflation had been undermined by the dismal experience of the 1970s, but most academic research on the subject was careful to differentiate between short-term and long-term effects. In the short run, distortions to profits caused by inflation, and tight money policies designed to stanch inflation, could do great damage to stock prices. But in the long run, shares that represented ownership in ongoing businesses almost by definition had to appreciate, when valued in currencies themselves depreciated by inflation.[1]

An important test of this theory came in the United States. On October 6, 1979, Federal Reserve Board chairman Paul Volcker installed a harsh regime of monetary restraint, similar to that already in place in Britain. The American economy was laboring through a four-year expansion beset with foreign trade imbalances, weakness in the dollar, large federal budget deficits, high interest rates, and persistent inflation. Volcker took it upon himself to clean up the mess. He hiked the discount rate a full percentage point to an unprecedented 12 percent and placed curbs on the ability of banks to issue additional credit. His message was clear: the Fed was slamming on the brakes. Volcker believed that in the past the Federal Reserve had eased up prematurely in attempts to combat inflation, allowing the inflationary forces plaguing the economy to remain unextinguished. This time the Federal Reserve would persist in the unpleasant task until the job was finally done.

The drastic Fed action precipitated what was called the "October massacre" in the American financial markets. Stocks and bonds dropped sharply; over the ensuing two weeks the Dow Jones Industrials fell nearly 10 percent. *Barron's* termed the market action "a controlled panic." By untimely coincidence, the drop occurred almost exactly fifty years after the 1929 crash. The press was of course full of predictable comparisons.

But beneath the cataclysmic headlines lay another story. The stock market reaction to the new Fed policy was not as bad as had first appeared; in fact, the market regained all its losses in the months immediately following the October Massacre. When compared with the severe slides the market had taken earlier in the decade, the 1979 drop was relatively mild. American stock prices dipped early in 1980, but then recovered again. Prescient observers noted that at last the market seemed to be acting as the inflation hedge it was supposed to be.[2]

The mid-November 1979 decision by the Bank of England to raise the discount rate to 17 percent would prove to be the nadir of the British stock market; from that point, a long bull market began that would more than quintuple prices over seven years. The turn in the American market took longer, not arriving until August 1982, when the success of the Federal Reserve's anti-inflation policy finally allowed the central bank to ease monetary policy. It was at this point that the record-shattering American bull market of the 1980s and 1990s commenced. The impressive rises in both the U.K. and U.S. markets were made possible by monetary easing, which permitted the economies of the two nations to grow again, after inflation had been squeezed out. But also very important was the widespread acceptance of the new theories of market risk and efficiency, which encouraged a massive influx of pension and retirement money into equities. Just as government policy in Britain and the United States was radically reshaped by the pro-market ideology of economists like Milton Friedman and Friedrich von Hayek, world stock markets were rejuvenated by the not unrelated series of ideas that formed modern portfolio theory.

The widespread acceptance of modern portfolio theory made the abrupt elimination of foreign exchange controls in Britain in 1979 even more significant than it otherwise would have been. British stockbrokers and fund managers, who for an entire generation had relatively little experience investing in overseas markets (because capital controls prevented them from doing so), suddenly found that the entire world was open to them. A growing body of evidence indicated that movements in foreign stock markets were not well correlated (meaning that overseas markets did not tend to move up or down together). This implied that an acceptable level of risk could be achieved, even in a portfolio that had a great deal of exposure to relatively volatile foreign markets, if proper diversification between markets was maintained.

U.K. stock prices actually fell on the news of foreign exchange decontrol, because it was assumed (correctly) that portfolio managers would now invest more money overseas rather than in domestic British stocks. It was generally believed that only 2 to 4 percent of the assets of institutional portfolios were invested in foreign stocks at the time exchange controls were abolished. The expectation was that that figure would quickly rise to 10 percent or more, depriving the domestic stock market of buying power.

This issue was extremely controversial in 1980, when tight money was causing much hardship in British industry. Labour politicians complained bitterly at the surge of overseas investment at the very time when factories were closing almost daily. But the new breed of fund managers, armed with modern portfolio theory and the free-market ideology of the Thatcher government, insisted that they had a fiduciary duty to their clients to seek the best rate of return on their investments, commensurate with risk, even if that meant investing outside the United Kingdom. Foreign markets inevitably offered some opportunities for growth that British markets lacked, particularly in industries like electronics, information technology, and utilities. In addition, with exchange rates no longer fixed, investing overseas made it possible to hedge the risk that the British pound might depreciate relative to other currencies.

The downward pressure on U.K. stock prices resulting from the elimination of exchange controls was short-lived; the potential for improved corporate profitability under the Thatcher regime was too great to ignore. In fact, the abolition of capital controls likely helped the British stock market more than it hurt, because it gave non-British investors the confidence necessary to invest in Britain at the same time it made it possible for Britons to invest abroad. The huge amounts of money invested in American mutual and pension funds dwarfed the equity holdings of British institutions. Even a relatively small percentage of this American money, flowing into the London stock market, could and did have a dramatic impact.

A comparison of P/Es in the London market provides a measure of how much investor confidence, both foreign and domestic, increased during the first Thatcher term. When Thatcher first became prime minister in 1979, the overall P/E for the U.K. market was about 8 to 1. When the Tories sought and won reelection in 1983, corporate earnings were up only marginally (about 1 percent), but the market P/E had expanded to 12 to 1.

Ironically, just as British and American portfolio managers came to embrace modern portfolio theory, academic researchers began to raise questions about it. Initially, the objections centered on two issues. First, did the measure of risk (the so-called beta factor, which distilled the riskiness of an individual stock down to its volatility compared to the overall market) adequately encompass the full range of risk factors that affect stock prices? And second, were the stock markets of the world truly "efficient" in the sense that Fama described it? If either of these two crucial assumptions could be shown to be false, the entire theory could be called into question.

UCLA finance professor Richard Roll led the attack on the beta approach to risk analysis. Roll argued that risk in the stock market was related to a number of factors—such as currency fluctuations, interest rates, and inflation—that could not be captured by a single coefficient (beta) applied to a single market index (such as the Standard & Poor's 500). Roll went so far as to say that the concept of beta analysis, as it was currently used, was meaningless. In 1980, drawing largely on Roll's research, *Institutional Investor* published an article with the provocative title "Is Beta Dead?"

Other critics came forward, publishing studies showing that beta analysis did not accurately forecast stock market performance. They showed that beta factors tended to vary over time, and that the risks not measured by beta analysis were often very significant and were not eliminated by diversification. One of the most appealing elements of beta analysis was its simplicity. But it was this very simplicity that, according to the critics, made it deficient. They argued that other variables must be included to properly assess risk. These included such factors as asset replacement cost, credit risk, cash flow, unfunded pension liabilities, and changing rates of growth in the economy.

The reaction to the new research critical of beta analysis was mixed. One American portfolio manager commented, "I think Beta has some important information in it. But it may be such an imprecise measure of risk that we have to be very, very careful how we use it."[3] A proponent of beta accused critics of a more general resistance to the application of mathematics to finance, warning, "People who have been antagonistic to using the highest scientific standards in finance could use Roll's work to throw us back into the stone age."[4] But a beta critic scoffed, "If Roll is right, advanced mathematics will become to investors what the *Titanic* was to sailing."[5]

Beta was not the only component of modern portfolio theory to come under assault. Troubling empirical evidence contradicted the crucial assumption of the theory that the market was efficient—that all public information is reflected in stock prices, making it impossible for people to consistently beat the market by buying or selling stocks that they believe are priced incorrectly. When Eugene Fama defined the concept of the "efficient market," he argued that the market could be assumed to be efficient if no system of trading could be devised that consistently outperformed the market. Scholars took him up on this challenge, and many seemed to find anomalies that undermined Fama's theory.

One of the first to do so was finance professor Fischer Black, who took the straightforward approach of tracking the results of stock recommendations published in the *Value Line Investment Survey*. Writing in the *Financial Analysts Journal* in 1973, Black demonstrated how an investor who followed *Value Line*'s advice would have outperformed the market to a statistically significant degree. Black commented, "It appears that most investment management organizations would improve their performance if they fired all but one of their securities analysts and then provided the remaining analyst with the Value Line service."

Black's article was particularly troubling for proponents of the efficient market. The *Value Line Survey* was widely disseminated and could be obtained by any investor. If it was so easy to beat the market, how could the market be said to be efficient?

Other studies following Black's work found evidence of further anomalies. Wharton professors Marshall Blume and Irwin Friend, examining data from 1928 to 1968, discovered that the returns for stocks of small companies were greater than the returns for stocks of large firms, even after adjustments were made for the additional risk inherent in smaller firms.[6] This implied that small-capitalization stocks were not priced as efficiently as large-capitalization stocks.

Research also showed that stocks tended to perform differently on different days of the week. A 1977 study of low P/E stocks concluded that they tended to do better than the rest of the market, indicating that they were priced inefficiently.[7] But by far the most significant challenge to the efficient market concept came from Yale professor Robert Shiller, who compiled data on dividends and earnings from 1871 to 1979 and found that the stock market fluctuated far more than could be justified by changes in dividends.[8]

How could the market be truly efficient if it bounced around much more than changes in the underlying fundamentals (dividends paid to shareholders) justified? Shiller reasoned that this "excess volatility" was caused by the irrational behavior of stock market participants, meaning that the market was not efficient at all. In effect, Shiller provided intellectually rigorous support for the age-old idea that markets were subject to dramatic distortions caused by excess speculation and other nonrational patterns of behavior.

The work of Shiller and others who challenged the efficient market theory provided cover for many investment professionals who had chafed under the notion that the market could not be beaten, even by professionals such as themselves. Academics who continued to support the efficient market theory were derided as "eggheads," or "zealots." A story was often told about an imaginary University of Chicago professor who noticed a $100 bill lying on a sidewalk. The professor refused to believe the bill was really there; if it was, he said, someone would have grabbed it already. According to this professor's profoundly "rational" view of markets, phenomena like speculative bubbles could not occur.

Although the academic debate on the question of market efficiency was occurring almost exclusively in the United States and Britain, it would be the Japanese stock market that would provide the most pronounced example of what many observers believed to be "bubble" behavior. In December 1980, Japan followed Britain's example and finally eliminated exchange controls that had hindered foreign investment in Japanese stocks. Under the new Foreign Exchange and Foreign Trade Control Law, the treatment of investment from overseas entities was changed from a policy of "prohibition in principle" to "freedom in principle."[9] This was part of a broader plan to gradually deregulate Japanese financial institutions and to open up Japanese markets. According to one contemporary Western writer, the "leading Japanese financial institutions border on the feudal compared with their Western counterparts."[10] Presumably foreign competition would force hidebound Japanese banks and brokerage firms to shape up.

Much of the pressure for reform in Japan came from Western countries, particularly the United States, that had bought into the newly fashionable pro-market ideology. But despite well-publicized steps to open up markets in Japan, external pressure never fundamentally altered the traditionally close relationship between the government and business that had existed ever since the mid-nineteenth-century Meiji decision to use the power of government to drag Japan forcibly into the modern world.

The Japanese economic model differed greatly from Western concepts of laissez-faire capitalism. The Ministry of International Trade and Industry, acting as a national planning board, directed the economy through "administrative guidance," an approach that relied more on traditional relationships and patterns of behavior than on overt legal mechanisms. The MITI, as it was called, often made major decisions as to which technologies would be developed and which industries would be favored by government policy. It rationed foreign exchange, determining what could and could not be purchased abroad. In the financial sector, the Ministry of Finance coordinated overall industrial policy with the MITI, directing the activities of banks, insurance companies, and brokerage firms. This was relatively easy, given a securities industry dominated by the big four and a banking industry consisting of only about 150 banks, compared to the approximately 14,000 banks in the United States. The Ministry of Finance would communicate its policy decisions informally to the top executives of a few large financial entities, and those decisions would be obeyed.

The result was that the Japanese stock market continued to evolve as a curious hybrid. Its basic structure had been established by the American occupying authority after World War II, but the Americanized system of rules and regulations coexisted with uniquely Japanese practices. A securities industry catering to middle-class investors had flourished, while still allowing traditional patterns of corporate cross-holdings typical of old *zaibatsu* arrangements. Rules forbidding manipulative practices by individuals were on the books, and sometimes enforced, while at the same time the Ministry of Finance itself routinely engaged in operations designed to "direct" the market in ways favored by government policy. Most fundamentally, the financial markets were organized to provide cheap capital to Japanese businesses, at the expense of investors. Interest rates paid to thrifty Japanese savers were set by fiat at very low levels, and high stock prices, with very low dividend payments, were a goal of government policy. High stock prices made it possible for Japanese firms to sell their shares at very attractive levels. But conversely, the implied return to be received by investors who bought those expensive shares would not be very good.

Easy credit was an essential element of Japanese economic policy. The Bank of Japan pursued an expansionary monetary policy; as late as 1989, after years of rapid growth in the Japanese economy, its basic lending rate was a mere 2.5 percent, less than half what it had been earlier in the decade. Prime corporate clients could borrow from banks at 4 percent. The government directed banks to lend in excess of actual economic needs, providing cheap capital for business. The loans were collateralized by land or stock and were usually never paid off, being rolled over year after year. High land and stock prices were thus essential to the government's economic strategy; inflated real estate and equity values provided the collateral upon which the aggressive lending policy could be based.

During the 1980s the Japanese model seemed to be a smashing success. Westerners had long admired the ability of Japan to mobilize and direct its resources to accomplish national goals. The *Financial Times* looked back with approval to a book that had been written in 1905 by the British journalist Alfred Stead, entitled *Great Japan: A Study of National Efficiency*. The original edition of the book had included a preface by a former British prime minister, Lord Rosebery, proclaiming, "Japan is indeed the object-lesson of national efficiency, and happy is the country that learns it." References to the "Japanese miracle" were common in the West. A book entitled *Japan as Number One* became a best-seller in both Japan and the United States. The Japanese stock market, measured by the Nikkei average, skyrocketed over the decade of the 1980s, up nearly 600 percent to almost 39,000 in 1989. Price-earnings ratios jumped from under 25 to 1 in 1980 to nearly 60 to 1 by the end of the decade. (P/Es in the United States and Britain averaged under 20 to 1 in 1989.)

While Japanese authorities made superficial changes in the 1980s to open up and liberalize the market, it was still a game dominated by a relatively few players, acting in collusion with the Ministry of Finance to achieve government policy objectives of promoting growth by making cheap equity capital available for Japanese business. High stock prices meant that Japanese firms could raise capital by selling their shares very dearly, with trivial dividend rates that, at the height of the boom, averaged only about 0.5 percent. (This compared with U.S. dividend rates of about 3 percent at the stock market peak in 1987.) Obviously, Japanese firms with such a low cost of capital had a big advantage over their foreign competitors. They could afford to spend massive amounts of money to modernize facilities and engage in research and development, financed on the backs of Japanese investors who received minimal dividends and interest rates on their invested savings.

How were such high stock prices maintained? Ultimately, it was the *kieretsu* system of corporate cross-holdings, combined with overt market support schemes orchestrated by the Ministry of Finance, that sustained the stock market boom. In the early 1950s, shortly after the American occupying authorities had forced the dissolution of the *zaibatsu* conglomerates, roughly 70 percent of Japanese stocks had been held by individuals. By 1989 this condition had been completely reversed, with 70 percent of listed shares in Japan now held by other listed corporations, banks, and insurance companies. In effect, Japan, Inc., owned 70 percent of itself.

Most of these holdings were tied to business relationships. For example, it would not be unusual for a company that made parts for an automaker to own stock in that automaker. Likewise, the automaker could (and likely would) also own stock in the supplier. These cross-holdings had the effect of cementing long-term business relationships, and were often required if one company wished to do business with another. In October 1989, when Japan's four largest steel companies (Nippon, Kawasaki, Sumitomo, and Kobe) announced that they were establishing pension funds for their employees, they stipulated that any trust bank or life insurer seeking a role in managing the new funds must buy at least ten million shares in the respective steel producer to gain the business. An institution that wanted to handle the lucrative administrative work for the funds would be required to purchase fifty million shares. Steel stock prices were slumping due to market concerns that steel prices were coming under competitive pressure. Knowing that further equity financings would be required in the future, the steel companies saw a need to support their share prices, and openly sought to do so by using the pension management contracts as leverage.[11]

The large banks were inextricably tied into the *keiretsu* system. The Japanese banking system was divided into three distinct groups. First were the three Credit banks: Industrial Bank of Japan, Long-term Credit Bank, and Nippon Credit Bank. Since 1945 these banks, originally established with close government cooperation, had implemented the government's industrial policy by making long-term strategic loans to favored industries and companies. The second group of banks—the so-called City banks—were the main shareholders of the various *keiretsu* groupings. (The six largest City banks—Sumitomo, Mitsubishi, Mitsui Taiyo Kobe, Dai-ichi Kangyo, Sanwa, and Fuji—were the core entities in the six largest *keiretsu*.) The third grouping was the so-called Trust banks. Only these banks were permitted to handle trusts and estates for individuals and manage corporate pension funds.

Unlike in the United States, where banks were forbidden to own stocks directly, almost every major Japanese bank held a large portfolio of equities. The major banks usually owned substantial blocks of stock in their customers, and were in turn largely owned by their customers. The percentage of shares in these banks owned by individual investors was tiny. In 1989 only 2 percent of Industrial Bank of Japan shares were owned by private investors. The comparable figure for the Long-term Credit Bank was 3 percent, 4 percent for Nippon Credit, and an average of less than 5 percent for the major City and Trust bank shares.[12] Most of the banks' shares were owned by corporations that were clients of the banks.

The banks could and did turn to their corporate shareholders frequently to secure additional equity financing. Industrial Bank of Japan was a prime example. Although its profits were not large and its dividend payouts were quite low, IBJ shares rose 1,800 percent between 1984 and 1989, largely due to the fact that so few free-floating shares were available and because its core corporate customer-investors kept on buying. Despite a P/E ratio of 80 to 1, the bank was able to call repeatedly on its shareholders when needed to buy new issues of still more shares.

Similar concentrated corporate shareholding existed among major industrial firms. Sony's top ten shareholders in 1989 (all of which were corporations) held 40.7 percent of its shares; only 13.1 percent were considered to be floating shares, available for trading in the marketplace. For Nissan, 33 percent of shares were owned by the top ten stockholders, with only 8.7 percent of the total outstanding free-floating.[13] Overall, for stocks listed on the Tokyo Stock Exchange, only about 25 percent of all shares were not owned by long-term corporate, banking, or insurance holders, most of whom had business relationships with the companies in which they owned shares.

Compare this distribution of share ownership to that which existed in the United States. It is true that the percentage of publicly traded shares held by individuals in American markets fell from nearly 80 percent after World War II to 71 percent in 1980 and

58 percent in 1989, and would continue to decline in the 1990s. But most of the difference was taken up by institutions (such as mutual funds and pension funds) acting as proxies for individuals, rather than by industrial corporations, banks, and insurance companies, as in Japan. It is relatively rare for publicly traded American corporations to own large blocks of stock in other publicly traded firms. The American stock market continued to be a market in which individuals, either directly or through institutional proxies, were the dominant participants.

The cash returns (dividends) shareholders received in both markets declined in percentage terms in the 1980s, continuing the trend toward lower dividend payments that had accompanied the abandonment of traditional standards of valuation based on current dividends in favor of standards based on future earnings potential. But significantly, in the United States shareholders were partly compensated for the lesser dividends through the mechanism of stock buybacks, where companies would repurchase their own shares in the open market. This had the effect of putting money directly into shareholders' hands, and increased the earnings per share of the companies by reducing the number of shares outstanding. No such offset to lower dividend rates existed in Japan, where major companies were forbidden by law from repurchasing their own shares.

Japanese firms instead plowed excess funds into *keiretsu* investments in other listed corporations. Since these purchases were made for business relationship reasons and not evaluated as stand-alone investments, the corporate purchasers were not especially concerned about the rates of return they would receive. This system was ideal for maintaining artificially high stock prices, which, in turn, provided a ready source of cheap capital for companies that wished to issue equity.

During the 1960s, before equity financing had become widely accepted, Tokyo exchange-listed companies had raised a mere 4 trillion yen through equity issuance. This figure increased to 11.6 trillion yen in the 1970s and to 73 trillion yen in the 1980s. (A phenomenal 25 trillion yen in new stock was sold by exchange-listed firms in 1989 alone, an amount equivalent to 6.3 percent of Japan's gross domestic product.)[14] During the 1980s in the United States, by contrast, net new stock issuance was actually negative, as American companies bought back a net amount of nearly $500 billion in equities through stock repurchases, leveraged buyouts, and mergers. Over the decade of the 1980s, Japanese companies increased their equity base by $1 trillion relative to their American counterparts.

The high prices in the Japanese stock market in the late 1980s did seem to deter foreign investors. Fujitsu carried twice the P/E of IBM, Kawasaki Steel was valued at seven times the P/E of Bethlehem Steel, and Nippon Telephone and Telegraph was valued three times higher than AT&T, despite the fact that NT&T earned 40 percent less than AT&T. Japan's sixteen largest commercial banks had a market capitalization six times greater than the combined market capitalization of the fifty largest American banks. After foreign exchange controls were liberalized in 1980, overseas investment in Japanese stocks initially increased. But the flow of funds into Japan peaked in 1983, when 6.3 percent of all listed stock was owned by foreigners, and then fell. By 1989, foreigners owned only about 4 percent of all Japanese listed stocks. Overseas investors could find much more attractive opportunities in other countries. The fact that foreigners were net sellers during the late-1980s boom tended to reinforce the belief on the part of Japanese corporate managers that foreign investors were undesirable, because they would quickly sell out when prices appeared to be too high or when conditions temporarily worsened.

Critics of the Japanese "bubble economy" of the 1980s (a term that came into wide usage only during the Japanese economic decline of the 1990s) cited seemingly absurd stock market valuations and the easy money policy that presumably helped create them as evidence that Japan was caught up in the late 1980s in a classic speculative bubble. By implication, both Japanese investors, and foreign investors newly permitted into the Japanese market, were overcome by an emotional enthusiasm for the success of the Japanese economic model, an enthusiasm that expressed itself in the same type of speculative excess seen so often in stock markets in the past.

Unfortunately, as is frequently the case with conventional wisdom (and popular mythology) about "bubbles," a closer examination of the facts casts doubts on this widely accepted interpretation. A comparison with the so-called South Sea and Mississippi bubbles of 1720 is in order. In those instances, stock prices thrust upward to astronomical heights, far beyond what was justified by the fundamentals of the companies involved, only to come crashing down later. But in both cases the heavy hand of government played a decisive role. John Law in France openly proposed to "fix" the price of Mississippi Company shares at 10,000 livres, in order effectively to set interest rates at the low level of 2 percent. Likewise, in Great Britain, the directors of the South Sea Company, assisted by allies in Parliament, blatantly attempted to manipulate South Sea share prices higher. Investors who sought to profit from these actions could not be described as "irrational" or "foolish"; they were simply hoping to benefit from a manipulated stock market that was in no way free.

Similar circumstances exisited in the Japanese stock market of the 1980s. Government policy mandated high stock prices to fortify Japanese companies with cheap capital, so that they could better compete in the world arena. With 70 percent of the market owned by corporate "relationship" investors who were not likely to sell at any price (and in fact often bought more), the task of maintaining high stock prices was not nearly as difficult as it would have been in a totally free market.

It was the individual Japanese investor who was made to bear the burden of this rigged market system. The Ministry of Finance protected the small investor from outright fraud, but beyond that the brokerage industry, and the entire stock market, was structured to minimize internal competition and channel funds to industry. Officials of the securities bureau of the ministry were usually highly protective of the companies they were supposed to regulate. In part the close relationship between government bureaucrats and brokerage firm officials was related to the practice, widespread in all ministries, of *amakudari*, whereby government bureaucrats would routinely retire at age fifty-five and "descend from heaven" to a lucrative position in the private sector. Regulators expecting to eventually "descend from heaven" would be unlikely to take actions that would damage their future employers.

Despite the preponderance of corporate cross-holdings in the market, however, individual investors were still quite important. If

Japanese brokers had been merely divisions of universal banks (as in Germany), other issues, such as corporate control and lending, would likely have taken preference over stock market activity. But since the brokers, separated from the banks by virtue of American-imposed law, derived their profits from the stock market, a viable market was essential to their success. Because corporate cross-investors held stocks for the long term and thus seldom traded, stock prices were set at the margin largely by the actions of middle-class investors, who also generated much of the commission income important to the brokerage industry.

Stock brokerage was the most profitable industry in Japan in the 1985–89 period, with returns on equity averaging 21 percent. Nomura had the largest profits of any company in 1987, and ranked third behind Toyota in 1989. In 1989, 38 percent of brokerage firm revenue came from commissions, 14 percent from equity underwriting, and 15 percent from trust fund management.[15] Individuals accounted for 23 percent of the 673-trillion-yen turnover of the largest brokers and for 30 percent of the commissioned trades.

The sad experience of the Japanese investment trusts in the 1980s indicates how individual investors were often badly mistreated. As stock prices soared over the decade, shares became prohibitively expensive for many small investors. At the end of 1989, for example, the average share price of Tokyo Stock Exchange stocks was 1,867 yen, with a minimum trading lot of 1,000 shares. At this level a single transaction would cost the average worker three months' pay. Unlike their Western counterparts, Japanese companies rarely split their shares to accommodate small investments. To get around this problem, major brokerage firms created investment trusts, which were somewhat like American mutual funds.

Investment trusts became an affordable way to play the market; due to aggressive sales efforts by stockbrokers, investments in equity investment trusts rose from 5.8 trillion yen in 1985 to 22.3 trillion in 1987. Unfortunately, the returns generated by the trusts were dismal. Throughout the 1980s, when Japanese stock prices (including dividends) grew at an annual rate of 21 percent, trusts returned only 3.8 percent annually. Trusts held 3.4 percent of all equities over the period 1981–89, but accounted for 8 percent of turnover.[16] The high turnover rate suggests that they were churned mercilessly to benefit the brokers operating them, who received both management fees and commissions on transactions executed for the trusts.

Investment trusts could only be offered by fifteen brokerage firms licensed by the government, and thus had very limited competition. The four largest trusts, tied to the big four brokers, had nearly 75 percent of the total business and usually turned in the worse performance. Trust shares typically could not be redeemed for the first two years after purchase; quite often, immediately after the two-year period lapsed, holders would come under intense pressure from salesmen to cash out of funds and invest in new ones, thus generating more sales commissions. Trusts also often became a convenient repository for low-quality new stock offerings the managing brokerage firm was otherwise unable to sell, and trust funds were used shamelessly by their broker-managers to support the stock prices of client companies.

It should be evident by now that the Japanese stock market of the 1980s was very different from its Western counterparts, even though the framework under which the market nominally operated was similar to that of the American market (and in fact had been patterned after it). The central objective of the Japanese stock market was to provide cheap equity capital for Japanese industry, in order to make Japan more competitive internationally. As one writer put it, "The Japanese stock market can best be described as an inadequately regulated exchange controlled by a cartel of brokers and run for the benefit of listed companies."[17] The "benefit" received by the listed companies was access to cheap capital, through the sale of their stock at high prices.

It is thus clearly incorrect to describe, as so many analysts have done, the Japanese stock boom as an irrational bubble, inflated by investors acting on emotion rather than reason. High stock prices were *institutionalized* in Japan, as a direct consequence of government policy.

Furthermore, while Japanese stock prices certainly were "high" in the late 1980s, they were not as outrageous as the bubble theorists insist. The practice of companies making cross-investments in each other, for business relationship reasons, creates an issue of double-counting in the denominator of the earnings-per-share ratio, which is in turn used to calculate P/Es. If Company A owns shares in Company B while Company B also owns shares in Company A, in theory these cross-holdings should cancel each other out. If cross-holdings are eliminated, the number of shares used to calculate earnings per share declines, meaning that the earnings-per-share ratio goes up. And obviously, if the earnings-per-share figure used in the denominator of P/E ratios increases, the P/E ratio itself declines proportionately. The best estimates are that the true P/E ratios for the Japanese market in the late 1980s are literally cut in half by eliminating cross-holdings from consideration. Japanese shares, while still quite expensive by non-Japanese standards, were not nearly as overvalued as they appeared to be.

In addition, because Japanese managements were under little pressure from their stable shareholder base to report high profits in the short run, they often understated profits to minimize taxes. Japanese companies routinely used accelerated depreciation in reports to shareholders, which tends to reduce reported profits for capital-intensive firms. (In the United States, on the other hand, companies only use accelerated depreciation for tax purposes, reporting to shareholders earnings figures based on straight-line depreciation.) Japanese firms also tend to take much larger reserves for contingencies, which has the effect of depressing reported profits. Some analysts have suggested that the net effect of these accounting differences was to cause reported Japanese earnings data to be understated by 40 percent relative to U.S. figures. This estimate may well be exaggerated, but it illustrates the problems involved in making apples-to-apples comparisons of valuations across the two markets. Obviously, lower reported profits make P/E ratios appear to be higher, further exacerbating the apparent overvaluation of Japanese equities.

Another very important advantage of the *keiretsu* system of corporate cross-holdings, as far as Japanese managements were concerned, was that it made hostile takeovers virtually impossible. In Anglo-American markets, hostile takeovers were a blunt-force method of making management accountable to shareholders. In theory, if a company's stock price languished because of poor management, an outside party could buy up the shares, oust the management, and then proceed to run the company in a manner designed to maximize "shareholder value."

The antics of colorful characters like Charles Clore in Britain in the 1950s gave hostile takeovers something of a bad name. That image was reinforced in the 1980s, when both the American and British stock markets were repeatedly rocked by hostile takeover bids from corporate "raiders" who sought to acquire companies with undervalued assets or, as the raiders would claim, underperforming managements. Hostile takeovers were often messy, controversial affairs that, if successful, could provide unseemly profits to the acquirers while at the same time forcing the acquired firm to restructure in a way that cost many employee jobs.

Corporate raiders such as T. Boone Pickens, Carl Icahn, and Sir James Goldsmith became household names. The "raiders" defended themselves by arguing that they were simply agents of the marketplace, disciplining recalcitrant managements who had not done well for shareholders. When Pickens attempted a hostile takeover of Gulf Oil Company, he noted that Gulf's oil reserves were worth more than $100 per Gulf share, at a time when Gulf's stock was trading around $47. Pickens believed that Gulf shareholders would be better off if the company was dismantled and the reserves sold off. Pickens bluntly stated that the difference between the stock price of Gulf Oil and the value of the company's reserves represented what he called "the negative contribution of the management."[18]

Overall, Pickens and other raiders like him were quite successful. Goldman Sachs estimated that a major portion of the American stock market's rise in the mid-1980s came from the anticipation of takeover bids.[19] By 1987 the annual value of merger activity in the United States reached nearly $300 billion; close to half of all large American companies received a takeover offer during the 1980s. (Pickens later ran into difficulty, however, when he sought to expand his field of activity to Japan. Attempting a hostile takeover of Koito, a firm in which Toyota had substantial cross-holdings, he discovered that corporate shareholders of Koito were not about to abandon their traditional relationships to sell out to a foreign raider, regardless of the potential profit a hostile offer might entail. The Koito bid failed.)

The Thatcher liberalization in Britain created an open season for hostile takeovers, with both foreign and domestic companies participating. Takeover activity hit a record £16.55 billion in Britain in 1986, dwarfing previous totals. As hostile bids grew more acrimonious, it was not uncommon for contending parties to use negative advertising campaigns to disparage opposing bidders. A low point was reached in the bitter struggle between Guinness and Argyll for control of Distillers. Guinness eventually won out, but several executives were later subject to criminal prosecution when it was revealed that an orchestrated effort had been made to manipulate the price of Guinness shares, which were to be used to buy Distillers stock.

This was not a pretty picture, but advocates of the Anglo-American model of equity markets argued that such unpleasant eventualities were necessary to ensure that managements were responsible to shareholders. If a management team did not run its company in a manner that produced value for stockholders, someone else could step in, buy up the company, and replace the team with people who would. This brutal mechanism was abhorrent to Japanese, and many Continental European, executives. The very stability and long-term orientation that seemed to make the Japanese and German economies successful were at stake.

Ironically, the system of stable cross-holdings that protected Japanese managements from hostile takeovers made them vulnerable in other ways. Because so few shares were actually available for public trading, it was much easier for various unsavory market operators to manipulate prices, even of stocks of major companies. In many instances, speculators would attempt to "corner" the floating supply of shares, with the idea that they would cause trouble for management until a profitable buyout of their interests (usually by one or more of the firm's stable shareholders) could be arranged. Another scheme would be to reduce the floating supply of shares so much that the company would face delisting from the Tokyo Stock Exchange, an embarrassing consequence all managements wanted to avoid. In many ways these practices were not unlike incidents of "greenmail" in the United States and Britain, in which corporate raiders would buy up a percentage of a company's shares, threatening a hostile takeover, hoping to be bought off by the target company's management through the purchase at a higher price of the shares the raider owned.

An official Japanese study conducted between April 1987 and March 1989 found 128 instances of share "cornering." In 1988 alone, there were 95 such cases, compared with only 25 five years earlier. In 32 of these instances, share prices rose four to six times, and in 9 cases share prices jumped over ten times.[20]

Even more disturbing were the notorious activities of the *sokaiya*—literally, individuals whose business it was to attend shareholder meetings. Before the war, *sokaiya* were routinely hired by managements and paid a small honorarium to make sure stockholder meetings ran smoothly. After the war, the practice evolved into something like a protection racket, where many *sokaiya*, often associated with organized crime, became extortionists, disrupting meetings if they were not paid off by management in advance. In one instance, *sokaiya* tied up the 1984 annual Sony shareholders' meeting for thirteen hours with their disruptive tactics. Worse, *sokaiya* sometimes threatened corporate officials with blackmail or physical injury. Many companies preferred to pay the relatively small amounts involved rather than deal with the consequences of not paying.

If *sokaiya* were compensated, as they often were throughout the 1980s, they would then become ruthless allies of management. It was not uncommon for *sokaiya* to shout down or physically intimidate dissident shareholders. For this reason the practice was illegal; prosecutions of management officials for paying off *sokaiya* became increasingly common, with several resulting scandals. By the end of the decade, many companies had had enough. Embarrassed by negative publicity and threatened with legal sanction, on June 29, 1989, 694 exchange-listed companies held their shareholder meetings at the same time to prevent *sokaiya* from attending more than one. By the 1990s, the practice of simultaneous shareholder meetings had become the norm.

The willingness of Japanese managements to tolerate the *sokaiya* is indicative of how little importance those managements attached to shareholder relations. The Anglo-American notion that managements should work primarily to enhance shareholder value was fundamentally inimical to the way most Japanese corporations were run.

The Japanese openly derided such concerns as "short-termism," preferring instead to concentrate on long-term growth in sales and market share without being troubled by the need to generate short-term earnings and dividends for shareholders. Of equal importance was the strong desire to preserve the practice of "lifetime employment" in major firms, which had become the indispensable foundation for the social compact between Japanese labor and management.

The idea that employees should be given lifetime tenure by employers had actually originated in many of the old *zaibatsu* organizations before World War II. The period immediately after the war, when the *zaibatsu* conglomerates were broken up, was one of great labor unrest. Newly organized labor unions, sanctioned by the American occupying authority, quickly came under Communist influence. After much turmoil, the unions were tamed, but only through the acceptance by employers of a broad range of reforms that effectively made blue-collar Japanese workers the equal of white-collar employees. The distinctions between management and labor were intentionally blurred to achieve social peace. In this system, the job of every employee was equally important, and every worker was an integral part of the greater organization. Workers would subordinate their individual interests to the overall interests of the firm, if, at the same time, the firm recognized that it had an almost paternal obligation to its employees. If its workers were like "family," dismissals or mass layoffs were out of the question.

Japanese firms were expected to retain all their employees, regardless of economic conditions. This inevitably led to what would in the West be called "redundancy," and depressed profits when economic growth was slow. An American or British firm would likely respond to adverse economic circumstances by laying off workers. Furthermore, the big American and British mergers in the 1980s often resulted in slashing reductions in staffing levels, as a means of ruthlessly cutting costs to facilitate carrying the heavy debt load that the merger required. But Japanese firms could not really consider mass firings, not so much because of explicit labor legislation but rather because of the stigma that would be attached by Japanese society to such actions.

Clearly a conflict could (and often did) exist between maximizing shareholder value and maintaining lifetime employment. It is here that the cross-shareholdings system and lifetime employment were inextricably linked. The fact that most managers expected to be employed by one firm for their entire working life meant that those managers who were responsible for making cross-holding investment decisions could afford to take a long-term view. They did not need to press for maximum returns on their firm's cross-holding investments, instead concerning themselves more with the long-term relationships those investments represented. At the same time, the existence of stable "relationship" shareholders, who did not press managements to maximize short-term earnings or dividends, meant that managements had the necessary leeway to sacrifice short-run profits to maintain employment levels, allowing for the very lifetime tenure that made cross-holding investments possible.

Significant financial innovations were not likely to occur in the heavily structured Japanese markets. Hostile takeovers as a means of disciplining managements were virtually unknown. Despite the Japanese stock market boom of the 1980s, management responsiveness to shareholders was not much better than in Continental European countries, where equity markets had traditionally played much smaller roles. This was illustrated by a study conducted by the Investor Responsibility Research Center in 1989. The study ranked countries on the basis of four standards: disclosure, voting rights, the ease with which shareholders could introduce corporate resolutions, and the manner in which shareholders were notified of important meetings and proxy votes. Scores were calculated: the United States received a rank of 100; Japan only rated a 48, on a par with France and Germany.[21]

For most of the 1980s, the Japanese system seemed to be working. Stock prices rose at an annualized rate of 21 percent per year, despite the fact that operating profits per share for Tokyo exchange-listed stocks grew only 2.8 percent per year. (Net income for these firms rose at a 5 percent rate, but the heavy issuance of new shares reduced the increase in profits per share to only 2.8 percent.) It was thus the expansion of valuations—P/E ratios—that provided most of the gain in stock prices.

As in Britain and the United States, falling interest rates justified some of the rise in valuations. Government bond yields in Japan fell from around 10 percent in 1980 to 3.5 percent in 1987; declines in the Anglo countries were of comparable magnitude. But these interest rate reductions were nowhere near large enough by themselves to justify the expansion of Japanese P/E multiples during the decade, particularly considering that the multiple expansion continued after interest rates began to rise again in 1987. The Japanese market divorced itself from valuation concerns, especially during the later years of the 1980s. It was an *administered* market, directed by government policy and cozy corporate relationships, not the free interplay of supply and demand.

As the Japanese market boomed, its defenders became openly disdainful of critics, usually from outside Japan, who questioned the seemingly stratospheric valuations. One Japanese analyst wrote that P/E ratios "should not be allowed to act as an undue discouragement from purchasing Japanese equities because, in some senses, the idea of a price-earnings ratio imposes Western concepts of value on stocks that are not subject to Western market conditions."[22] Nomura, the largest Japanese brokerage firm, ran a two-page advertisement in 1988 headlined "Copernicus and Ptolemy." Nomura compared its bullish view on Japanese equities to the ideas of Copernicus, who first calculated that the earth revolved around the sun rather than vice versa. The skeptics (those with bearish views) were compared to Ptolemy, whose belief in an earth-centered universe was consigned to the dustbin of history. Nomura's advertisement concluded with the phrase: "Copernicus or Ptolemy? Enlighten yourself."

Even some Japanese investors, however, preferred to hedge their bets, not fully accepting the oft-repeated justifications for high domestic stock prices. There was a surge in overseas investment by Japanese individuals and institutions in the mid-1980s. Most of this money went to the United States; in 1986, for example, fully three times as much Japanese money went to purchase American stocks as went into European equities.[23] A measure of the interest in foreign securities can be seen in the activity of the Foreign Section of the Tokyo exchange, which had begun operations in 1973. The Section started very slowly, initially hamstrung by foreign exchange controls and suspicion of foreign investments in general. By 1984 only eleven non-Japanese stocks were listed.

But then it took off. By the end of 1987, eighty-eight companies were traded in the Foreign Section, and the volume of trading in foreign stocks skyrocketed. Turnover jumped in 1985 to fully nine times the 1984 level, and the 1985 number itself was quadrupled by 1987. Foreign stock prices appeared to be quite cheap by Japanese standards, the vigorous incantations of the Tokyo market bulls notwithstanding.

Other than high valuations, there were warning signs that the Japanese system of administered stock prices was shakier than it appeared to be. An increasingly large share of earnings reported by Japanese corporations was coming from gains in their *keiretsu* stock holdings, as opposed to profits from actual operations. Nowhere was this more evident than in the banking system, where a deterioration in the economics of the banking business was disguised by stock market profits.

The deregulation of the financial sector in the 1980s had hurt major banks in two ways. First, large companies now had other options when they needed to borrow money; because they could go directly into the international financial markets, they were no longer tied to domestic banks. Second, the interest rates banks paid their depositors, which had been fixed by law at very low levels, rose as these rates were decontrolled. Thus many banks were squeezed from two sides. Their cost of funds was greater, while much of the most profitable business of loaning money to top corporate clients was taken away by new competitors.

Ominously, in 1989 42 percent of profits of Japanese City banks came from gains on securities, not from their regular business. Dai-Ichi Kangyo Bank, Japan's largest City bank, actually realized 60 percent of its profits from selling shares for capital gains. A study by the consulting firm McKinsey and Company revealed that between 1984 and 1990, Japanese banks reported annual profit increases of 13 percent. But, the survey also revealed, if stock market gains were excluded, profits had grown at only a puny 1 percent rate.[24]

To make matters worse, stock market profits often resulted from what was in reality merely paper shuffling. The banks would take gains by selling some of their long-term stockholdings to inflate reported profits, in the process incurring a burdensome tax liability, but would then have to repurchase most of the shares they sold to maintain their *keiretsu* relationships. Nothing had really changed. The banks also took advantage of high stock prices to aggressively sell more of their own shares, as discussed earlier. In effect, they were able to use the rising stock market to provide more capital, which could in turn be used to loan more money to client companies, much of which would then be recycled into the stock market through *keiretsu* investments. This whole process made the banks dangerously dependent on rising share prices. It was a corroding weakness that would have devastating consequences for the Japanese banking system in the 1990s.

All major stock markets registered impressive gains in the 1980s. Even though the Japanese market boom has often been referred to as a bubble, the fact is that the British market, in percentage terms, racked up comparable gains during the period 1980–87. But the primary difference was that the British (and American) bull market(s) were based on rapid increases in corporate earnings (at least after 1982) and massive increases in individual participation, either directly or indirectly through mutual funds and pension funds. Japanese share price gains occurred at a time when corporate profits were growing only slowly, and individuals, while increasing their participation in absolute terms, represented a steadily shrinking share of a market increasingly dominated by incestuous corporate cross-investments.

During the bull market of the 1980s, the concept that long-term investment in stocks was a reliable means of building wealth finally became broadly accepted by middle-class Britons and Americans, and by many middle-class Japanese. In the United States and the United Kingdom, important changes in the pension laws encouraged a move away from traditional defined-benefit retirement plans (where employers guarantee a specific level of pension benefits, regardless of the performance of their pension fund investments), toward defined-contribution plans (where employers make fixed contributions to a retirement plan, with the actual amount of benefits paid to be determined by the returns generated by plan investments). The conventional wisdom, repeated over and over again, was that a steady policy of investing pension money or individual savings in a diversified portfolio of stocks would enable the average investor to achieve solid returns with an acceptable degree of risk.

The stock market thus became increasingly important to average citizens. In the early 1980s less than 20 percent of American households and less than 15 percent of British households had significant exposure to stocks. These percentages would steadily increase over the 1980s as more money poured into defined-contribution retirement plans and as individual investors gained confidence in stocks. Similarly, millions of Japanese became equity investors, demonstrating that the stock market could play a significant role in a non-Anglo economy. A few academics, such as Robert Shiller, were beginning to chip away at the widely accepted notion that markets were inherently rational and efficient. Nevertheless, by 1987, when most stock exchanges were hitting new highs almost daily, the stock market was more important to the lives of more people than it had ever been before.

VOLATILITY

WHEN ALAN GREENSPAN took over as chairman of the Federal Reserve Board in 1987, he confronted an immense stature gap. His predecessor, Paul Volcker, had become a larger-than-life figure who had succeeded in vanquishing inflation where so many others had failed. Greenspan's measured, professorial demeanor paled by comparison with Volcker, whose earthy disdain for the bland protocols of central banking had become famous. But appearances aside, Greenspan was well aware of the challenges ahead and was prepared to face them.

Shortly after assuming office at the Fed, Greenspan initiated a secret study designed to anticipate future crises and to develop contingency plans for meeting them. Greenspan was most concerned with identifying specific "flash points"—such as a major bank failure, the collapse of the dollar in foreign exchange markets, or a stock market crash—that could imperil the financial system. His aides immediately went to work on the project. Neither they nor Greenspan himself had any inkling of how soon it would be needed.

One source of concern to the Fed was entirely new, a consequence of radical new financial technologies that had only recently been developed. In the 1970s and 1980s a new theory of pricing options had made possible a huge market in *derivative securities*, defined as securities whose price was derived from relationships with other securities. Greenspan and his aides fretted that the rapidly growing number and size of derivative transactions threatened the stability of the markets and the entire financial system.

The breakthrough in options-pricing theory had been made by Professors Fischer Black and Myron Scholes in 1973. As they pertain to the stock market, options are contracts that enable the holder to purchase (or sell), at his discretion, a given stock at a given price (called the "strike" price) within a given amount of time. The advantages to the option buyer are that he can benefit from the movement of a stock without actually having to put up the full amount of money necessary to purchase or sell short the stock, and that his potential loss is limited to the amount he pays for the option.

Options on major stocks were traded sporadically in the 1960s. Market professionals thought that speculators paid too much for them, and therefore the professionals usually preferred to sell options to individual buyers. Because no options valuation model existed, the price of the options was determined on an ad hoc basis, based on the length of time the option would exist and the level of interest rates. (The higher the interest rate, the greater the value of the option, because the option holder effectively acquires a claim on a stock's prospective returns by making an investment smaller than would be required if he actually bought or sold the stock itself, thereby freeing up money that can be put out at interest elsewhere.)

But Black and Scholes recognized (as had others before them) that the ad hoc approach to valuing options was missing a crucial element. Some account had to be taken of the likely price movement of the particular stock on which the option was written. Theorists had previously struggled to incorporate some notion of the stock's expected returns into an options-pricing formula without success. The Black-Scholes insight was that the value of the option did not depend on the expected return of the underlying stock, but instead on the *volatility* of that stock, defined as the expected range (up or down) through which the stock price tended to move over a given period of time. The more volatile the stock, all other considerations being equal, the more valuable the option.

For example, assume an investor wished to purchase options on two stocks, both trading at $50 per share. The first stock is a relatively stable (nonvolatile) utility that tends to move slowly over time. The second stock is a highly speculative technology company subject to sharp price moves based on rapidly changing investor expectations. Each option gives the option buyer the opportunity to buy the underlying stock at $50 for three months. Clearly the option on the technology stock would be worth more, because the likelihood of a substantial rise in the price of the technology stock sometime during the three-month life of the option is much greater than the chance of a big gain in the utility stock. (The chance of a large loss in the technology stock is also much greater, but of little concern to the option buyer because the most he can lose is the amount he pays for the option, regardless of how far the technology stock falls.)

A colleague of Black and Scholes, Dr. Robert Merton, then took the idea one step further, developing the concept of a "replicating portfolio." Again take the above example of options to buy one hundred shares each of two stocks at $50 per share, with each stock trading at $50. Assume, for simplicity, that the nonvolatile utility stock could either rise to $55 or fall to $45 over the life of the option, while the volatile technology stock could either rise to $70 or fall to $30 over the same period.

Merton deduced that the seller (writer) of the options could "hedge" his risk by purchasing fifty shares of each stock and charging a price (premium) for the option that would completely insure him against loss. The fifty shares of stock, combined with the amount of the premium, would "replicate" the value of the option. If the utility stock rose $5 to $55, the option buyer would exercise his option to buy one hundred shares at $50. Since the hedged option seller would own only fifty shares of stock, he would then go into the market, buy the other fifty shares at $55, and then deliver them to the option holder at $50, taking a $250 loss. However, if the seller of the option had charged the buyer of the option a premium of $250, he could exactly offset his loss.

Likewise, if the utility stock fell $5 to $45, the option seller would lose $250 on the fifty shares he owned but have no other obligation since the option buyer would not exercise his option to buy the stock at $50 if it was selling in the market at $45. Again, an option premium of $250 would exactly offset the option seller's loss on the hedge.

The reasoning is exactly the same in the case of the technology stock. However, the fair price of the option is quite different. Since the technology stock is much more volatile (moving up or down over the period $20 per share rather than just $5 in the case of the utility), the option premium necessary to indemnify the option seller against risk would be $1,000 per hundred-share option rather than $250 (using the same assumption that he buys fifty shares of stock at $50 to "hedge" his risk.)

Obviously these examples greatly oversimplify reality. There are many more than two discrete prices at which any given stock can trade at in the future. To deal with the different scenarios, Merton made a crucial assumption—that *continuous*, efficient markets would allow the option seller to constantly modify his "hedge" as the stock price moved around, so that he could protect himself in all eventualities. The hedge would "replicate" the movement in the option's value as the stock moved up or down. This assumption seemed quite reasonable on the academic drawing board. But, unknown to Merton and others at the time, it would prove to be fatally flawed. It was a ticking time bomb destined to explode disastrously in the future.

In the short run, however, all was well. By coincidence, the Chicago Board of Trade inaugurated trading in stock options the same year that Black and Scholes presented their new model for pricing options. Option traders routinely made use of the Black-Scholes model to price, and hedge, their transactions. Many more complicated derivative securities would soon come into being, all having the Black-Scholes model as their theoretical underpinning.

Hayne Leland, a professor of finance at UCLA, soon spotted what he thought would be an important application of the Black-Scholes theory. He would create a "put option" on the entire market that would enable portfolio managers to protect their holdings in down markets without having to dump their entire portfolios. (A put option enables its holder to sell a specific stock at a specific price during a specified period of time.) To create such a marketwide option, Leland employed Merton's idea of a replicating portfolio. By using a package of stocks that would exactly replicate the price movements of a put option, Leland believed it would be possible to hedge a portfolio in the same way the option would.

Leland's strategy would soon come to be called "portfolio insurance." By a fortuitous coincidence, a market in stock index futures was created in 1982, which made Leland's idea much easier to implement. Stock index futures contracts enabled portfolio managers to buy or sell an entire market index—such as the S&P 500—without being required to buy or sell every stock in that index. Equity index futures were like the commodities futures contracts that had existed for generations, with the important distinction that while commodities contracts required the seller to actually deliver the commodity in question to the buyer, equity futures contracts were settled in cash. The cumbersome necessity of delivering the precise numbers of shares of the many stocks that made up the index was avoided.

A manager seeking to "insure" his portfolio would sell futures contracts in an amount indicated by the Black-Scholes model. Continual adjustments were required; the replicating (hedging) process necessitated that additional futures contracts be sold if stock prices fell, and that contracts be repurchased if prices rose. In a volatile market where prices bounce around a lot, this hedging process could be costly, as the manager would be required to sell contracts when prices fell and then buy them back when prices rose. In effect, this loss was the premium that was being paid for the portfolio insurance.

Leland's portfolio insurance depended on the same crucial assumption Robert Merton had made. In order that managers be able to make the constant hedge adjustments required, the prices of index futures contracts had to continuously track the prices of the stocks that made up the market index. Theoretically, arbitrageurs would ensure that this occurred. Seeking to profit from any discrepancies between index futures prices and the prices of the stocks that made up the index, these professional traders would sell the stocks in the index while buying the index futures if the futures price was too low, and do the reverse if the futures price was too high. Computerized trading systems, which made it possible to simultaneously buy or sell large numbers of stocks, would facilitate the arbitrage process (hence the terms "computer trading" and "program trading").

Advocates of portfolio insurance were very successful in convincing managers to employ this technique; by 1987 nearly $100 billion of institutionally managed equity money was insured in the United States. Critics fretted that portfolio insurance strategies might exacerbate a market decline because they required that more futures contracts be sold when prices fell. But most managers who had "insured" their stock portfolios were confident that they had protected themselves from a sharp market drop.

The explosive growth of new derivative securities in the United States, based on the new options-pricing theory, could not have occurred without a concurrent reform in the way stocks were traded—the abolition of fixed commission rates. Under pressure from the Securities and Exchange Commission (SEC), on May 1, 1975 (nicknamed "May Day"), the New York Stock Exchange reluctantly abandoned its long-standing practice of fixing minimum commission rates which member firms were required to charge customers for the execution of stock transactions. Institutions, which had the most leverage to negotiate lower rates because of the volume of business they did, were the first beneficiaries. Within a few months, commission rates on large trades fell 40 percent, and would continue to decline over time. Eventually, individuals also benefited; the low-cost Internet trading prevalent today could not have come into being without a negotiated rate structure. In addition, the large volume of transactions necessary to hedge derivative contracts (and to constantly adjust the hedges as the underlying stocks moved, in line with Miller's dynamic hedging process) would not have been possible if those transactions had to be executed at pre–May Day commission rates.

The abolition of fixed commission rates in the United States created an environment in which exotic new equity-linked derivative securities could thrive. The same breakthrough occurred in Britain in 1986, as the Thatcher government forced the London Stock Exchange to implement what became known as the Big Bang reforms. These changes began with the same premise as the May Day reforms in the United States—that fixed commissions were anticompetitive and should thus be eliminated. But the result in Britain was more far-reaching than in the United States, revolutionizing stock trading in a way that quickly led to the abandonment of the hallowed trading floor of the London Stock Exchange and its replacement by an electronic system linking dealers together, the Stock Exchange Automatic Quotation System (SEAQ). Within a few months, practices that had evolved over three centuries were swept away.

How would the radically reshaped market for equities hold up in a crisis? This was a question that perplexed market participants and government authorities (such as Alan Greenspan). They would soon find out firsthand.

On Monday afternoon, October 19, 1987, Greenspan was on an airplane bound for a speaking engagement in Dallas. Before his departure, the Dow Jones Industrials had been down 200 points, nearly 9 percent, but appeared to be stabilizing. Immediately after disembarking in Dallas, Greenspan asked how the market had finally closed. When told the Dow had ended down "five-oh-eight," he at first breathed a sigh of relief, assuming the response meant 5.08 points. He was quickly disabused of that notion.

Hurrying to consult by telephone with other Fed officials, Greenspan moved to implement the contingency plan just developed to deal with such a catastrophic event. He issued a terse statement declaring, "The Federal Reserve, consistent with its responsibilities as the nation's central bank, affirmed today its readiness to serve as a source of liquidity to support the economic and financial system."[1] This announcement served notice that the Fed would reverse what had been its policy of monetary restraint and flood the banking system with liquidity. At the same time, in private conversations with major banks, Federal Reserve officials pressured the banks to provide loans to distressed stock market dealers who had been forced to take on large inventories during the precipitous market drop. The Fed invited the banks to borrow as much as they needed from its "discount window" in order to make such loans, and "encouraged" the banks to look at the broad picture—the need to protect the entire financial system—rather than their own narrow interests.

The Fed's actions seemed to accomplish their immediate objective. Major brokers and dealers got their loans and short-term interest rates actually declined (from 7.5 percent to 6.75 percent) as the Fed pumped money into the banking system. This was a textbook response to a major market collapse, not unlike that pioneered more

than a century earlier by the Bank of England in the Overend Gurney panic. But Greenspan and the other regulators knew that they
faced further perils that would be more difficult to deal with. What
would be the effect of the huge weight of derivative contracts, including portfolio insurance programs, that overhung the market?
And could the Federal Reserve, as an American central bank, forestall what was a truly worldwide panic in an era where new commu-
nications technologies made possible the instantaneous transmission
of violent market forces across national borders?

The Crash of 1987 had actually begun overseas. Prices fell sharply
in East Asia on the morning of October 19, with the notable exception of Japan, where the decline was only moderate. As the sun
moved west, the panic spread to Europe, with all European markets
registering sizable losses well before American exchanges opened.
The equity futures market on the Chicago Mercantile Exchange,
where trading commenced prior to the New York Stock Exchange
opening, was quickly convulsed by the spreading crisis. The futures
contracts traded on the "Merc" were the vehicles by which the massive portfolio insurance programs were implemented. Within sec-
onds, prices on the most widely traded Standard & Poor's 500 index
futures plunged dramatically.

Hayne Leland and other developers of portfolio insurance had assumed that index futures contracts would move in lockstep with the
actual, or "cash," stock prices on the New York Stock Exchange.
Normally, when confronted with a large drop in futures prices, index
arbitrageurs would step in, buying futures with the intention of selling the stocks included in the index, locking in a profit if the price
they paid for the futures contract was less than the aggregate price at
which they sold the index stocks. But given the rapidly spreading
panic, no one knew with any degree of certainty where (or even if)
stocks could be sold in New York. The index arbs sat on their hands,
and the futures fell lower and lower.

The process fed upon itself as the day progressed. When the portfolio insurance computer models flashed signals requiring that more
futures contracts be sold, there was no one to sell to, and futures
prices collapsed. This led to big gaps between the actual futures
prices and the theoretical prices derived from available stock quota-

tions, making it appear that the futures market was "predicting" further sharp declines in stock prices. This encouraged more selling of stocks, both by index arbs who wanted to sell stocks first so they could then buy the "cheap" futures and by other traders who feared that the depressed futures prices presaged lower stock prices. As the market decline accelerated, the futures-cash relationship quickly spiraled out of control.

When the New York Stock Exchange closed at 4 p.m., the Dow Jones Industrial Average was down nearly 23 percent, the worst single-day drop on record. (The decline was nearly twice that of the worst day of the 1929 crash.) Because of time differences, all European and Asian markets had closed much earlier than New York, before the full extent of the New York collapse was evident. As Greenspan struggled to stabilize the American network of broker-dealers and inject liquidity into the banking system, he knew that Asian markets would be opening within hours. All indications were that the panic would accelerate overseas, threatening again to pull down the American market.

Far Eastern stock markets sold off sharply on the morning of Tuesday, October 20. Even Japan, which had been relatively unscathed on Monday, did not escape the stampede to sell. As on the nineteenth, the selling quickly spread to Europe as those markets opened. Traders around the world waited apprehensively for trading to commence in New York. Although the Japanese stock market, in terms of total market capitalization (counting all the interwoven cross-holdings of Japanese stocks), was nearly as large as the American market, the U.S. economy was still by far the world's biggest, and the Federal Reserve the most influential central bank. Would Greenspan's forceful actions be sufficient to halt the collapse?

At first they seemed to work. The market opened up sharply (with the Dow Jones Industrials rising 200 points), allowing many dealers to unload their bloated inventories of stocks. Unfortunately, the rally soon ran out of steam, and the market slipped into reverse. Prices fell at an accelerating pace, forcing the New York Stock Exchange to halt trading in major stocks because of "order imbalances." Sellers overwhelmed the few buyers attempting to stand against the onslaught.

The Exchange shut down the automated order entry system that index arbitrageurs used to sell many different stocks simultaneously. While this temporarily reduced pressure on Exchange-traded stocks, it also eliminated the mechanism used to keep index futures in line with stock prices. Without any bids from arbitrageurs, futures entered a free fall.

By noon the stock market had ceased to function. Major brokerage firms secretly proposed closing the Exchange, to prevent further losses. Felix Rohatyn of Lazard Frères later admitted, "Tuesday was the most dangerous day we had in fifty years. I think we came within an hour [of a complete meltdown]."[2]

Trillions of dollars' worth of stocks, and perhaps the entire international economy, hung in a suspended state. The most powerful Wall Street banks, and even the Federal Reserve itself, seemed powerless. But, as had often happened in the past, at the very depth of the crisis, the market reversed itself. Perhaps all the sellers who wanted to sell (or who had been forced to sell) had done so. Perhaps they simply gave up trying. Whatever the case, the market sputtered, then began to rise, gradually gaining strength. When the closing bell sounded, stocks were still strong. The end of the trading day was greeted with an almost audible sigh of collective relief.

Why did the market turn around Tuesday, just when unmitigated disaster seemed unavoidable? One crucial source of buying came from the many large corporations that hastily announced plans to buy back large quantities of their own stock at the new, drastically lower prices. Another explanation could be that the decision of the New York Stock Exchange to shut down its automated order system removed burdensome index arbitrage selling at a crucial point. Both these explanations probably have some validity; regrettably, however, the true story of October 20, 1987, will always remain a mystery.

As foreign markets opened on Wednesday, October 21, they followed the lead of New York and traded significantly higher. But after Wednesday, the trend of most foreign markets diverged from that of the U.S. market. Major foreign stock exchanges (except Canada's) resumed their declines on the twenty-second, and continued to fall for most of the rest of the month, while the American market stabilized and actually rose slightly over the same period.

All major world stock markets ended the month sharply lower; the crash was truly a worldwide phenomenon. The drop in the American market was more concentrated, occurring primarily on one day, October 19, while the foreign declines were spread over several days. Austria was best performer in October, down only 11.4 percent in U.S. dollars, while Japan generated the second best results, down only 12.8 percent. (Since both the Austrian and Japanese currencies appreciated against the dollar, however, the declines in these markets were worse when expressed in terms of their own currencies.) Hong Kong was the worst performer worldwide, down 45.8 percent in U.S. dollars.[3]

The decline in the American market for the entire month was right in the middle of the pack, ranking as the eleventh least severe out of twenty-three world stock markets. The rank of the U.S. market actually improves from eleventh to fifth least severe when expressed exclusively in terms of dollars, because the dollar depreciated against most currencies during October.[4] Even though the collapse on October 19 itself was sharper in the United States than elsewhere, other markets subsequently caught up with the American decline. By the end of the month, stock prices in New York, while down sharply, had actually held up better than prices on most foreign bourses.

Given the worldwide collapse in equity prices in October 1987, it is interesting that most explanations advanced for the crash in the United States focused primarily on domestic factors. In particular, attention quickly focused on a high-profile culprit—index arbitrage—and more specifically, portfolio insurance. The chairman of the New York Stock Exchange, John J. Phelan, had previously expressed concern that options and futures trading based on indexes could exacerbate a market downturn. On the evening of October 19 he said that such a "waterfall" effect seemed to have occurred.[5]

A subsequent SEC report examining the causes of the crash focused on this issue. The report concluded that up to 20 percent of the volume on October 19 in the stocks making up the Standard & Poor's 500 index was created by portfolio insurance selling through the futures markets. More ominously, during the fateful 1–2 p.m. time period when the market really began to disintegrate, portfolio insurance selling may have accounted for as much as 40 percent of the total volume. In this view, the final resounding crash in the last hours of trading on October 19 might not have occurred if portfolio insurance selling had not pushed the market over the cliff.

Most other countries where stock prices also plunged, however, did not have active "portfolio insurance" programs; many didn't even have developed futures markets. Computer-directed futures trading was prevalent only in Canada, France, Japan, Britain, and the United States in 1987. These five countries experienced an average decline of 21.25 percent in October, while eighteen countries without widespread computer futures trading were down 27.89 percent.[6] Obviously portfolio insurance and/or computerized futures arbitrage was not the source of the worldwide market drop.

But while portfolio insurance and futures trading strategies did not cause the 1987 crash in the United States, they most likely exacerbated it. This may well account for the fact that most of the October collapse occurred in one day in New York, while it was spread over longer periods in foreign markets. The large futures-related selling volumes identified in the SEC report were certainly of sufficient magnitude to do great damage very quickly to a market that was already extremely fragile. One market analyst said, "I don't know if Monday's drop would have been 50 points or 400 points without portfolio insurance, but it definitely made things worse."[7] The market decline was so severe that many "insured" accounts at first couldn't execute their insurance strategies effectively, then were forced to unwind their mangled positions at a loss when prices rebounded. One "insured" portfolio manager admitted that it was "questionable how well portfolio insurance worked this week." An investment banker predicted (correctly) the "end of portfolio insurance as a strategy. It's really turned out to be portfolio destruction."[8]

An official British inquiry into the October 1987 crash failed to reach definitive conclusions about the cause of the drop. The futures market in London was small both relative to volume in London equity markets and to the American futures market. Average London trading volume in equity futures contracts was only equal to about 20 percent of the overall value of the London equity market, whereas in the United States index futures trading averaged *two times* the volume of cash equity trading in the period leading up to the October crash. In addition, portfolio insurance had never caught on in

Britain; there was relatively little in force when the market break occurred.

Since it was not really possible to blame program trading or portfolio insurance for the London market drop, the inquiry focused on
other potential causes. The most prominent possibility was that selling from foreign markets had been responsible for knocking the London market down. But ultimately, no real evidence was found to
support this or other suggested explanations. The investigation failed
to reach any conclusive judgment on the cause of the London market
drop.

Ironically, the Japanese market, which appeared to be significantly
more overpriced than other stock markets in mid-1987, held up better during October. The financial apparatus of Japan, Inc., swung
into action to minimize the damage. The Ministry of Finance held
"consultations" with the leading Japanese brokerage firms, which in
turn aggressively bought stocks with their own capital to hold up
share prices and pumped out relentlessly optimistic market commentaries to retail customers. Stable *keiretsu* stockholders were pressured
to buy still more shares, providing further crucial support for the
market.

Nothing was more indicative of the collective efforts to stabilize
Japanese stock prices in 1987 than the manner in which the high-
profile partial privatization of the government's interest in Nippon
Telephone and Telegraph was handled. The original plan had been to
sell the shares in tranches over several years, until half the government's holdings were disposed of. The first tranche had come to market in early 1987 at an initial offering price of 1,197,000 yen per
share, or seventy-seven times projected 1988 earnings. Because of
huge public demand, the shares were sold by lottery, with more
than 10 million Japanese investors submitting applications. The new
stock eventually opened for trading at 1,600,000 yen and soared to
3,180,000 nine weeks later; at its peak, the stock traded at a P/E of
204, which valued the entire company at 50 trillion yen. This was an
immense number, more than the total capitalization of the German
stock market *and* the Hong Kong stock market (the largest in Asia
outside Japan) put together.

NT&T shares fell in October 1987 during the worldwide market crash, imperiling the government's plans to dispose of more of its holdings. On cue, the big four brokers stepped in to support the price, finally stabilizing it at 2,600,000 yen per share, setting the stage for the sale of the next tranche. But this time there was little public interest. Instead, shares had to be forced into the hands of companies and institutions with which NT&T did business. In this manner the NT&T offering was finally completed and termed a "success."

More than a decade after the 1987 crash, no one has been able to point to a single decisive news event that could or should have caused the precipitous worldwide fall in prices. This has caused considerable embarrassment to advocates of the efficient market theory, which allows for major market moves only in response to significant news. Eugene Fama, who had originally coined the phrase "efficient market," admitted his "frustration," which, he said, came "from not being able to identify the news that gave rise to" the 1987 market drop.[9]

William Sharpe, another of the godfathers of the efficient market hypothesis, admitted he was "perplexed" by the market's volatility. "It's possible that a well-informed forecast of future market events moved the market as it did," he said; "you can't prove it one way or the other. On the other hand, it's pretty weird."[10]

Fischer Black pointed to increased volatility in the stock market in the months preceding the crash. He reasoned that this might have caused investors to perceive markets as being more risky, and thus caused them to demand a higher "risk premium." In this scenario, investors would have sold stocks down to levels where expected future returns were high enough to compensate for the new level of perceived risk. But Black admitted, "The only insight that the [efficient] market theory provides is that stock prices are going to be more volatile than they have been. But, we don't know in what direction."[11]

How could a truly "efficient" worldwide stock market lose roughly one-fourth of its value over such a short period? Since no news development can be identified that could have so decisively changed investor expectations over so short a time span, it seemed intuitively obvious that the overall market must have been badly mispriced, either before or after the crash. This is the essence of the case made by critics of the efficient market hypothesis. It is based on the same reasoning employed by the economist Robert Shiller, who found in his 1980 study that stock prices have been far more volatile over time than can be justified by changes in underlying fundamentals.

After the 1987 crash, Robert Shiller wrote scathingly that "[the] efficient market hypothesis is the most remarkable error in the history of economic theory. This is just another nail in its coffin." Harvard professor Lawrence Summers, later to be Treasury Secretary, agreed, noting that "if anyone did seriously believe that price movements are determined by changes in information about economic fundamentals, they got to be disabused of that notion by Monday's 500 point movement."[12] The reasoning of Shiller and Summers has been expanded on by other scholars, who seek to replace the efficient market theory with what can best be called behavioral explanations of market movements.

Shiller, Summers, and other "behavioralists" argue that patterns of behavior by investors that are not entirely rational influence stock prices in ways inconsistent with the efficient market hypothesis. The behavioralist approach was built on academic research in the 1970s that discovered "anomalies" seeming to contradict the efficient market hypothesis. As previously discussed, these ranged from Fischer Black's 1973 study showing that *Value Line Investment Survey* recommendations could have been used to outperform the market to studies indicating that basic data like P/E ratios, book values, etc., had significant predictive capability. The implication of these studies—that it was possible to beat the market using only publicly available data—meant that the market could not be efficient. And, the behavioralists argued, if the market was not efficient, some other theory to explain market movements—particularly wild, irrational gyrations like the Crash of 1987—would have to be found.

Shiller's 1980 work on stock market volatility gave important traction to the behavioralist argument, although the term "behavioralist" was not yet in use. By demonstrating that stocks were much more volatile than they theoretically should be, Shiller implied that the market could not possibly be an efficient mechanism that perfectly responded to all relevant information.

Shiller's critique touched off a flood of research in the 1980s and 1990s that sought to find other anomalies undermining the efficient market theory. But these studies, commonly accessible only in scholarly journals, received little mainstream notice until the 1987 crash dramatically called attention to the behavioralist case. Even advocates of the efficient market hypothesis had difficulty explaining how such a sudden collapse could occur in an efficient market.

Behavioralists like Shiller think that investors act on the basis of many influences beyond hard factual information. They describe this extraneous activity as "noise trading." Fischer Black coined the term "noise" in 1968, defining it as background static (such as rumors, uninformed guesses, etc.) that causes investors to act on something other than the solid data actually useful in evaluating stocks.[13] Because it is often hard to distinguish between noise and good information, investors trade too much, and for the wrong reasons. Black felt that markets would be much less active if participants were not distracted by noise.

Because it is so difficult to separate noise from hard information, investors are forced to develop rules of thumb—ways of behaving in a confusing environment. Behavioralists see similarities between these behaviors and patterns observed by psychologists in the general population. Behavioralists seek to use the science of psychology to better understand how noise trading affects the market.

In effect, behavioralists say that investors make many mistakes. They overreact or underreact to news on the basis of stereotypical assessments of individual stocks. They are sometimes overconfident, exaggerating their ability to predict the future, and at other times lack confidence, becoming paralyzed by their past mistakes. They are unwilling to take losses when they should, and often fail to recognize how inflation distorts the measurement of stock market performance.[14]

One of the most significant studies supporting behavioralist theory, covering a period going back to 1933, was conducted in 1985 by Werner De Bondt and Richard Thaler.[15] For each year studied, De Bondt and Thaler searched out the best- and worst-performing stocks over the preceding three-year period. They then observed how

these best- and worst-performing stocks did in the five years following the year in question.

De Bondt and Thaler found that the worst performers did better
than the best performers, going forward, by a substantial margin,
even when the results were adjusted for beta risk. This demonstrated,
the behavioralists believed, that investors overstate the importance of
past performance, shying away from stocks that have not done well
in the past and overpaying for stocks that have done well. Thus, the
"losers" become too cheap and the "winners" become overpriced.
Over time—when the market finally adjusts to economic realities, as
opposed to investor psychology—the "losers" bounce back (outperform), while the "winners" lag (underperform).

This conclusion hit hard at the efficient market hypothesis. It implied that buying stocks on the basis of their past performance could
enable investors to substantially outperform the market, something
that should not be possible if the market was truly efficient.

Additional research revealed other cases of apparent nonrational
investor behavior. Stocks that announced positive earnings "surprises" tended to outperform the market for lengthy periods, while
the reverse was true of stocks that announced disappointing earnings.[16] The efficient market theory assumes that all information is instantly built into stock prices; it does not allow for a predictable drift,
set in motion by unexpected news. Behavioralists theorize that this
drift occurs because investors systematically fail to adjust their expectations to earnings "surprises." Thus, they are likely to be surprised again when the next quarterly earnings come out, resulting in
a further price move in the same direction.

Perhaps most important, behavioralists think they have found evidence that irrational bubbles exist in the stock market. One well-
publicized study showed that stock price moves tended to feed on
themselves over three- to five-year periods, then reverse.[17] This
meant that stocks often moved dramatically away from fundamental
values over several years, only to fall back eventually, just as would
presumably occur in a speculative bubble.

Surprisingly, Eugene Fama, who invented the term "efficient market," published research in 1992 that seemed to undermine his own

ideas.[18] He and a colleague determined that the ratio of a company's book value (its assets minus its liabilities) to its stock price could be used to predict the future stock price. They also found that the stocks of smaller companies tended to do better than those of large companies, even when adjusted for risk. Like the results of other studies, this conclusion tore at the basic assumption of the efficient market hypothesis—that publicly available data such as a company's size and the book-to-market ratio could not be used to beat the market.

How did Fama respond to the empirical evidence (including his own) that contradicted his theory? He went on the offensive, publishing an article in 1998 entitled "The Attack of the Anomalies."[19] He observed that some research (like the winners-losers overreaction study) implied that the market overreacts to news, while others (like the earnings "surprise" research) showed that the market underreacts. Considering all the public data, Fama argued that the instances of overreaction and underreaction cancelled each other out. The efficient market hypothesis, he noted, did not rule out the possibility that the market could overshoot or undershoot. It only required that the errant moves be random, and hence unpredictable.

Fama also had a simple explanation for why his own 1992 work did not contradict the notion that markets are efficient. He believed that stocks of small companies and companies with low book-to-market ratios seemed to beat the market because they were more risky than the market. (In an efficient market, expected return is a function of risk. The more risk an investor is willing to take, the greater his expected return.) Fama had already adjusted his 1992 results for beta risk. But he was now arguing that beta alone was not a good enough measure of risk. (Recall that beta is a measure of how volatile a stock is in comparison to the entire market.)

Fama's explanation seems plausible. Firms that have low book-to-market ratios are usually companies whose stock has declined, meaning that the firm is probably not doing well. Likewise, small companies tend to be either relatively new entities or established firms that have run into difficulty. In all these cases, it seems reasonable to assume that these companies (and their stocks) are riskier than the large firms that make up most of the capitalization of the stock market.

Fama went further, raising the possibility that proper risk adjustments could explain away other "anomalies" used to support behavioralist theory. In particular, could the strong performances of the "loser" stocks in the 1985 De Bondt–Thaler study not be accounted for by the extra risk inherent in those stocks? As even Professor Thaler admitted, "It's scary to invest in these stocks. When a group off us thought of putting money on this strategy last year, people chickened out when they saw the list of losers we picked out. They all looked terrible . . ." Professor De Bondt agreed, saying, "The theory says I should buy them, but I don't know if I could personally stand it."[20]

Do improper risk adjustments explain away the behavioralist anomalies? Regrettably, there is no way to answer this question precisely. No other consensus measure of risk has emerged to replace the simple beta approach, making the assessment of risk maddeningly complex. It is impossible to verify the existence of an "anomaly" (or to verify the efficient market theory itself) without resolving this issue.

Common sense tends to support the behavioralist contention that some investors behave irrationally. Professor Shiller and others have conducted surveys that support this belief. Efficient market advocates counter that many of these nonrational behaviors, over a large population of investors, cancel one another out, and when they don't, better-informed market participants will step in to take advantage of the resulting misvaluations, thus eliminating them. The difficulty of properly adjusting results for risk, and other statistical obstacles, make it impossible to resolve this debate definitively.

Efficient market proponents claim that the extreme volatility evidenced in 1987 (and in so-called speculative bubbles) should be viewed as an inevitable consequence of the new forward-looking methods of valuing stocks that had replaced the traditional reliance on dividend rates. The stream-of-future-income model used to price stocks is very sensitive to slight changes in assumptions for future corporate growth rates and interest rates. As an example, the economist Merton Miller calculated after the 1987 crash that a reduction of 0.5 percent in the assumed annual growth rate of earnings/dividends and an increase of 0.5 percent in predicted interest rates justified a

25 percent decline in stock prices in October 1987—almost exactly what actually happened. Nobody can explain why investors would suddenly have changed their collective assumptions on one day, October 19. Nevertheless, this example does show how extreme stock price moves can result from seemingly minor changes in predicted future conditions.

The efficient market theory was not the only new idea that came under fire after the 1987 crash. Modern portfolio theory had encouraged investment managers to make diversified investments across many volatile foreign markets, based on past data indicating that movements in those markets were poorly correlated with one another. Proper diversification would presumably cancel out much of the risk of foreign investing. Prior to the October 1987 crash, this had generally held true. Movements in stock markets around the world were poorly correlated with one another, meaning that declines on stock exchanges in some countries would be offset by rises on other exchanges in other countries.

Suddenly, in October 1987, all stock markets moved together in one direction—down. This was an unprecedented development and caused a great deal of consternation. As will be discussed in detail in the next chapter, many new stock markets had "emerged" in the 1980s in countries that had previously not had any equity markets to speak of. Much of the investment flowing into these markets came from countries with "developed" markets, such as the United States, Britain, and Japan, and was made on the basis of the principles of diversification inherent in modern portfolio theory. Even conservative investment managers were willing to invest in volatile overseas stock markets, secure in the knowledge that cross-market diversification would limit the overall risk in their portfolio to acceptable levels. But the traumatic events of October 1987 called this crucial assumption into question.

The 1987 crash had another effect that garnered a great deal of attention at the time. Because the Japanese stock market declined significantly less than the U.S. market, and because the U.S. dollar depreciated against the Japanese yen during 1987, by the end of the month of October the total dollar capitalization of the Japanese market, in dollar terms, for the first time exceeded that of the American market. Stunningly, Japan, with a real economy about half the size of the American economy, now had the world's largest stock market. For many observers, this was just one more confirmation that Japan was now really number one.

Japan's apparent success was quite unsettling to many Anglo-American observers. Although tentative steps to deregulate the Japanese economy had been taken, the Japanese economic system remained decidedly different from the freewheeling laissez-faire capitalism of the United States and Britain. The Japanese equity market was still an administered market, tightly bound by traditional government-to-business and business-to-business relationships. How was it possible to explain its apparent success without undermining faith in the very free-market principles on which Anglo-American markets were based?

Equally disquieting was the new academic research by Shiller and others that questioned one of the key presumptions of modern economic theory—that markets were inherently rational. The notion that markets are efficient is essential to the belief that free markets (including free equity markets) are the best means of allocating resources in the economy. If the critics were correct in arguing that financial markets are subject to disruptive speculative movements based on nonrational investor behavior patterns, the case for free markets becomes less clear. Government intervention might be necessary to ameliorate damaging market inefficiencies.

By the 1990s equity markets were more important than ever before. The equity culture, already potent in the United States, Britain, and Japan (although in very different forms), was spreading to other countries in Europe, Asia, and Latin America. But troubling questions remained. Were unfettered markets truly the most efficient means of allocating resources in the economy? Were there other models, such as the Japanese, that might be better adapted to local conditions than the laissez-faire approach employed in the United States and Britain? And finally, what would be the effect of newly freed markets on many developing countries that had little or no experience in dealing with them?

EMERGING MARKETS

IN 1984 the first book on the subject of "emerging markets" was published. The author of *Emerging Securities Markets*,[1] Antoine W. van Agtmael, stated unambiguously that his purpose was to show "why investment bankers, investors and development experts can no longer ignore emerging markets . . . viewed by many as too small and irrelevant to warrant much attention . . ." He went on to predict, "The frontiers of international investment are beginning to push toward the major emerging markets . . . This trend is likely to accelerate."

Since the Depression, most economists and government officials had seen little role for equity markets in developing economies. Stock exchanges were viewed as sideshows at best and gambling dens at worst, which performed no useful economic function and often actually damaged the real economy by creating instability.

The Bretton Woods articles contained a clause listing local capital-market development as an important objective. But this was largely ignored until the 1970s, when World Bank president Robert Mc-Namara set up a division in the International Finance Corporation to focus the bank's attention on this issue. Even then, equity markets took a back seat to debt markets. Most economists did not recognize any difference in the "quality" of capital used to develop a country; a project financed with short-term loans was seen as essentially identical to a project financed by equity. Since it was far easier to negotiate loans from a few major international banks than to go through the arduous process of establishing the institutions and rules necessary for a viable stock market, debt financing became the preferred vehicle by default.

During the 1980s, the free-market ideas that had gained ascendancy in London and Washington spread to the developing countries of East Asia and Latin America. The result was more open economies, greatly reduced tariff and trade barriers, privatization of many state industries, and unprecedented reliance on market forces. But these years were also a period of great turbulence; markets were often volatile and always unpredictable, causing great discomfort to governments that were much more familiar with managing closed economies. A number of countries, particularly in Latin America, soon found themselves overburdened with debt, in what became known as the 1980s debt crisis. Some (like Mexico) were forced to default. Chastened by this experience, the idea of permanent capital—in the form of equity, not debt—became very appealing to countries that feared losing control of their economies to foreign banks or institutions like the International Monetary Fund.

As curbs on foreign exchange transactions and prohibitions on foreign investment were dismantled, overseas pension and mutual fund managers began to look at the emerging stock exchanges in a new light. Stock markets in countries like Mexico, Brazil, Malaysia, and South Korea were no longer seen as exotic and risky; instead, modern theories of portfolio diversification implied that these markets, with great potential for rapid growth, could be invested in safely. Furthermore, because much academic research indicated that developed domestic markets in countries like the United States and Britain were relatively efficient, meaning that it was difficult (or impossible) for professional managers or individual investors to consistently outperform the market indexes, it appeared to make sense to search overseas for stock markets that were not so efficiently priced. Under these circumstances, how could investment managers do their fiduciary duty if they did not seek out opportunities in emerging economies?

By the 1980s, after capital controls were eliminated in most first-world countries, cross-border equity investment between developed markets had become commonplace. The Wall Street firm Salomon Brothers estimated that worldwide investment in foreign shares totaled nearly $2 trillion in 1991, the large majority going into developed stock markets. More than one equity transaction in every seven had a foreign investor on at least one side. Greenwich Associates estimated that American corporate pension fund managers had increased the international equity portion of their total assets to 5.6 percent at the end of 1990, representing a doubling in only three years. (This percentage would double again over the next two years.)

Foreign investment in emerging markets, while still small compared to total cross-border equity investment, grew even more rapidly. The total investment in emerging equity markets by foreign institutional investors had been a mere $500 million in 1984. By 1991 that figure had ballooned to $25 billion; it is estimated to have reached $100 billion by the end of the 1990s.[2]

The rapidity with which this change occurred is startling. As recently as 1970 only a handful of developing countries even possessed functioning stock markets. Only six of these countries had any cogent securities regulation, and only two—Argentina and the Philippines—had securities regulatory commissions. By the early 1990s over fifty developing countries had viable stock markets, and twenty-one of these nations had established securities commissions. These markets had become an important source of capital; it was estimated that net new equity issues approximated 3 percent of GDP annually during the late 1980s and early 1990s in these emerging economies, three times the OECD average for developed countries.[3]

The transformation in the role of equity markets in less developed countries directly paralleled the change in the perception of stock markets worldwide. It was driven by the same constellation of ideas—the free-market concepts of economists such as Milton Friedman, combined with modern portfolio theory and the notion that markets are efficient mechanisms to allocate capital—that had rejuvenated Anglo-American stock markets. In previous decades, newly independent developing countries had sought to establish state airlines as a measure of national prestige. Now many of these countries rushed to set up stock exchanges so as to participate fully in the new global market economy.

Evidence seemed to suggest that countries that embraced free-market economics and developed strong equity markets prospered, while nations pursuing more traditional mercantilist policies did not. Brazil was a textbook case. In the mid-1960s, before equity markets were in vogue, the Brazilian finance minister Octavio Gouvea de Bulhoes implemented a series of reforms designed to establish a strong stock market. A mechanism for the self-regulation of stock exchanges was established, and innovative tax incentives were created allowing up to 12 percent of income tax owed to be invested in equities, providing funding for companies that wished to go public. Rules to set up fully funded pension funds, which could be invested in stocks, were laid down.

The Brazilian economy boomed in the 1970s, with real fixed capital investment exceeding 25 percent of GDP and an impressive growth rate of 8 percent per annum. The Brazilian stock market became the largest outside the developed countries, with active exchanges in both São Paulo and Rio de Janeiro. But the "Brazilian miracle" did not last. Inflation and political instability in the late 1970s led to a reversal of the government policy favoring free markets; coincidentally or not, the economy fell into severe recession in the early 1980s and lagged other emerging economies in recovery. Many proponents of equity financing pointed to the weakening of the Brazilian stock markets as an important drag on the country's economic performance.

The contrast with other countries was striking. By the mid-1980s South Korea had surpassed Brazil as the developing country possessing the largest stock market. Only a few years earlier, the Korean stock market had been a sleepy backwater of little significance to either domestic or foreign investors. But by 1990 it had grown larger than some long-established European markets, such as those in Switzerland and Belgium, and was bigger than all Latin American stock markets combined.

This growth was no accident. The South Korean government had been pushing pro-equity market policies for some time, although it

initially encountered substantial resistance. Much like Japan, the traditional South Korean economy was dominated by large business
conglomerates. These were called *chaebols*, and were each usually
controlled by one family. By 1980 the *chaebols* produced more than
90 percent of South Korea's GDP, and were financed almost exclusively by bank loans. The South Korean government wished to reduce the economy's dependence on bank financing and at the same
time wanted to diffuse the ownership of the *chaebols*. Forcing the
chaebols to go public, through the sale of stock, seemed like an ideal
way to accomplish these objectives.

In 1972 the government enacted the "Going Public Encouragement Act." The term "encouragement" was a euphemism; in reality
the act empowered the Ministry of Finance to require large companies to sell shares to the public. By the early 1980s, in response to this
pressure, most major South Korean companies were listed on the
stock exchange and had made pro forma public offerings. But little
had actually changed. A large majority of shares were still closely
held, and trading volume was minimal. Valuations were generally
cheap, with P/E ratios of 4 to 1 and 5 to 1 quite common. At these
prices, equity financing was simply not attractive to Korean business.

Like many developing countries, South Korea delayed in removing all foreign exchange controls even as it liberalized its economy
and markets. As South Korean export industries boomed, the resulting large trade surpluses were locked into South Korea; they could
not be recycled into foreign capital markets. Much of this money
went into the equity and real estate markets, pushing up prices dramatically. By 1987 P/E ratios had expanded to an average of around
15 to 1. With even blue-chip Korean companies forced to pay 15 percent interest rates for bank financing, selling stock became a much
more appealing means for Korean businesses to fund themselves.

As late as 1985, only 2 percent of the South Korean population
owned stocks. One authority calculates that by the end of the decade
this figure had jumped to an incredible 45 percent.[4] While this estimate may be high, there is no question that a remarkable change in
attitude transformed the South Korean equity market, and the economy, in the space of only a few years. Almost overnight, the stock

market had become an integral component of the South Korean economy.

The contrast between the fates of Brazil and South Korea was striking. The conclusion seemed obvious. Strong capital markets could be a powerful engine of economic growth even in countries (like South Korea) that had very little experience with financial markets. On the other hand, nations (like Brazil) that failed to nurture viable capital markets risked falling by the wayside. Japan by the late 1980s had the largest stock market in the world and arguably the most successful industrial economy. The Japanese example seemed to demonstrate that it was apparently not necessary for nations to make radical changes in the structure of their economies to successfully utilize equity markets. Countries like South Korea and Japan were very different from the United States and the United Kingdom, but this did not stop them from using equity markets as an engine for economic growth.

Unfortunately, the nations hosting the bustling new equity markets did not have the benefit of many decades of experience in developing legal and regulatory structures for their new bourses, as the United States and the United Kingdom did. They lacked populations that had, over generations, become accustomed to equity investing. The new markets were hastily cobbled together with very limited oversight, then thrown open to legions of wholly inexperienced investors. It was an incendiary mix.

Nowhere did this state of affairs produce a more fiery display than in Taiwan. At first glance, Taiwan might appear to have been an unlikely site for an equity market boom. An island nation of approximately twenty million people, Taiwan had become in 1949 the place of exile for Nationalist forces fleeing the Communist takeover on the mainland. It had long been dirt poor; as late as 1960, Taiwan's per capita income ranked between Zaire and the Congo.[5] A long economic boom, driven by cheap labor for export industries, commenced in the late 1960s, and by the 1980s had produced a strong industrial economy. But Taiwan, like many emerging economies, lacked a correspondingly strong financial sector. Most Taiwanese companies, because they lacked access to capital markets, were financed almost exclusively by bank loans, and were highly leveraged. Financial reporting was opaque at best. These primitive conditions contributed to a disquieting run of corporate bankruptcies in the mid-1980s, which were referred to collectively as the Cathay crisis.

It seemed a very inhospitable environment for a stock market boom. But a boom nonetheless commenced; in 1986 the Taiwan Stock Exchange Index broke through the symbolic 1,000 mark, and over the ensuing months subsequent millenary marks fell like rows of dominoes. By 1989, incredibly, the index shattered 12,000. It had taken twenty-five years since the inception of the stock exchange for the market to reach 1,000. It took just three more years to multiply that by a factor of twelve.

How was this parabolic rise possible? In large part it could occur because, as in Japan and South Korea, the floating supply of shares was so small. Many companies that went public sold only 5 to 10 percent of their shares, allowing the existing (usually family) ownership to retain the balance. Other companies that sold more of their equity did so through the same types of cross-holding arrangements that existed in Japan, usually to corporate buyers with which they had long-standing business relationships. Firms that held shares in one another formed groups that were called *bang*; the owners of *bang* firms were usually families that had come from the same regions of mainland China. *Bang* shares rarely if ever came onto the market. In addition, the government and the governing party, the Kuomintang, held significant stakes in various businesses.

There was virtually no publicly disseminated research material available on the Taiwan market or on individual stocks. Corporate reporting requirements, by Western standards, were nonexistent. As in the early postwar stages of the Japanese stock market, very unsophisticated means were used to value stocks, with judgments often based on nominal price levels rather than P/E ratios or other tools for making assessments of relative value.

This environment was clearly rife for manipulation. Thinly traded stocks, with little or no reliable public information and a population of inexperienced investors, provided endless opportunities for unscrupulous market operators to make money. Surprisingly, most investors were not deterred by the knowledge that stock prices were often and obviously manipulated. As in the American stock market of the nineteenth century, attention was not focused on the fundamentals of the underlying businesses represented by the shares being traded. Instead, the objective of many investors was to determine what "big players" were active in a given stock and to ascertain what they were attempting to accomplish. By so doing, the thinking went, many average investors could hope to mimic the success of these "big hands."

The antics of the "big players" were followed intently. The press delighted in reporting the latest moves of "Grasshead" Tsai, "Exorcist" Yu, "Little Boss" Weng, "King of the Monster Bulls" Cheng, "Chili Pepper" Chiu, or "Big Tuna" Chaung. Stocks were believed (correctly in many cases) to move in response to their machinations. The "big players" were presumed to be ruthless and powerful. Connections with gangsters were not uncommon; an official of the largely impotent Taiwan securities regulatory commission suffered numerous stab wounds in an attack presumably precipitated by an action the commission had taken. Much was made of a report that a restaurant owned by "Big Tuna" Chaung had allegedly refused to allow customers who had not yet paid their bills to leave when a fire broke out, resulting in the incineration of several unfortunate patrons. The restaurant was back in business in a few weeks.[6]

Convenient targets of manipulation were the shares of small shell companies and moribund firms with tiny floats. One such company, Hsin Chi Woolen Mills, was nearly bankrupt and trading below NT$7 in March 1989 when it was chosen as a trading vehicle by several operators. Its share price shot upward; during one period of twenty-five trading days, the stock jumped the 5 percent daily maximum change permitted by the exchange twenty-two times. Over the three months during which the manipulation occurred, the stock gained 209 percent, or 46 percent per month compounded. Small shell companies as a group, often possessing little intrinsic value, actually outperformed blue-chip Taiwan stocks during the boom years.

A relatively small number of blue-chip stocks dominated the Taiwan Stock Exchange Index, the most widely followed measure of market activity. The index, like most modern market indexes, was weighted to reflect the market capitalization of its component stocks.

Thus the largest Taiwanese company—Cathay Life Insurance—represented over 8 percent of the total index weighting. The top three companies totaled 24 percent and the top ten totaled 42 percent. But because many shares, even of the large blue-chip firms, were closely held and thus not publicly traded, very small floats existed even for these dominant firms. It was therefore possible for market operators to move the stock prices of the large-capitalization companies that dominated the index by buying or selling relatively small numbers of shares. A common scheme would be to accumulate shares in smaller companies, then "ramp" the shares of index stocks to create the impression that the overall market was booming. The small stocks would then look to be lagging by comparison, and attract buying attention.

As in Japan, many investors believed that the market would never be allowed by the government to fall dramatically. In fact, the Koumintang Party had used the success of the stock market in its advertising during the previous election. An oft-repeated slogan promised "Big Profits and Great Prosperity."[7] The newly legalized opposition Democratic Progressive Party was not to be left out; one of its leaders predicted in early 1990 that the stock market would hit 15,000 by June of that year. The politician, Jo Gao-jeng, observed that there was just so much money around that it had nowhere else to go.[8]

The government had in the past actively intervened to brake market declines. At the time of the worldwide 1987 crash, Taiwanese premier Yu Kuo-hua explicitly directed Taiwan Stock Exchange president Chao Hsiao-feng to organize a market rescue effort including important "big players." Chao complied, conspicuously inviting several notorious "big hands," including "Chili Pepper" Chiu, "Thunderclap" Lei, and a shadowy figure known as "Ahbula" to a conclave. Coincidentally or not, the Taiwan Stock Exchange Index jumped more than 2,000 points in slightly over a month after the meeting took place.[9]

Individual investors streamed into the market. The number of active brokerage accounts reached 4.6 million in 1989. Adjusting for the fact that some investors maintained more than one account, it was estimated that about one in every three adults was involved in playing the market.[10] Despite the highly publicized role of "big players," small investors accounted for an astounding 90 percent of all market activity.

Government policy encouraged individual participation in the market. Unlike in Anglo-American markets, the prices for new stock offerings were set by the state, based on arbitrary formulas that usually resulted in pricings below the market clearing level. The result is that most offerings were massively oversubscribed, and represented a form of "free money" for small investors, because prices almost always jumped to a substantial premium above the offering price. (Institutional investors were prohibited from purchasing new issues.) A lottery system was set up, requiring prospective buyers of new offerings to send in their applications by postcard. So great was the demand that requests for postcards soared by a factor of six during the late-1980s bull market, exceeding the capacity of the Directorate General of Posts to produce them.[11]

In effect, the practice of artificially underpricing new stock offerings was a means by which the Kuomintang could curry favor with small investors, who were also voters. It is another example of how the success of average investors in the market became inextricably linked to the success of the governing party. The Kuomintang saw a booming stock market as a good way to retain power in an era during which it was being forced to open up the political system through democratic reforms. It hoped to create a nation of prosperous investors who would remember where their newfound wealth came from.

By the late 1980s, the policy seemed to be almost too successful. Private employers complained that they had difficulty finding people to fill positions because prospective employees preferred speculation to working. There were widespread anecdotal accounts of government offices remaining vacant until the stock market closed at noon, as clerks took the time to trade shares. Turnover on the Taiwan Stock Exchange (the number of times an average share changes hands in one year) was in 1989 roughly 600 percent, meaning that the average share was bought or sold six times per year. Even the 600 percent turnover figure, high as it was, actually understated reality because the calculation was based on the total number of shares outstanding, including the majority of stock that was closely held and never really available for trading. Once stocks held by controlling owners, and cross-holdings, were excluded, the actual turnover figure approached something like 2,000 percent. This meant that a typical share would change hands every fifteen to twenty business days. (By comparison, the highest annual turnover ever recorded on the New York Stock Exchange was 319 percent in 1901; the figure fell to as low as 15 percent at midcentury.)

As might be expected, valuations were astronomical. By the final quarter of 1989, investors were paying P/E ratios averaging close to 100, roughly double the stratospheric P/Es of Japan and six times the P/Es of American stocks. One of the largest and most respected Taiwanese companies, the International Commercial Bank of China, attained a market capitalization at the end of 1989 of $21 billion in U.S. dollars (although only a small fraction of its shares were actually free to trade). This amount equaled the total market capitalizations of J.P. Morgan, Bank America, Bank One, Wells Fargo, and First Wachovia. ICBC's earnings, however, were less than 7 percent of the combined earnings of the five big American banks.[12] At the market peak in early 1990, Taiwan's stock market capitalization approached that of Germany, a country with a vastly larger economy.

When Western observers in Taiwan raised questions about these seemingly absurd valuations, they were often met with a pained, patronizing response. "You do not understand our market" was a common refrain. There were a number of reasons why, in the view of most Taiwanese (and some foreigners), the Taiwan market was "different" and subject to its own unique rules. First and foremost was liquidity. Taiwan's booming export economy had produced a great deal of money, and it had to go somewhere. Another explanation given was that stock valuations were not really as high as they appeared, because most Taiwanese companies possessed substantial undervalued assets, such as real estate and cross-stockholdings, that were carried on the books at original cost, not at current market values. Taiwan companies were therefore worth more than they first appeared, if these undervalued assets were appraised correctly. (In this way, a rising stock market created something of a self-fulfilling prophecy. The market's rise increased the value of a company's shareholdings in other firms, thus making the company itself worth even more, and so on.)

Taiwanese investors were also supremely confident that the "big players" and the government would never allow the market to collapse. They were quick to point out that the Kuomintang itself had holdings in a major brokerage house and indirect holdings in two large investment management companies. Much as in Japan, the interests of major business leaders and politicians seemed to come together in the stock market. As Taiwan bulls never tired of mentioning, Westerners had also been predicting for years that the "overpriced" Japanese market would collapse, and it had not yet done so.

But the Taiwan collapse did come. The market peaked on February 19, 1990, and then commenced a zigzag course downward, accelerating over time. The government seemed paralyzed, with the president declaring that the legislature must act, while legislative leaders deferred to the executive. The decline was shocking to an investing public whose short experience had only witnessed rising prices. Medical personnel reported sharp increases in hyperactive and melancholic behavior.[13] The number of psychiatric patients confined at Taipei Municipal Sanitarium jumped 75 percent over the previous year.[14] Looking for positives in an otherwise depressing picture, one manufacturing executive quipped, "The continued downward trend will prompt workers [who had quit to take up speculation full time] to return to their jobs to ease the labor shortage."[15]

The small stocks and shell companies that had been the favorites of manipulators and speculators were virtually wiped out. On one of the worst days, in August 1990, 202 of the 207 issues traded on the Taiwan Stock Exchange fell the maximum amount permitted, down 7 percent on the day. The rout continued until October, when the market mercifully bottomed at 2,560, a drop of fully 80 percent from its high eight months earlier.

The "big hands" who had only months earlier been lionized by the press and public now sought to separate themselves from the debacle. "Big Tuna" Chuang's Hai Ba Wang Group, which operated seafood restaurants and had diversified into stock brokerage, was plagued by rumors that customer funds had been embezzled and that stock-trading losses threatened the survival of the organization. Chuang angrily denied the reports, claiming, "My family and I have never bought stocks. How is it that you can go to jail for printing counterfeit money, but not for printing stock certificates? Stocks are things that can cheat people."[16]

On the surface, the Taiwan experience would seem to be a classic speculative bubble, as defined by Kindleberger and others. Innovative new ideas—in this case the development of the stock market itself—combined with easy money liquidity and a new population of eager investors to create an unsustainable boom that rocketed stock prices to levels unjustified by underlying fundamentals. Inevitably, the bubble burst and the market collapsed.

But the problem with applying this model to markets such as that of Taiwan (or Japan, as discussed previously) is that it makes no allowance for markets that are not truly free. The Taiwan market was in fact very thin, with most shares locked away, and was subject to manipulation by "big players" and by the government and the governing party, who had strong reasons to push for higher prices. Prices unquestionably rose to "irrational" levels. But many factors were responsible for this rise; as with most so-called bubbles, crazy speculation was not the only force behind the boom.

Surprisingly, the Taiwan market debacle had little effect on the overall Taiwanese economy, perhaps because it was in so many ways divorced from that economy. Economic activity slowed substantially in 1990 but quickly recovered. The fact that the economy was largely export-driven undoubtedly played a big role. Demand for Taiwanese products was more dependent on economic conditions overseas.

The boom-and-bust cycle evidenced in Taiwan would occur in other emerging stock markets. The ingredients were usually the same: imperfect market mechanisms, a very limited floating supply of shares, little transparency of information, overt efforts (often by governments) to manipulate prices, and inexperienced investors. One of the most serious crises would hit in Mexico, a country that had often been troubled by financial instability. A large spike in the price of oil in the 1970s had enriched the country, creating a boom that attracted foreign capital, largely in the form of foreign bank loans. No real

Mexican equity market existed at that time. Unfortunately, however, the worldwide credit crunch in 1979–81 led to Mexican debt defaults in 1982, followed by a long siege of capital flight and depression. Between 1983 and 1986 annual amounts equivalent to nearly 6 percent of Mexican GDP were sucked overseas, mostly to service the oppressive foreign debt.

A financial restructuring and recovery were finally achieved by the end of the decade. In the early 1990s the economy boomed; inflation fell from nearly 160 percent in 1987 to 7 percent in 1994, much industry was privatized, the government deficit was eliminated, and rapid GDP growth resumed. The government actively pursued a policy to keep the Mexican peso strong. Once again, foreign capital flooded in; because a Mexican stock market now existed, funds poured into equity as well as debt securities. Large capital inflows enabled Mexico to sustain a substantial trade deficit. But the country was totally at the mercy of foreign investors. If the torrential inflow of capital were ever to dry up, the peso exchange rate and much of the stability of the Mexican economy that had been built around a sound currency would collapse.

This is precisely what happened in 1994, as overseas investors turned cautious on Mexico. Unfortunately, the Mexican government, beset by election year pressures, preferred to ignore the problem. Rather than raising interest rates to choke off demand for imports, it pursued an easy credit policy, exacerbating the trade imbalance. At the same time, the government still sought to maintain the value of its currency, declaring repeatedly that the peso would not be devalued. When it was unable to roll over its peso-denominated foreign debt, the government made the fateful decision to issue debt in U.S. dollars (called tesobono bonds). Mexico's external peso debt in 1994 actually dropped from $20 to $3 billion, but was replaced with U.S. dollar debt (tesobonos) that jumped from $2 billion to $29 billion.[17]

Time was running out. Mexico was experiencing an $18 billion annual trade deficit; with little new outside capital coming in, foreign reserves were drawn down rapidly. Savvy Mexicans began to ship money overseas; they had seen such foreign exchange crises before, and were not about to get caught again. By December 1994 dollar reserves were only one-third of the amount of the outstanding dollar-denominated tesobonos, which of course would eventually have to be repaid in dollars.

On December 16, Mexico was forced to devalue the peso, announcing a 15 percent reduction in its official value against the dollar. But this only made matters worse, as foreign investors completely lost confidence in Mexican policy makers. Within a few days the government capitulated and let the peso float; the currency immediately slid to roughly half its previous value.

Because of the use of the tesobonos, which still had to be paid back in dollars, not depreciated pesos, the Mexican government debt ballooned in peso terms to unsustainable levels. The IMF hastily assembled a $16 billion rescue package, but it was soon apparent this was not nearly enough. President Clinton proposed an additional $40 billion loan, but it did not clear Congress. In desperation, Clinton then made use of $20 billion from an exchange stabilization fund, even though the fund had not been created for this purpose.

Foreign investors suffered losses of about $30 billion during the December 1994–January 1995 Mexican meltdown. The bulk of the losses, however, were concentrated among creditors, not equity investors. Mexican stock prices (expressed in pesos) adjusted upward, partially offsetting the devaluation; stock prices acted as the hedge against inflation that they were supposed to be. The advantages of permanent equity capital, as opposed to short-term debt, as a means of financing developing countries, became even clearer.

Another, more unsettling conclusion could also be drawn from the Mexican debacle. In the previous debt crisis of the early 1980s, Mexico's foreign investors had largely been confined to a few large international banks. To resolve the crisis, it had only been necessary to assemble the various banks and negotiate an acceptable arrangement. This is precisely what occurred in the 1980s, under the auspices of U.S. Treasury Secretary Nicholas Brady, after whom the so-called Brady plan to restructure Mexico's debt was named. By 1994, however, the big banks had been replaced as foreign investors by thousands of institutional and individual investors, primarily mutual funds and pension funds. When this diverse "herd" decided to get out, they did so in a stampede. Mexico was now confronted with a crisis driven by the infinitely larger, anonymous group of players who make up a modern capital market. As David Hale, the chief economist for Zurich-Kemper Financial Services, put it, the Mexican peso crisis was "the first great liquidity crisis to result in part from the rise of mutual funds as important global financial intermediaries."[18] The Mexican government, much to its chagrin, could not negotiate with "the market."

The Mexican GDP contracted by a painful 7 percent in 1995, with imports falling dramatically as the depressed economy choked off demand. For the first time in years, Mexico registered a net trade surplus, of $7.4 billion, representing a $25 billion swing in just one year as the cheap peso stimulated exports and restrained imports. By 1996, the domestic economy had turned the corner; GDP growth picked up to 7 percent in 1997 and 4.6 percent in 1998.

Although Mexico, aided by the American bailout, recovered fairly quickly from the 1994–95 crisis, troubling issues remained. Open markets meant that emerging economies were entirely at the mercy of the whims of portfolio managers in North America and Europe. If these institutional investors, who were very sensitive to short-term rates of return, decided en masse that a particular country was no longer attractive, they could devastate that country's capital markets and economy by suddenly pulling out their money. Market volatility induced by rapid-fire portfolio investment decisions resurrected the same concerns that had caused economists like John Maynard Keynes to be deeply suspicious of unfettered international capital flows.

Countries that were not dependent on potentially capricious foreign capital inflows—such as Japan—had much more leeway to deal with economic difficulties. Unfortunately, in the Japanese case, this may have been a mixed blessing. Japan was able to muddle through its economic decline in the 1990s without being forced by the discipline of the capital markets to take unpopular corrective measures. The result was the longest bear market in Japanese history.

As discussed previously, the growth in Japanese corporate earnings in the 1980s had lagged well behind the impressive growth in stock prices, resulting in the uncomfortably high valuations of the end of the decade. When the economy stalled at the beginning of the

1990s, the traditional system of administered stock prices could not be maintained and caved in under its own weight. Rising prices had created gains for the banks and corporations that owned large cross-holding positions, enabling them to inflate their earnings from operations with profits from stock transactions. The market decline reversed this pleasant illusion, resulting in losses on equity holdings that exacerbated the already weak earnings performance of Japanese companies and financial institutions.

This is not to imply that traditional *keiretsu* and government efforts to support stock prices were abandoned. As the stock slide continued into 1992, the government launched a series of what were euphemistically referred to as "price-keeping operations," a play on the term "peace-keeping operations," which came into common usage after the Gulf War.[19] The first such overt attempt, in late 1992, involved regulatory changes that made possible the investment of an additional 2.82 trillion yen ($24 billion) of the massive government-administered postal savings and pension funds in stocks. When this failed to stem the long-term decline, loud attempts were made by bureaucrats to "jawbone" the market, and further strategically timed buying by public pension funds was authorized.

Despite these efforts, by the end of the decade the Nikkei average of 225 stocks had dropped by two-thirds. Trenchantly observing the failure of Japan, Inc., to halt the decline, Garry Evans, a market strategist at HSBC Securities in Tokyo, noted, "As a whole, artificial things don't work. It's like a pressure cooker: You can keep a lid on it, but the steam's going to come out somewhere."[20] In fact, many analysts argued that efforts to support share prices did more harm than good by preventing the market from finding a true equilibrium level from which a legitimate recovery could begin. Unlike in emerging economies, where crises would hit with the severity of a typhoon, then pass, allowing a recovery to set in, in Japan the collapse was stretched out over years in a painfully slow process, and was never really allowed to come to resolution.

The Ministry of Finance estimated that Japanese banks held a combined 76.7 trillion yen in bad loans. As a percentage of GDP, the net liabilities of bankrupt Japanese companies were far higher than the liabilities of bankrupt American companies had been at the depth of the Great Depression. If anything, the true extent of the problem was probably understated, because of the common practice of hiding insolvent debts on the books of financial institutions.[21]

On November 4, 1997, Sanyo Securities failed. It was the first Japanese brokerage firm to seek bankruptcy protection since World War II, and its collapse marked the end of the finance ministry's patched-together "convoy system," in which troubled firms had been merged into or assisted by other, stronger firms. But this time, ominously, other firms refused to help bail out Sanyo. Most of them had severe problems of their own.

One of those firms, Yamaichi Securities, itself soon went under. The fourth largest brokerage house in Japan, it was the biggest firm ever to be forced into receivership. In a dramatic public apology, the head of Yamaichi wept openly at a press conference: "I express deep regret, and I really feel sorry for our employees. I sincerely hope you will give them support to find new jobs."[22] In a grim reminder of the personal toll the financial crisis was taking, it was reported that a thirty-eight-year-old accounting section chief at Yamaichi died after working nonstop for fourteen days. The Japanese media had a word for what had happened: *karoshi*, death from overwork.

Yamaichi had been crushed by an 80 percent drop in its share price, which it had struggled futilely to support, and $23.6 billion in debts. Much as in other Asian countries where "crony capitalism" was rampant, stories soon began to emerge of questionable (and outright illegal) activities. Payoffs to racketeers were exposed, as were off-balance-sheet liabilities exceeding $1.58 billion arising from unlawful trading practices in which brokers arranged dummy transactions to prevent favored clients from having to report losses. This practice of effectively indemnifying clients against loss, known as *tobashi*, benefited a number of prominent politicians.

The head of the Bank of Japan, Yasuo Matsushita, admitted that the Japanese financial system had been severely threatened by successive collapses of large financial institutions. Falling stock prices made the situation worse, because of widespread equity cross-holdings in which many companies held stock in customer firms and suppliers, and vice versa. When stock prices declined, the value of important assets held by these business also declined, weakening them financially. In early 1998, prominent officials of Japan's dominant political party (the Liberal Democratic Party, or LDP) began still another overt campaign to "talk up" the Japanese stock market, in an effort to take pressure off beleaguered institutions hurt by falling stock prices, and hopefully to point the way for a sustained market recovery throughout East Asia. The explicit target was 18,000 on the Nikkei stock average by March 31, the end of the fiscal year for most Japanese companies.

Leaks to the press hinted at a large economic stimulus package to be announced soon. In addition, the government disbursed nearly one trillion yen to investment managers who ran public funds, in the belief that the managers would pump the money into stock investments. Unfortunately, as in the case of so many prior clumsy attempts by the government to manipulate the market, the plan failed. The Nikkei actually dropped 1 percent from the time the publicity campaign began until the March 31 target date.[23]

Individual Japanese investors, who, more than any investors outside the United States and Britain, had come to embrace long-term stock ownership, retreated from the market. At the height of the boom, more than 20 percent of the savings of the notoriously thrifty Japanese had been invested in equities. By the year 2000 that proportion had fallen to a puny 6 percent (compared to 35 percent in the United States). Most Japanese preferred to keep their savings in "safe" savings and time deposits, even though the interest rates paid were next to zero.

To many Japanese, the stock market is thoroughly discredited, and is widely assumed to be routinely manipulated. The presumption of chicanery is so pervasive that commonly used terms have evolved to describe different types of manipulation: one refers to price-rigging by speculators and another to manipulation by politicians. Even the politicians who spent their time devising schemes to bolster stock prices rendered a negative vote on the market with their personal money. The average member of the upper house of Parliament had only 4 percent of his assets invested in stocks at the end of 2001.[24]

As Japanese banks, corporations, and individuals unloaded their stocks, foreigners were the principal buyers. A British economist observed, "The Japanese are permanent sellers, and the market only goes up when foreigners buy."[25] By 2000 foreigners held more than 20 percent of all Japanese stocks (up from less than 4 percent ten years before), and actually accounted for over half of the total share turnover on the Tokyo Stock Exchange.

The decade-long collapse of the Japanese stock market—and the much more abrupt crash in the Taiwan market—are similar in one important respect. Both markets were never truly free. The stunning booms that had occurred in the 1980s were fed by elaborate systems of cross-holdings and by government policies deliberately designed to produce very high prices. In Japan, the objective was to create a source of cheap capital for Japanese business, effectively at the expense of the individual Japanese investor. In Taiwan, the objective of the governing party and its cronies was to co-opt the citizenry into a booming market as a means of securing political support. Excessive speculative ebullience on the part of many inexperienced investors undoubtedly played a role in the booms (and subsequent busts) of both markets. But to characterize the resulting collapses purely as examples of irrational speculation gone astray, without recognizing the extent to which the markets were subject to manipulation by powerful institutional forces, is to badly misinterpret what actually occurred.

In the space of less than two decades, equity markets had become widely accepted around the world as an indispensable tool for economic growth. But many of these markets were at best primitive mechanisms, lacking the accumulated years of institutional experience that had helped perfect Anglo-American bourses. Academic theories of behavior, such as the efficient market theory, that were developed primarily from research on much more transparent, developed markets in the United States, were of limited value in explaining market activity in countries like Taiwan and Mexico (and even Japan). In addition, the inherent instability of poorly developed markets was greatly magnified by unpredictable international capital flows. Governments (and investors) had little real experience coping with the radically new environment. The true consequences of the worldwide sprint toward open markets could not yet be foreseen.

CONTAGION

ON SEPTEMBER 15, 1998, an extraordinary article appeared in the *Wall Street Journal*. The subject was the tumult sweeping through international financial markets, and the author was none other than the legendary investor George Soros. For most of his career Soros had shunned publicity, operating in the secretive netherworld of offshore "hedge funds." In spite (or perhaps because) of the mystery surrounding him and his methods, Soros attained near-mythical status as a brilliant but amoral master strategist capable of shifting massive amounts of investment capital around the globe at a moment's notice in search of quick profits, regardless of the consequences his actions might have on local economies.

Soros had achieved his greatest fame as the man who "broke the Bank of England" in September 1992, pummeling the British currency by selling billions of pounds in foreign exchange markets until the government in London was forced into a humiliating devaluation. Soros and his fund made an overnight profit of nearly $1 billion on what became known in the currency markets as Black Wednesday. Unapologetic, Soros lectured both government officials and private economists on the dogma of modern market economics, claiming that he was only the instrument through which markets disciplined governments that refused to accept economic realities. In an era of global capitalism, Soros was both the high priest and avenging angel.

It is from this perspective that Soros's article in the *Wall Street Journal* was so remarkable. The man who more than anyone else personified global financial markets now warned that the international economic order was in trouble. "The global capitalist system," wrote Soros,

> is coming apart at the seams. The current decline in the US stock market is only a symptom, and a belated symptom at that, of the more profound problems that afflict the world economy. Some Asian stock markets have suffered worse declines than Wall Street's crash of 1929, and their tumble has been followed by economic collapse. In Indonesia, most of the gains in living standards that accumulated during the [past] 30 years . . . have disappeared. Japan, the world's second largest economy, has reported an annualized 3.3% decline in economic activity for the second quarter. Russia has undergone a total financial meltdown. It is a scary spectacle, and it will have incalculable human and political consequences.

"There is an urgent need to recognize," Soros went on, "that financial markets, far from tending toward equilibrium, are inherently unstable. A boom/bust sequence can easily spiral out of control, knocking over one economy after another. Thus, in finding a remedy, 'market discipline' may not be enough. There is also the need to maintain stability in financial markets."

Soros noted that within the United States the Federal Reserve had assumed the role of "lender of last resort," providing crucial support to the financial system at times of severe stress, such as the stock market crash of 1987. But there was no such international institution capable of stabilizing the global markets that had little respect for national borders. The International Monetary Fund, with inadequate resources, had tried to do so but failed. The implications for investors, both domestic and overseas, were ominous. Financial storm clouds could suddenly brew up in a faraway place of seemingly little significance, only to wreak havoc on unsuspecting markets half a world away.

Exactly this seemed to be occurring in the fall of 1998. For the first time since 1914, a foreign financial crisis threatened to cause an

American stock market crash. Headlines and leads from the *Wall Street Journal* told the story: "Stocks Plunge Again—Dow drop wipes out 1998's gains. On Nasdaq, it's worse." "Fear swept through the stock market yesterday, triggering frenzied selling that drove most market measures into the red for the year." "Big U.S. Stocks Fall on Foreign Pressures." Thomas Galvin, chief investment officer of Donaldson, Lufkin & Jenrette, commented on the intensity of trading. "You could see the whites of people's eyes. There was relentless and indiscriminate selling taking place."[1]

David Komansky, chairman of Merrill Lynch, observed, "What we're seeing is the dark side of a truly global marketplace. Going forward, this is what a global, wired economy will look like during a market correction."[2] Max Chapman, Jr., chairman of Nomura Securities' three regional units outside Japan, commented: "It's not like in '87 when the market plunged and by 5 pm you knew what your losses were. This one is more insidious. It's getting you from all places. If you're a global payer, you get kind of dizzy." And Greg Hopper, portfolio manager at Bankers Trust Global Investment Management, described the market rout this way: "The whole world was on one side of the ship for three years, and now they wanted to go to the other side of the ship all at once."[3]

Treasury Secretary Robert Rubin compared the decline to the 1973–74 bear market, the worst stock market drop since the 1930s. In 1974, Rubin noted, "the difference between the people who were smart and shrewd, and the people who weren't smart and shrewd [was that] [t]hose people who were really smart and shrewd lost a lot of money. Those people who weren't smart and shrewd got wiped out." Rubin said the United States must respond to "enormous forces" as best it can. "Success" came when "you managed extremely difficult forces well enough . . . to come out the other end."[4]

But the U.S. economy in 1998, unlike 1974, was booming, with low inflation and low unemployment. In fact, Federal Reserve Board chairman Alan Greenspan labeled the economy's late-twentieth-century performance "the best I have seen in my lifetime," a far different set of conditions from those in the dismal days of 1974. Other economists noted the divergence between the stock market and the domestic economy. Stating that the market had become "delinked" from the economy, James F. Smith, Jr., professor of finance at the University of North Carolina, said, "the stock decline is not telling us a thing about the US economy. There's hardly anything wrong with the US economy today that you can't solve with lower interest rates."[5]

The American stock market appeared to be delinked to the domestic economy because it had become far more closely linked to the world economy. The culmination of two decades of economic liberalization and the end of the cold war had created a truly worldwide equity market. But, as Soros noted, as equity markets became more important, and as the elimination of cross-border barriers allowed them to become interlinked, a disturbing instability had been introduced into the economic system. In essence, Soros was repeating the age-old case against excessively volatile speculative markets. It was the same argument used by critics of the South Sea Bubble and "overspeculation" in nineteenth-century railroads. It was very similar to the concerns of the architects of Bretton Woods, who were deeply suspicious of unrestrained speculative capital flows. And it was an argument that was central to the academic research of economists like Robert Shiller and others who in the 1980s and 1990s found that stock markets were often driven to "irrational" extremes by the emotional behavior of participants.

The crisis that triggered Soros's concerns actually began in the spring of 1997, as a series of destabilizing events first spiraled out of control in Thailand, ultimately engulfing the world's financial markets in what President Bill Clinton termed "the worst financial crisis in fifty years." In many ways Thailand symbolized the uneasy mix of influences that characterized the so-called Asian Tiger economies. Neither completely Eastern nor Western, it occupied a no-man's-land between alien cultures.

Thailand was synonymous with the "Asian miracle"; despite frequent changes in government, it had through a series of liberalizations succeeded in developing an open-market economy based on free enterprise. The country had sustained an annual growth rate of 8 percent in the ten years preceding 1997, and from 1985 to 1995 had been the fastest-growing economy in the world. Many Thai businesses had been built on the assumption, not at all atypical in East

Asia, that this impressive growth would continue indefinitely. But by 1997 the economic boom had run out of steam, and Thailand was in trouble.

One analyst estimated that between 25 percent and 50 percent of the loans made by Thai banks and finance companies were nonperforming, meaning that the borrowers were unable to make the required interest and principal payments.[6] Financial institutions had become the unwilling owners of an uncomfortably large number of foreclosed or repossessed properties, from gleaming (often empty) office towers to luxury cars and expensive townhouses. Numerous loans collateralized by Thai stocks were also in jeopardy, given the steady slide that had sliced nearly two-thirds off the market's value since its peak in early 1994.

In addition to the problem of loans that were now nonperforming, Thai banks and finance companies were being squeezed relentlessly by rising interest rates. They, like most financial institutions, borrowed money short-term to fund their lending activities, but short-term interest rates had jumped from 9 percent to 25 percent as the Thai central bank (the Bank of Thailand, or BOT) had been forced to raise rates in response to pressure in the foreign exchange markets. The crux of the problem, which would soon recur in distressingly similar forms throughout East Asia, was that the Thai government had committed itself to a policy of "pegging" the Thai currency, the baht, to a basket of currencies heavily weighted to the U.S. dollar. But as the dollar rose in value in the mid-1990s relative to the currencies of Thailand's principal trading partners (Japan and China), the baht rose as well, creating a trading imbalance. Thai goods and services became too expensive to compete in international trade. More money was flowing out of Thailand to pay for imported goods and to service existing foreign debt than was coming in in payment for exports. This imbalance in what economists call the current account could only be made up by flows of foreign investment money into Thailand. Unfortunately, in times of uncertainty, such foreign investment would only be provided at interest rates that were excruciatingly painful for domestic Thai businesses and consumers.

As conditions worsened, the Stock Exchange of Thailand was hit by a heavy selling that forced the exchange to suspend all trading in shares of banking and finance companies, which represented 50 percent of the total market capitalization. The crisis quickly spread beyond the Stock Exchange, with "runs" developing at many financial institutions as worried depositors scrambled to withdraw their money. The panic was on.

It was an isolated panic, however, largely ignored in the rest of the world. A perusal of the financial press in New York, London, and Tokyo at the time reveals only limited coverage of the developing Thai crisis. Thailand was only one small country, far away, and the rest of Asia seemed to be doing pretty well. The American stock market continued its steady advance; market participants were more interested in debating the merits of Federal Reserve Board chairman Alan Greenspan's concern, voiced a few months earlier, that the market might be "irrationally exuberant." Michel Camdessus, the chairman of the International Monetary Fund, reproached lax Thai regulators but went on to say, "I don't see any reason for this crisis to develop further."[7] Severe financial dislocations in countries like Thailand had happened before and had never seemed to have much impact on markets in the rest of the world.

The Thai baht came under increasing pressure as money flowed out of the country (holders selling baht to obtain other currencies), forcing the Bank of Thailand to buy baht continually to support its price. The man on the front line of the currency war was the bank's assistant governor, Siri Ganjarerndee, who spent much of his time studying a computer screen monitoring foreign exchange rates. The central banker was acutely aware of who the enemy was. "Most of the activity is from hedge funds abroad," he said. "They want to test the determination of the BOT to defend the exchange rate system."[8]

Central bankers like Siri Ganjarerndee often developed a bunker mentality as they battled to defend their country's currency. While an academic economist might define the root causes of foreign exchange crises in dry terms such as current account deficits, overvalued currencies, and inappropriate monetary policies, central bankers often saw the conflict in highly personal terms—us versus them. And the "them" was the so-called currency speculators, usually hedge funds, who sought to reap exorbitant profits from the economic distress of entire nations.

The first hedge fund was formed in 1949 by former journalist and academic Alexander Winslow Jones. Jones observed that all economic sectors and markets did not move in unison; rather, some did well while others did not. He therefore hit upon the idea of creating a fund that would buy stocks in companies and sectors that he believed would do well, while simultaneously selling short stocks in companies and sectors that he felt would do poorly. This scheme had the advantage of protecting the fund from a sharp decline in the entire market that would presumably drag down all stocks together. Since the fund would be short roughly as many stocks as it owned, the losses sustained in an economic downturn on the stocks it owned would presumably be offset by the profits made on the stocks it was short. Hence the fund's risk was "hedged."

Raising money from small groups of wealthy individuals and institutions, hedge funds operate outside of the securities laws designed primarily to protect small investors. The rich individuals and institutions that invest in hedge funds are presumed to be sufficiently sophisticated so as not to require the protection of government regulators. Thus hedge funds could, and do, engage in an almost unlimited number of exotic transactions free from virtually any government oversight.

As the most famous hedge fund operator and currency speculator in the latter half of the twentieth century, George Soros was immediately presumed by many observers to be behind the attack on the Thai baht. (Rumors had circulated for some time that Soros had also been involved in a 1996 speculative raid on the baht that cost the Bank of Thailand $4 billion.) In person, Soros didn't really look the part of a notorious currency speculator; small of stature, with wire-rim glasses and a wrinkled brow, he appeared to some acquaintances to resemble an economics professor. Others, noting his squat, rugged build, tan complexion, and the fact that he appeared to be ten years younger than his actual age, likened him to a ski instructor. All agreed, however, that he comported himself in a courtly, restrained manner; he neither smoked nor drank and was certainly not flamboyant.[9]

Soros's Hungarian father, Tivadar Soros, had been taken as a prisoner of war in Russia in 1917, only to escape later during the turbulent years of the Russian Civil War. It is perhaps from his father that young George acquired his steely pragmatism. Tivadar described to George how, while on the run in Siberia, pragmatism had been essential. As George put it: "What side of the revolution was he on? Oh, both sides of course. He had to be, to survive."[10]

Growing up in Budapest in the 1930s, Soros seemed to be a normal child, with many friends and a keen interest in sports. But there was another side of his personality that he kept hidden from his acquaintances. As he later wrote in one of his books, "If truth be known, I carried some rather potent messianic fantasies with me from childhood, which I felt I had to control, otherwise they might get me into trouble."[11] In another book, *The Alchemy of Finance*, he disclosed how painful it had been for him as a youngster to carry around such beliefs:

> I have always harbored an exaggerated view of my self-importance—to put it bluntly, I fancied myself as some kind of god or an economic reformer like Keynes or, even better, a scientist like Einstein. My sense of reality was strong enough to make me realize that these expectations were excessive and I kept them hidden as a guilty secret. This was a source of considerable unhappiness throughout much of my adult life. As I made my way in the world, reality came close enough to my fantasy to allow me to admit my secret, at least to myself. Needless to say, I feel much happier as a result.[12]

As his wealth and power increased, Soros had less reason to conceal his inner feelings of superiority. His right-hand man in the 1980s, Jim Marquez, observed, "It was very easy for him to lose his temper. He had a way of looking at you with such penetrating eyes that you felt you were under a laser gun. He could see straight through you . . . almost like you were a lesser being."[13]

Messianic visions aside, Soros was successful in large part because he was one of the first investment managers who understood how markets in different regions of the world were linked together. A colleague said, "George was one of the early ones who could figure out that you had to be global in your thinking rather than just being parochial . . . You had to know how an event here would effect an event there . . . What he took was information from various sources and kind of mulched it in his mind. Then he would come up with a thesis that most of the time was valid."[14]

Hedge fund operators tend to be secretive by necessity, but as Soros became more successful in the 1990s he recognized that it was no longer possible to escape public scrutiny. He decided to make himself available to the media, offering comments about markets and providing unsolicited advice on issues like NATO and Bosnia. Unfortunately, his newfound openness backfired; to many suspicious observers his public remarks had an air of hubris about them, or, even worse, they hinted of a hidden agenda. The master manipulator of markets now seemed to be seeking to extend his nefarious activities into the realm of public policy.

Rumors of Soros's involvement in selling Thai baht were widespread, but could not be proven. By late June 1997, with or without Soros, the situation was critical. The Thai minister of finance was fired, and the new minister, Thanong Bidya, made a big show of going in person to the central bank to demand detailed figures on the foreign exchange crisis. There he "discovered" that most of the country's foreign currency reserves ($30 billion worth) had already been tied up in forward currency contracts in a frantic effort to defend the baht. The true reserves actually available to the bank had dwindled to only $1 billion. Within a week, on July 2, 1997, the government abandoned its long-standing policy of pegging the baht to the dollar. It was an abrupt, de facto devaluation that left government policy in a shambles.

How had the Thai version of the "Asian miracle" collapsed so abruptly? One Singapore-based economist said the crisis resulted from too much "silly money" flooding into Thailand after the government removed restrictions on capital flows in the early 1990s.[15] Domestic entities were allowed access to relatively cheap foreign capital; high interest rates in Thailand made it attractive to borrow overseas in foreign currency at lower rates, and then to convert that currency into baht. As long as the Thai government was able to maintain the value of the baht, there was little risk involved in these borrowings. But if the government was unable to hold up the price of the baht, many domestic borrowers would face disaster. Their debts, denominated in foreign currency, would, after a devaluation, automatically become much larger when translated back into baht. Many Thai individuals and firms would likely be bankrupted as a result. Thus the central bank struggled to artificially support the baht as long as it could, until it simply ran out of resources. From that point on, the end came quickly and painfully.

Thailand's rush to liberalize its markets in the early 1990s had exposed many weaknesses. In particular, the opening of domestic markets to global capital flows revealed flaws in the Thai legal and regulatory systems that invited cronyism and corruption. One foreign telecom executive said, "Everyone says that the absence of rule is the rule itself. But when you open to the world, it sticks out like a sore thumb."[16] Thailand was simply not ready to deal with large, cross-border capital flows. The country threw open the doors of its economy to the global marketplace, but was unprepared for the consequences.

Shock waves from the sudden Thai devaluation reverberated through other Asian countries that market participants feared were similar to Thailand—specifically Malaysia, Indonesia, and the Philippines. It was not at all clear that these nations would suffer similar fates. After all, experts pointed out, Thailand had borrowed much more short-term money as a percentage of its economy than had the other countries; at the end of 1996, interest payments on Thai debt equaled 25 percent of GDP, double the level in Malaysia and the Philippines, and almost three times that of Indonesia. Malaysia and Indonesia received substantial revenue from oil exports, which Thailand did not. Malaysia and Indonesia also employed more flexible exchange rate mechanisms that allowed their currencies to depreciate slowly, hoping to reduce the pressure for a sudden devaluation. And in the Philippines, bank credit was only about 36 percent of GDP, compared to over 100 percent in Thailand, while the Philippine current account deficit was 4 percent of GDP, half that of Thailand.[17] For these and other reasons, the chief economist at Deutsche Bank AG in Tokyo voiced a commonly expressed opinion when he said, "I think it's wrong to lump the four together."[18]

The markets ignored the opinions of the experts. In the days immediately following the Thai devaluation, the stock and currency markets in Malaysia, the Philippines, and Indonesia were pummeled. A Malaysian official said plaintively, "We have been telling people that we are not Thailand, but they still believe we are . . ." When asked why local funds had not supported the stock market as foreign investors fled, he admitted, "This is not really a mature market."[19]

Central banks in the afflicted countries battled mightily to fend off the onslaught. On July 8 alone, six days after the Thai devaluation, the Malaysian central bank, Bank Negara, bought between $1 billion and $2 billion worth of the Malaysian currency, the ringgit, to support its value. And the Philippine central bank increased its overnight interbank borrowing rate to 32 percent annualized, the highest ever. But stock prices continued to fall. A trader in the Philippines, stunned by the chaos in the stock market, said, "It's very bloody and the fight [over the Philippine peso] doesn't seem to be over, so it's anybody's guess where the market will go from here."[20]

The Philippines was the first country, after Thailand, to capitulate. Less than three weeks after the Thai devaluation, the Philippine central bank rolled back its high interest rates and allowed the peso to "float"—or, more aptly, to sink—to whatever level market forces dictated. But Malaysia was determined to fight on, led by its feisty prime minister Mahathir Mohamad.

No stranger to controversy, Mahathir possessed a stern determination belied by a cherubic face that made him appear much younger than his seventy-one years. Born in a small village in a rural Malayan state, he was the son of the colony's first non-British headmaster of a secondary school. He was acutely aware of how the colonial British "looked down upon" Malays; he would carry this sense of resentment with him throughout his adult life.

When Japan conquered Malaya in World War II, Mahathir was reduced to hawking coffee, cake, and bananas on the street to survive. After the war he was able to wrangle a scholarship to medical school; there he received his degree, but decided to enter politics instead of medicine in the postcolonial period. He quickly became an ardent advocate for the ethnic Malays, who felt victimized both by their British colonizers and by the Malayan Chinese minority, which dominated the business world.

In 1970 Mahathir published an incendiary book, *The Malay Dilemma*, which was immediately banned by the government. In it he characterized the Malays as long-suffering victims of injustices imposed upon them by others, who sought to exploit them and encouraged their gentle "character," which allowed them to become victims. Describing the interactions of ethnic groups, he wrote, "The Jews are not merely hook-nosed, but understand money instinctively. The Europeans are not only fair skinned, but have an insatiable curiosity. The Malays are not merely brown, but are easygoing and tolerant. The Chinese are not just almond eyed people, but are also inherently good businessmen . . . The possession of these characteristics means little until different races come into contact with each other." When the "races" did come together in Malaysia, Mahathir felt, the Malays were the losers.

When Mahathir became prime minister in 1981, he promptly undertook the task of reforming the character of the Malays. Through various affirmative action schemes and high-profile government projects, he sought to raise up native Malaysians in the estimation of themselves and of outsiders. An Australian anthropologist, Clive Kessler, compared Mahathir's showy projects to the actions of tribal Malaysian chieftains who sought to "create reality." A chieftain would build an elaborate, highly visible balcony on his house rather than something more practical that could not be seen. "The whole national development policy," Kessler said, "is about putting up extra balconies, filling plots of land and really showing that Malays are 100% stakeholders in the global economy."[21]

Mahathir was quick to react to perceived affronts from foreigners. In the 1980s he imposed an embargo on British goods following a series of incidents that upset him, and he later chilled relations with Australia after Prime Minister Paul Keating referred to him as being "recalcitrant" on certain diplomatic issues. But there was always something of a dichotomy in Mahathir's thinking: he very much wanted foreign investment but feared that such investment could make Malaysia subservient to foreign interests.

Mahathir was not about to knuckle under to what he believed was a new, insidious form of colonialism—global free-market capitalism. Behind the financial crisis that threatened to swamp his ambitious plans he saw not the impersonal workings of the market, but instead deliberate attacks on the Malaysian people by unscrupulous individuals. Foremost on the list of enemies was George Soros. In late July Mahathir described the currency crisis as a "well planned effort" to undermine the Malaysian economy.[22] Over the next several weeks he would brand foreign currency traders, specifically including Soros, as "international criminals" bent on destroying emerging economies. He called Soros a "moron . . . with a lot of money," and infuriated U.S. Secretary of State Madeleine Albright at a regional security conference in Kuala Lumpur by publicly insinuating that Americans such as Soros were conspiring to sabotage Southeast Asian economies, and that Western states were "oppressing" developing states with human rights demands. Mahathir vowed to protect Malaysians from an open global economy, which he described as "a jungle full of roaming ferocious beasts," warning that "we will learn how to live in the jungle and we will develop the skills to handle the wild beasts."[23]

In early August Mahathir was told that Soros wanted to meet him. "We'll find out what he wants to explain," the prime minister announced peremptorily.[24] The meeting never came off, and both the ringgit and Malaysian stocks continued to fall; on August 5 Malaysian shares suffered their largest one-day drop since 1995. Finally, on August 8, Mahathir announced that Malaysia would no longer defend the ringgit. Trying to put the best possible face on matters, he predicted, "Even if the value falls, we will do nothing, because we are confident it will recover." He also warned that as long as traders such as Soros can "interfere" with currencies, "no country is safe."[25]

There was much talk of a flight of capital from Malaysia, in part because of Mahathir's harsh rhetoric. Overnight interest rates shot up to 50 percent annualized, from 9 percent before the crisis. Meanwhile, in spite of a hastily announced $16 billion aid package from the IMF, the Thai baht continued to slide lower. Then on August 14 Indonesia finally abandoned its efforts to support its currency, the rupiah, allowing it to float. Far from playing itself out, the crisis only seemed to get worse.

One man who thought he had seen it all in Indonesia, and East Asia, was Stephen Swift, chief of investments of Credit Suisse Asset

Management's Indonesia Fund. But nothing had prepared him for the drubbing he and his fund took in Indonesian stocks in 1997. "I've been through Asian crises before," he said, "but Indonesia's was like no other to date for its speed and devastation. Crashes occurred simultaneously in both the foreign exchange and stock markets. Liquidity just dried up. The rupiah lost 40% of its value in US dollars. With Indonesia it was contagion, pure and simple."[26]

As in Thailand, Malaysia, and the Philippines, the falling rupiah abruptly increased the size of loans denominated in dollars. Although many companies were "public," meaning that shares were held by numerous investors and were listed on the Indonesian Stock Exchange, the amounts of their foreign currency liabilities were often not disclosed, because of lax reporting standards. Their share prices plunged when the true extent of those liabilities belatedly became evident. Highlighting a problem of transparency that existed in many Asian countries, Swift remarked, "I've always said there are no public companies in Asia—only private companies with public quotes."[27]

He went on to point to the essential "difference between an emerging market and a developed market," which, he said, was the lack in emerging markets of "the varied buying and selling patterns that provide depth. All investors tend to move the same way in emerging markets." Tan Min Lan, senior economist in Singapore for Merrill Lynch, agreed: "There is a complete loss of confidence in the region. We have large sell orders from our clients who want to cut back their exposure to Asia."[28]

Prime Minister Mahathir of Malaysia refused to accept the explanation that the crisis was being driven by impersonal market forces. After a particularly brutal week on the Kuala Lumpur Stock Exchange in late August, he stunned investors by blasting foreign fund managers as "stock manipulators." He then announced an array of measures to prop up prices on the Kuala Lumpur exchange, including a ban on short-selling and a pledge to use billions of ringgits in state-managed pension funds to buy stocks. Loosely veiled threats were made that Malaysia's tough antisubversion law could be used to arrest those who sought to "sabotage" the economy. Once again, Mahathir singled out George Soros as the principal villain, claiming he had "evidence" Soros was behind the stock market decline. But his accusations seemed to do more damage than good, frightening away legitimate foreign investors. Reuters reported that Morgan Stanley had suspended all trading in Malaysian stocks. An official at Morgan Stanley was quoted as saying, "There are enough problems in these markets as it is without authorities changing the rules of the game . . ."[29]

By September a thick, choking haze had descended over much of Malaysia, the product of pollution, a stifling drought, and wide-spread forest fires in nearby Indonesia. The airborne muck seemed to symbolize the blight that had fallen over the economy, blotting out the spectacular successes of previous years. Even the world's tallest buildings—the Petronas Twin Towers—were invisible only a few blocks away. To fight the smog, Malaysians tried everything from spraying water off the tops of tall buildings to cloud seeding, but the haze was often so thick they had trouble even finding the clouds. A government official proposed that the country employ new Russian technology that reportedly could create man-made cyclones to flush the pollutants out of the air. Unfortunately, nothing seemed to work. One wealthy Malaysian bemoaned the financial turmoil that made it impossible to escape the soupy smog. "I lost so much money in the stock market," he complained, "otherwise I would be in England right now." He said he had dispatched his driver to buy surgical masks the government recommended for people who had to spend time outdoors.[30]

Prime Minister Mahathir continued to attack those he suspected were behind Malaysia's plight. He publicly voiced suspicions of a "Jewish agenda" behind speculative attacks on the currency and the stock market. "We are Muslims," Mahathir declared, "and the Jews are not happy to see Muslims progress. We may suspect that they have an agenda, but we do not want to accuse them."[31]

By this time George Soros had had enough. He blasted the Malaysian prime minister, declaring, "Dr. Mahathir is a menace to his own country . . . Dr. Mahathir's suggestion yesterday to ban currency trading is so inappropriate that it does not deserve serious considera-tion. I have been subjected to all sorts of false and vile accusations by Dr. Mahathir. He is using me as a scapegoat to cover up his own fail-ures."[32]

Mahathir's outspoken critique of the workings of global markets found little support from other Asian leaders. Much as they may have resented the harsh reality forced on them, they quickly realized it was a bitter pill they had no choice but to swallow. President Suharto of Indonesia warned that his countrymen must "understand [the] new realities and adjust to them," while Prime Minister Goh Chok Tong of Singapore said candidly, "I take the view that you can't fight the market."[33]

The "market" of the 1990s, however, was a vastly different entity from the one that existed only a decade earlier. In the Latin American debt crisis of the 1980s, for example, the principal players were the South American governments (the debtors) and the big American and European commercial banks (the creditors). Ultimately the crises were resolved by negotiations between the two groups, assisted at critical junctures by the U.S. government. But in the 1990s the explosive growth of mutual fund and pension fund investments in emerging markets created an entirely new dynamic. Just as in Mexico in 1994, it was no longer possible for the embattled nations of East Asia to sit down and negotiate with a few big banks; instead they faced panicky withdrawals by tens of thousands of individual investors who sought to pull their money out of funds that invested in emerging markets, in turn forcing the managers of those funds to dump emerging market securities (and currencies) to meet the redemptions. According to Salomon Brothers, the sixty-eight "Asian" funds registered in the United States experienced a net inflow of $2.2 billion in 1996. But by September 1997 those same funds had been hit with redemptions of over $2 billion, the first time net outflows had occurred since Salomon Brothers began tracking the funds in 1993. Even if the imperiled Asian nations had wanted to "negotiate" with their foreign investors, there was no single entity with which they could carry out such discussions. As one Salomon Brothers analyst put it, this was a "whole new ballgame."[34]

Arguably the spread of "bahtulism"—set off by the collapse of the Thai baht—should have stopped after Malaysia, Indonesia, and the Philippines succumbed. But on October 18, 1997, Taiwan stunned the financial community by also devaluing its currency. Taiwan possessed the third largest stockpile of hard currency reserves in the world, behind only China and the United States, and was running a substantial current account surplus, not a deficit like the other Asian victims. The government decided to devalue so that its exports would not be placed at a competitive disadvantage relative to those of countries that had allowed their currencies to drop in value. The specter of a never-ending series of competitive devaluations, much like those that had devastated the world economy in the 1930s, loomed.

If Taiwan could devalue, what currency was truly safe? Suddenly the larger and presumably stronger Asian economies of Hong Kong, South Korea, and even Japan were at risk. In the week immediately after the Taiwan devaluation, the Hong Kong stock market, which until a short time earlier had been the strongest in Asia, fell precipitously. Selling came both from investors who feared the spread of the "Asian contagion" to Hong Kong and from Asia-oriented mutual funds that were forced to sell relatively liquid Hong Kong stocks to raise the money necessary to meet investor redemptions. Overnight interest rates spiked briefly to 300 percent annualized as fears spread that the Hong Kong Monetary Authority, in spite of huge hard-currency reserves and a strict system of pegging its currency to the U.S. dollar, would be forced to devalue. "People smell blood," said an executive at a U.S. bank in Singapore. "This is the same as the Thai baht . . . Speculators have seen this before. Look at Thailand, Malaysia, Taiwan. Don't you see a pattern here?"[35]

The Hong Kong stock market break and concurrent severe declines in other Asian markets finally punctured the boom psychology on Wall Street. Caught up in the strong performance of the American economy, U.S. market participants had been slow to respond to the trouble in the Far East. But in October 1997 American stock prices were hit with a vengeance. The rout culminated in a 7 percent drop in the Dow Jones Industrial Average on Monday, October 27, the largest decline since the 1987 crash. The *Wall Street Journal* headlined its explanation for the market action "Hong Kong Stock Drop Spreads Worldwide."

Many American investors were surprised by the magnitude of the New York market decline, given the ebullient state of the American economy. As a parody of public attitudes, late-night talk show host

David Letterman referred to the Hong Kong market as "three old men and a duck," and professed shock that a decline in Hong Kong could have such a dramatic impact on U.S. stock prices. But Letterman's views, and public opinion in the United States, lagged substantially behind the pace of developments. The Asian markets were far more important and much more closely linked to the American market than most investors understood.

The Hong Kong stock market was the fifth largest in the world and the most important in Asia outside Japan. For the ten years from October 31, 1987, through September 1997, it was the world's best-performing equity market, up 25.9 percent per year, compared with 17.3 percent in the United States, which itself ranked fourth in performance for the period, behind Hong Kong, Holland, and Sweden.

The depth and breadth of public participation in the Hong Kong stock market also made the market important to the overall Hong Kong economy. A sharp drop in share prices could slow economic activity through the so-called wealth effect—whereby consumers, reacting to losses in their investment portfolios, spend less money—or by causing scared investors to transfer money overseas, thereby putting pressure on the Hong Kong dollar. It was this link between the Hong Kong dollar and the stock market, and the alleged manipulation of the link by sinister foreign speculators, that soon occupied the attention of Hong Kong authorities striving to deal with the spreading Asian crisis.

Given Hong Kong's rigid monetary regime, in which its currency was pegged directly to the U.S. dollar, selling pressure on the Hong Kong dollar automatically resulted in a reduction in the Hong Kong money supply. (This occurred because all Hong Kong dollars outstanding had to be backed up by U.S. dollar reserves; as those reserves were depleted by traders seeking to sell Hong Kong dollars in exchange for U.S. dollars or other hard currency, the volume of Hong Kong dollars outstanding by definition had to decline.) A contracting money supply meant higher interest rates, and higher interest rates typically caused stock prices to fall.

In a maneuver termed a "double play" by suspicious government authorities, speculators could theoretically profit by selling short both Hong Kong dollars and Hong Kong stocks. By selling short stocks, thereby forcing prices down, they might frighten investors into taking money out of the market and out of Hong Kong itself, putting pressure on the Hong Kong dollar. And by selling the Hong Kong dollar short, they would force interest rates higher, thereby causing stocks to fall. The speculators' bets thus reinforced one another, to the detriment of Hong Kong. One hedge fund trader essentially agreed that the government's suspicions were correct. "What [the speculators have] realized is that the way you get the [currency] peg is to go after the stock market."[36]

Hong Kong authorities, with the implicit backing of China, decided to fight back. The government intervened massively in the market, buying stocks to force prices back up and punish speculators who had been betting on a decline. Unlike similar efforts by officials to support prices in Japan, which never really succeeded in stemming the long-term decline, the Hong Kong intervention worked, aborting the decline, although only after the market had already fallen by two-thirds. The Hang Seng Index bounced back 8.47 percent immediately after the intervention began.

Tung Chee-hwa, the chief executive of Hong Kong, denied that the government had any intention "to artificially support the stock market." The authorities would, however, take "resolute action to reduce market distortion" caused by speculators. The Finance Secretary, Donald Tang, accused speculators of attacking the currency and the stock market with a "whole host of improper measures" including the spreading of "vicious rumors" about a possible devaluation and the condition of the banks.

South Korea, which had been one of the most successful economies in Asia, was not immune from the panic. By late fall 1997 the South Korean stock market had fallen to levels not seen since 1986–87; all the gains of eleven years had been wiped out in six months. The country's currency, the won, came under heavy pressure in foreign exchange markets. The familiar pattern of the smaller East Asian countries seemed to be repeating itself; first government officials would deny that a crisis existed, only to be forced by the worsening storm to reverse themselves. In late November a South Korean spokesman said there was "almost no chance" that the country would undergo the same kind of shakeup that had occurred else-

where. "Korea will never become another Thailand . . . ," he insisted.[37] A few days later, however, the government capitulated,
announcing that it planned to seek aid from the IMF. Economists
estimated that Korea might require as much as $100 billion, an
amount that would dwarf other Asian rescue packages.

The South Korean financial markets effectively seized up; for all
practical purposes they simply ceased to function. The market breakdown affected the entire business community. As one American investment banker in Korea put it: "Businesses are almost paralyzed.
They're not out there producing and marketing. They are just trying
to get liquidity."[38]

In the tense environment that existed in early 1998, any action
taken by the governments of the afflicted East Asian nations received
extraordinary scrutiny. President Suharto of Indonesia discovered
this in January, much to his chagrin. Suharto, who had ruled auto-
cratically for more than three decades, was accustomed to absolute
control of Indonesian economic policy. The results of that control
had for many years seemed to be positive; economic growth had
averaged 7.5 percent over the preceding ten years, lifting millions of
Indonesians out of poverty. But Suharto was now in for a rude
awakening. Within hours after he announced a budget plan on January 6, both the rupiah and Indonesian stocks plunged. Market participants perceived that Suharto was backpedaling on an austerity plan
he had agreed to under IMF pressure in October.

Calls immediately came in from important world leaders, to whom
the annual announcement of an Indonesian budget would be, under
normal circumstances, hardly worthy of notice. President Clinton
and U.S. Treasury Secretary Lawrence Summers telephoned, as
did German chancellor Kohl, Japanese prime minister Ryutaro
Hashimoto, and the top officials of the IMF. Within a few days a
chastened Suharto was forced to accept an IMF rescue plan of unprecedented scope, requiring broad reforms in the Indonesian economy that included the elimination of trade and manufacturing
monopolies, the removal of subsidies, comprehensive changes in the
banking system, and substantial budget cuts.

Still the rupiah continued to fall. It would eventually decline to a
ratio of 17,000 rupiahs to one U.S. dollar, down 85 percent from its

precrisis level. The remorseless decline in stock prices continued unabated; one analyst estimated that by early 1998 only twenty-two of
the nearly three hundred companies listed on the Jakarta stock exchange were actually still solvent.[39] Both the Suharto government
and the IMF came in for intense criticism from Indonesian dissi-
dents. Turmoil in global financial markets had forced Indonesia to
make painful changes, yet those changes had apparently not halted,
or even appreciably slowed, the decline in the economy or the markets. It was the worst of all possible worlds.

Suharto himself would soon pay with his job for the economic instability that swept through Indonesia like a sudden typhoon. In an
emotional confrontation with his vice president, B. J. Habibie, in
May 1998, Suharto was "persuaded" to relinquish power. It was a
humiliating end for a man who had for years been praised as "the father of development" in Indonesia.

Critics of the IMF's tough austerity plan argued that the conditions imposed by the fund often did more damage than good. And
inevitable questions were asked about the practices the World Bank
had employed in lending to Indonesia. Why had both institutions
failed to anticipate the crisis? Indonesia, which only months earlier
had been considered a great success story, was now a disaster area in
which a majority of the population had been plunged back into
poverty. World Bank president James Wolfensohn admitted that the
bank had been caught up in enthusiasm inspired by Indonesia's rapid
progress, causing it to overlook evidence of institutional weakness
and corruption in the Indonesian economy. "I [was] not alone in
thinking 12 months ago that Indonesia was on a very good path," he
said.[40] An economist who ran the World Bank mission in Jakarta described the dilemma bank officials faced this way: "In every country
we work in there is a tradeoff, shall we say, between being pure and
helping people. We deal in the real world." He conceded that the
bank had been willing to overlook endemic corruption and crony
capitalism in Indonesia, viewing it as a regrettable "tax" on the economy. After all, how could you argue with a sustained growth rate of
nearly 8 percent per year?[41]

Suharto was by no means the only government official to suffer the
consequences of economic failure. Kang Kyong Shik, South Korea's

finance minister from March to November 1997, was jailed in June 1998. His aides had urged him not to accept the job when it was first offered. "The economy was going bad," recalled Kang's chief of staff. "We knew we could get blamed." Kang was removed from his post in November 1997, two days before South Korea was forced to turn to the IMF. He was formally indicted in June 1998 for negligence of duty and abuse of power, for allegedly not informing the president of the magnitude of the crisis or of the decision to ask for IMF aid, and for improperly pressuring banks. His arrest was widely viewed in the West as an effort to find a scapegoat for the country's severe economic problems. Mr. Kang said simply, "I tried my best."[42]

The rest of the world seemed to shake off these events. North American and most European markets steadied in late 1997, then rallied substantially in the first half of 1998. Even more surprising, emerging markets elsewhere (such as Latin America and Russia) did not initially seem to be troubled by the Asian collapse. Funds flowed from Asian emerging markets into developing markets in Eastern Europe and South America; worldwide, emerging market equity funds took in a net of approximately $2.5 billion in 1997, despite Asian withdrawals.

But as 1998 advanced, non-Asian emerging stock markets began to stumble. By midyear, several Latin American markets had fallen substantially, although for the most part in an orderly fashion. It was in Russia, however, that the real catastrophe was to occur. The Russian stock market had been the best-performing equity market in the world in 1996 and 1997, shrugging off the turmoil in the Far East. In 1997 the Russian economy had posted its first positive growth since the disintegration of the Soviet Union. By the end of 1998, however, all would be in a shambles.

Russia had never really been much more than a poor stepchild among the world's emerging markets. Unlike the "Asian Tigers," which had lengthy histories of strong growth, often stretching back decades, the Russian economy had actually been contracting for most of the 1990s. In size it was smaller than the economy of the Netherlands. All the deficiencies of emerging markets—the absence of adequate legal and regulatory structures, primitive market mechanisms, and the lack of transparency—were painfully evident in Russia.

A designer of accounting software for a Western firm observed, "Russian profits are different from Western-style profits. The same data can give different results. It gets very complicated . . . Translation is sometimes difficult." An accountant at the Arthur Andersen office in Moscow admitted that Soviet-style accounting was "never designed to account for things like profit."[43] Rather, Soviet accounting procedures had been set up mostly to prevent employee theft. Although some large Russian companies were beginning to move toward adopting Western standards, most firms lagged behind. The man responsible for modernizing Russian accounting practices, Alexander Bakaev, head of the finance ministry's Department of Accounting Methodology, complained that Westerners were trying to push change too fast. "In my opinion, you should only move quickly when you need to go to the toilet," he said. "We can issue instructions, but, unfortunately, we can't control whether they ever get followed."[44]

According to a female professor of accounting, accounting in Russia had historically been a low-status job. Accountants used to be "fat women with big arms. No one wanted to be an accountant." The *Wall Street Journal* reported on a typical case involving a woman who was the chief accountant at the Moscow Electrode Factory. She had worked there for twenty years keeping books by hand in a white ledger, and had never been exposed to international accounting standards, much less to the tough generally accepted accounting principles (GAAP) employed in the United States. The dilapidated factory had trouble paying its 1,500 employees and had millions of rubles in unpaid energy bills. According to the figures produced by the chief accountant, however, it still earned a profit. When asked how this was accomplished, the plant director refused to answer, claiming, "This is a commercial secret."

By July 1998 the brief foreign fascination with Russian markets was fading fast. Stock prices slid steadily lower, and annual yields paid on short-term ruble-denominated government bonds, known as GKOs, shot up to triple digits as the prices of the bonds plummeted. It was estimated that foreigners held approximately $15 billion worth of the $49 billion in GKOs outstanding, the rest being owned primarily by newly established Russian banks. Rumors of a ruble devaluation and even of a possible government default were rife. Once again, as it had already done several times in Asia, the IMF was forced to step in with a $22.6 billion rescue package, designed to give Russia some vital breathing room. "They had created a Frankenstein monster," one foreign analyst said, referring to the high-yield treasuries the Russian government had issued. "Now they can cut off a couple of limbs. The monster is not quite dead yet, but they have provided the conditions under which it can be extinguished."[45]

Such optimism was short-lived. By mid-August the financial markets in Russia had essentially disintegrated; the prices of outstanding GKOs fell so far their yields reached 200 percent, and many Russian stockbrokers refused to trade with one another, fearing that their counterparties in any transaction might go bankrupt before the proceeds of the transaction were settled. One stockbroker admitted, "We are not participating in this madness."[46]

George Soros warned publicly that the financial meltdown in Russia had reached a "terminal stage," and recommended a measured 15–25 percent devaluation of the ruble. Little attention was paid to his proposal. As during the market turmoil in Asia, many observers harbored suspicions of a hidden Soros agenda. Earlier in the decade, Soros had complained that his opinions were routinely ignored by public policy makers. "I wish people would listen to me more. I've had very little impact on Western policy towards the Soviet Union," he told a reporter. "It's remarkable how the White House doesn't use one of the few resources it's got, which is me."[47]

Western officials may have ignored Soros, but they were quick to criticize the Russian authorities' handling of the crisis. A principal complaint was that the Russians didn't comprehend how serious the situation was. Many important Russians, ranging from central bank chairman Sergei Dubinin to President Yeltsin himself, were on vacation and seemed to be out of touch with events. A senior American official said many top Russians "don't fully understand how quickly domestic developments get linked to international events—and how quickly capital moves."[48]

Violent tremors from Russia reverberated through other markets. The Czech koruna fell more than 5 percent while the yield on long-term Polish government bonds rose by more than one-third to 9 percent. Farther away, yields on Venezuelan bonds jumped from around 8 percent to 11 percent, and stock prices fell across Latin America. Some analysts were baffled by the new contagion, given the relative insignificance of Russia in the overall global economy. Markets were now linked together in ways that would have been inconceivable only a decade before. Argentina's ability to defend its currency peg to the U.S. dollar might now depend on Hong Kong's ability to do the same. The fact that the IMF's announced rescue package had failed to prevent the debacle in Russia cast doubt on the ability of the IMF to intervene successfully elsewhere. Even the mighty U.S. stock market experienced a new skittishness as events unfolded overseas. Richard Medley of Medley Global Advisors took note of how unpleasant realities in distant countries had undermined the ineluctable optimism that had so long pervaded the American stock market. "This disputes the notion that we are in a smooth transition into the end of history," he observed tartly.[49]

What was particularly disturbing to adherents of modern portfolio theory was that correlations between movements in various emerging markets were increasing. The appealing notion that risk could be controlled by adequately diversifying across many different stock markets depended on the assumption that these markets would not all move together. But the 1987 crash, and now the 1997–98 emerging market crisis, undermined this belief, as panic spread quickly to different markets. The same institutional players (pension plans, hedge funds, and mutual funds) were now involved in all markets. Their decisions to buy and sell stocks were driven by influences that transcended national boundaries, inevitably increasing the degree to which different stock markets moved together. Ironically, the upsurge in cross-border equity investment that was in large part justified by the theory of diversification had the effect of undermining the very benefits of that diversification.

One piece of new research published in early 2002 confirmed this trend. The study found that the correlation among major existing international stock markets had increased markedly over the preceding three decades. In essence, major stock exchanges were becoming more closely linked, and thus more alike. But over the same period, many new markets had been created in developing countries, which still tended to fluctuate more based on local, rather than global, considerations. William Goetzmann of Yale, one of the authors of the study, observed, "The good news is, you can still get the diversification benefit. The bad news is, you have to risk your money in these fringe markets."[50] He did not comment on how long it might take the new emerging "fringe" markets to become more fully integrated into the world economy.

In the United States, the Federal Reserve Board struggled with the question of what to do about the turmoil in international stock markets. Prior to the eruption of the "Asian contagion," the Fed had been under pressure to increase interest rates in order to take the air out of what many perceived to be a dangerously inflating domestic stock market bubble. Nobel Prize–winning economist Paul Samuelson described the Fed's dilemma this way: "I define a bubble as a situation in which the level of stock prices is high because of a self-fulfilling prophecy in which people believe the market is going to go up. On that basis, I think there has been a bubble in the [U.S.] market for at least two years, possibly longer." By not acting to arrest the market's rise, Samuelson claimed, Fed chairman Alan Greenspan had "painted himself into a corner."[51]

Nearly two years earlier, in December 1996, Greenspan had coined the phrase "irrational exuberance" in discussing the performance of the stock market. On July 21, 1998, testifying before the Senate Banking Committee, he discussed what he called the "cross-currents" affecting the economic outlook. Greenspan admitted that the economy (and by implication the stock market) was growing too rapidly, and declared that "firming actions on the part of the Federal Reserve may be necessary" to ensure that the economic expansion could be sustained. But significantly, he also warned, "We need to be aware that monetary tightening actions in the U.S. could have outsized effects on very sensitive financial markets in Asia."

As the international market crisis worsened, pulling the American stock market down as well, Greenspan said that it was "just not credible that the United States can remain an oasis of prosperity unaffected by a world that is experiencing greatly increased stress."[52] In another speech Greenspan cautioned that fear and uncertainty were causing investors to "disengage" from financial markets, a trend that could have dangerous consequences.[53]

On September 29, 1998, the Fed acted, cutting the federal funds rate from 5.5 percent to 5.25 percent. Two weeks later, after the stock market had failed to respond positively, the central bank again cut short-term rates by 0.25 percent. One of the rationales given for the rate cuts was "to cushion the effects on prospective economic growth in the United States of increasing weakness in foreign economies . . ."[54] The second cut did the trick, triggering a substantial rally in American stock prices. Stephen Slifer, a Lehman Brothers economist, summed up the Wall Street reaction. "Without actually saying it," Slifer concluded, "Greenspan is saying 'We're going to supply liquidity to the system, and we're going to keep the U.S. economy out of recession.' "[55]

Nineteen ninety-eight was a defining year in the new era of worldwide equity markets. There were more active stock markets, which were more important, in more countries than ever before. The linkages among markets meant that shocks in one country—such as Thailand or Russia—could be quickly transmitted to other, seemingly unrelated, nations. Even the American economy and its booming stock market was not safe. For the first time since the pre-1914 era of international global markets, a crisis in foreign financial markets triggered a panic on Wall Street. The Federal Reserve Board itself had been forced to substantially modify domestic monetary policy because of an international market crisis. For better or worse, the wide acceptance of a free-market philosophy that emphasized the importance of equity markets had created an entirely new world financial order. But the consequences of that new order were only just beginning to be felt.

14

STOCK MARKET CAPITALISM

"EUROPE'S STAKEHOLDER CAPITALISM is under siege."

So declared Patrick Artus, an economic adviser to French prime minister Lionel Jospin, writing in the *Financial Times* in early 2002. "Across the continent," Artus warned, "the traditional model of consensual decision-making is retreating before the seemingly unstoppable march of Anglo-Saxon shareholder value. A once-unspoken fear is now openly raised: can a distinctively European economic system be saved?"

The advent of the new financial world order, with its vastly enlarged role for equity markets, has done more to radically reshape national economies than any event since the Great Depression. It has rocked many developing countries, which now find their fates tied inexorably to powerful and unpredictable external market forces. But even developed countries, such as Germany, France, and Japan, fear losing control of their own destiny. Their traditional social compacts—often referred to as stakeholder capitalism, where labor, creditors, local communities, and governments have an important voice in corporate decision making—are jeopardized by the newfound power of stock market investors who demand that managements concentrate first and foremost on maximizing profits and dividends. Can the "stakeholder" system survive in an era where from 30 percent to 50 percent of European stocks are held by demanding foreign investors, and over 50 percent of the trading on the Tokyo Stock Exchange originates overseas? The globalized equity market has become a battering ram knocking down resistance to an Anglo-American-style market economy.

In Germany, stakeholder capitalism is enshrined in law. Large German corporations have both supervisory and management boards (the latter selected by the former), with mandated representation for labor on the supervisory boards. In some heavy industries (primarily steel and coal), labor receives half of the seats on the supervisory board. In other large firms, the supervisory board is also evenly split, but with a chairman, elected by the shareholders, who can cast a deciding vote to break a tie. Mid-sized and many smaller firms are required to establish "workers' councils" in lieu of board representation for labor. German law sets out specific requirements detailing the types of management decisions that require "consent" by workers' councils and those that only require that the councils be "informed."

In Japan, unlike Germany, "stakeholder" restraints on the actions of managers have been a matter more of culture than of law. But the effect is the same; stockholder interests are checked by the interests of various other groups, particularly workers, who are perceived to have a stake in the firm. Most Asian and European countries possess forms of stakeholder capitalism that fall somewhere between the "cultural" Japanese practice and the "legal" German system. Increasingly, however, all varieties of stakeholder capitalism are coming under assault.

In 1999 Jack Welch, the chairman of General Electric, gave the keynote address at an international business forum that directly addressed these issues. Welch had become the poster boy for American stock market capitalism, creating value for his shareholders to such an extent that GE had become the largest corporation in the world in terms of stock market capitalization. Following Welch to the podium, however, the chairman of Toyota gave voice to a decidedly different perspective. He declared that Toyota would not abandon traditional practices like lifetime employment no matter how far Western credit agencies like Standard & Poor's lowered its credit rating, and no matter how many foreign institutional investors expressed their displeasure.[1]

In Germany the issue was brought home with force in 2001 by the successful effort of the British firm Vodaphone to effect a hostile takeover of the German firm Mannesmann. The protracted, highly controversial battle sharpened the issues as never before. (Only two other large hostile takeovers had ever been attempted in Germany. One, in 1990, failed, and the other, in 1997, started out hostile but ended up in a negotiated deal.) Mannesmann had only recently acquired a British firm through a similar hostile bid, with little objection in Britain, where hostile takeovers had long been routine. But such was not to be the case in Germany.

Even the shareholder representatives on Mannesmann's supervisory board were reluctant to define the issues simply in terms of shareholder interest, and the takeover effort met with condemnation from both the press and the German government. Britons, including Prime Minister Tony Blair, complained of a double standard. There was no objection in Germany to a German acquisition of a British company, but howls of outrage erupted when the tables were turned. (Prophetically, Vodaphone eventually succeeded in acquiring Mannesmann because nearly 60 percent of Mannesmann's stock was in foreign hands.)

In his *Financial Times* piece Artus cited Germany as the country where "the waning of the traditional model" could be most clearly seen. "Co-determination," where employees participate in corporate governance, appeared to be losing out to American-style management. The experience of the massive universal bank Deutsche Bank was a prime example. Within a short period of time the bank had restructured its management to concentrate power in the hands of a small number of people, moving away from the traditional broad-based management board—the *Vorstand*—where important decisions were made by consensus. The newly powerful Deutsche Bank executives came from backgrounds in investment banking and the financial markets. They represented, Artus claimed, an American "management culture." If present trends continued, Artus cautioned, efforts to preserve the European version of capitalism were "doomed to failure."

But not without a fight. Artus's boss, French prime minister Lionel Jospin, deliberately put himself out of step with the new global market order. Harkening back to a device originally proposed in 1971, Jospin floated the idea of a cross-border capital tax plan. Called the Tobin tax—after the American Keynesian economist James Tobin, who had first developed it—Jospin's plan called for a 1 percent levy on cross-frontier movements of capital to discourage speculative flows. It was as if Jospin was attempting to set back the clock to the Bretton Woods era, fifty years earlier, when distrust of international capital markets was pervasive.

In Germany, Chancellor Gerhard Schröder's government, galvanized by the Mannesman deal, which had shocked labor and much of the public, began to backtrack from market liberalizations favored by international investors. Previously, the government had passed a landmark corporate tax reform act that eliminated capital gains taxes on companies that sold cross-holding stakes in other companies. The stated purpose of the measure had been to encourage corporations with long-term cross-holdings unrelated to their basic business to sell those holdings, allowing for a more efficient use of corporate resources. Belatedly, unions and politicians recognized that the disposal of traditional cross-holdings would open up many more German companies to hostile takeover attempts by foreign firms, as those companies lost the protection afforded by stable shareholders. The government responded by hastily enacting a new law governing takeovers. Billed as a reform, it was greeted with dismay by U.S. and British institutional investors who complained that it actually provided new means by which German managements could shield themselves from unwanted suitors.

Critics of the German system of corporate governance argue that managements and cross-holding shareholders, insulated from the competitive pressures of the equity markets, are often unaccountable and, in many cases, incompetent. A series of corporate crises in the mid-1990s, including the bankruptcy of the Schneider group and the near-collapse of Metallgesellschaft, reinforced this opinion. A popular book by Gunter Ogger entitled *Nitwits in Pinstripes* attributed many of Germany's economic problems to "managerial failures, cosy back-scratching relationships and an entrenched system of block-shareholdings making hostile challenges [to management] virtually impossible."[2] The most intense pressure for reform came from foreign investors. "Above all," noted one German advocate of reform, "foreign investors in the German capital market found the German corporate system too complex and still lacking in transparency."[3]

Unfortunately, in the eyes of foreign investors, the new takeover law allowed German companies to enact so-called poison-pill provisions with the consent of 75 percent of shareholders; "poison pills" are designed to activate automatically in the case of an unfriendly takeover, creating such unpalatable burdens for the acquirer as to make the deal undoable. (Examples of poison pills include bylaws that rule out the use of debt to fund an acquisition, prevent the sale of key assets, and create prohibitively expensive golden parachutes for senior managers.) In addition, German companies, with only the approval of their supervisory boards, could now impose employment restrictions on acquiring firms that could last up to five years, tying the acquirer's hands by effectively preventing them from firing workers. One German investment banker warned that "capital markets will punish Germany and we will learn the lesson. Germany will find it difficult to attract institutional investors."[4] After German members of the European Parliament helped vote down a measure that would have restricted the use of poison-pill defenses, a former secretary of the U.K. Takeover Panel complained, "The message is that it is fortress Europe, and that European companies should be protected from overseas predators . . ."[5] Chancellor Schröder was not to be deterred. Despite his earlier efforts to make German markets friendlier to foreign investors, he now cautioned, "Don't count on me to Americanize German society."[6]

Schröder did remain committed to one important reform: a restructuring of the state pension system designed to encourage more equity investment by pension plans and by individuals saving for retirement. Starting in 2002, German savers were allowed to invest up to 1 percent of their income tax-free in insurance or mutual fund–based investment products; that amount rises to 4 percent by 2008. Anglo-American stock markets were driven by pension and retirement funds, the assets of which totaled well over half of GDP in the United States and the United Kingdom, compared to 4 percent in France and only a pathetically small 2 percent in Italy. In 2001 private pension assets averaged $23,780 per person in the United States, compared to only $3,800 per person in Germany and a mere $1,600 in France. Unfunded (pay-as-you-go) government pension systems accounted for 84 percent of all retirement benefits paid within the European Union.[7] As many observers saw it, the failure of European countries to develop large pools of retirement money that could be invested in stocks was a critical weakness of the European capitalist model.

A flood of pension and retirement money into equities had helped power the great bull markets of the 1980s and 1990s. During the 1990s global pension fund assets grew an average of 15 percent per year, from $4.6 trillion to $15.9 trillion. Equity holdings of those funds jumped from $1.6 trillion to $8 trillion, or from 35 percent to 51 percent of total assets. By the end of the decade, the stock holdings of retirement funds made up nearly one-quarter of total global equity market capitalization.

Over 80 percent of those shareholdings, however, were held by pension funds in the United States, Britain, and Japan, with the United States alone accounting for nearly 60 percent of the total. Increasingly, American pension money was finding its way overseas; one study of the two hundred largest defined-contribution plans in the United States found that their foreign equity holdings, as a percentage of total assets, increased from 12.1 percent in 1998 to 14.2 percent in 1999, and were projected to rise even more in future years.[8] Many Europeans feared that Anglo-American standards of corporate governance and shareholder value would inevitably follow in the wake of large Anglo-American institutional investors.

At times those investors espoused their cause with evangelistic fervor. In late 2000 an American lawyer named Ira Millstein led a team of American portfolio managers to Moscow. Their objective was to persuade senior executives of major Russian companies (who arrived at the meeting behind a phalanx of bodyguards) that it was in their interest to improve corporate governance and to provide better protection for minority shareholders. Russian stock market valuations lagged far behind those of Western nations, Millstein claimed, because Russia was not perceived as a friendly environment in which to invest. As an example, Millstein pointed out that the stock of Gazprom, the Russian energy monolith, traded at a price in 1999 that represented a total market capitalization of about $4 billion. If it had instead been valued on a P/E multiple typical of New York or London, it would have been worth a staggering $1.9 trillion. The entire Russian stock market, Millstein reported, was worth less than the Walt Disney Company (inadvertently hinting that Russia was a Mickey Mouse economy).[9]

Such remarks elicited some hostile responses; the manager of a heavy machinery company declared that he had not come to the meeting to be "taught how to wash his hands and brush his teeth."[10] Other attendees saw little value in equity markets, noting that at current valuation levels, Russian stock price levels were too cheap to make selling public equity attractive for Russian business. Nevertheless, most participants recognized that there was a positive return to be earned for good corporate governance. If Russian businesses wanted to raise the foreign capital they would need, at reasonable prices, corporate standards of behavior would at some point have to improve. One participant remarked that the sentiments expressed at the meeting reminded him of St. Augustine's prayer, "Make me chaste, but not yet."[11]

Unlike Lionel Jospin and Gerhard Schröder, who frequently sought to distance themselves from market-oriented reform efforts, Russian president Vladimir Putin embraced foreign equity investors enthusiastically. Foreign investment managers provided a convenient partner to help rein in the nefarious activities of the rogue oligarchs who dominated Russian capitalism in the early post-Soviet era. Putin had made an essential bargain with the oligarchs, allowing them to keep their wealth if they agreed to stop interfering in the government and to play by the rules of Western capitalism. As one Western portfolio manager put it, the oligarchs were "ceasing to behave as if they were temporary owners of the assets. They want to keep money in the company for reinvestment. They want to talk up the stock price. They want access to capital markets."[12] Many of the tycoons who ran big business in Russia were beginning to see themselves as part of the global equity market, a viewpoint that has revolutionary implications for the Russian economy.

A similar transformation has occurred in China, again largely driven by the need to attract foreign equity capital. In 2000 China began implementing new rules allowing private Chinese companies the freedom to raise capital through the country's stock markets; previously, only ponderous state-owned firms had been allowed to sell shares to the public. Under the new procedures, private investment banking firms, rather than the government, will decide which companies can issue new stock. The *New York Times* declared that this "simple reform could ultimately reshape China's economic landscape as radically as Deng Xiaoping's breakup of the communes did in the late 1970's."[13] The *Times* noted that the new stock market rules had political implications, in that successful private companies could become an increasingly powerful constituency that the government would find difficult to ignore. An economist from Morgan Stanley observed, "The rule of law and access to finance are the two things that will make China's private companies independent of political power."[14]

China originally created its stock exchanges in the early 1990s to provide an additional means of financing state enterprises. This plan was largely successful; within ten years, nearly one thousand state-run companies had sold stock to the public and listed their shares on the country's two exchanges, in Shenzen and Shanghai. The combined capitalization of China's stock markets ranks as the third largest in Asia, behind Japan and Hong Kong.

Unfortunately, the poorly regulated market has been plagued by many of the same problems that afflict other emerging bourses. It was frequently the subject of manipulation by both government and industry insiders. Transparency is very poor, with reliable data hard to come by. While millions of Chinese have engaged in trading stocks, most of them are short-term speculators, not long-term investors. Foreign investors, particularly foreign institutions, have been reluctant to get involved, both because of legal restraints on their ability to convert Chinese currency and the difficulty in securing solid information on Chinese companies.

The often blatant disregard for the rights of minority shareholders is a critical obstacle. One American investor interviewed by the *Wall Street Journal* cited the example of his investment in Shandong Huaneng Power Development Company. According to the company's annual report, the stock would provide safe, steady returns, with a great potential for growth thanks to surging Chinese demand for energy. But unexpectedly, Shandong Huaneng was taken over by a government-controlled power company at a bargain-basement valuation. Lawyers for the minority shareholders found little recourse, given China's primitive legal system. "We're getting stiffed," the American investor muttered.[15]

Sharp debates have occurred among Chinese authorities on how best to deal with the risk that the government's financial reform agenda will be obstructed by shortcomings in the equity markets. A senior government economist in early 2001 described the Chinese stock market as "worse than a casino," questioning whether it had been given too much of a role in China's economy.[16] At the same time, however, reformers committed to the use of equity markets to finance Chinese business defended the progress that had been made. "All countries have similar problems in the infancy stage of the stock market and they should not be exaggerated," argued one scholar who favored further reforms.[17] In fact, some progress has occurred, as Chinese regulators, seeking to prevent foreign buyers from losing confidence, have toughened disclosure requirements, launched prosecutions in cases of obvious manipulative activity, and required some firms to report earnings quarterly rather than semiannually.

Bill Kaye, a hedge fund manager familiar with investing in China, noted that there are many positives for the Chinese economy. "But," he warned, "the question is how much [potential investors] care about the fine print . . . There's nothing to stop these companies taking your money and walking off with it. You don't have any of the available exits . . . as a public investor [in China]."[18] The lack of board representation for minority investors, and a weak legal system, were the primary culprits.

According to Kaye, the critical issue going forward is whether Chinese companies will provide explicit commitments to deliver returns to shareholders in the future. He noted that even China Mobile, the company with the largest stock market capitalization in China, did not make any firm pledge to pay a dividend when it offered its shares. "The company does not expect to pay a dividend in the foreseeable future," Kaye quoted from the prospectus. He then commented, "I can tell you the Chinese concept of foreseeable is not the western concept—it means forever."

The total capitalization of the Chinese stock market in 2002 was approximately $650 billion, of which only one-third was free-floating, the rest still owned by the government. After an editorial in June 1999 in the Communist Party's mouthpiece, the *People's Daily*, endorsed rising stock prices, the government consciously pursued policies designed to attract more domestic investors, as well as foreigners, to keep the market strong. In late 1999, for example, the government announced a plan to tax interest payments on individual bank accounts, with the objective of prying billions hoarded by cautious savers out of banks and into the stock market.

As the *New York Times* noted, the potential effect of a burgeoning stock market culture on the Chinese economy and political system is enormous. China's entry into the World Trade Organization, setting a timetable for the gradual opening of the market to foreigners, should further accelerate this process. As one Chinese researcher, closely connected to the government, admitted, "We are obliged to open to foreigners. We should try to open domestically first."[19]

No country was immune from this pressure. Even a caustic critic of global financial markets like Malaysia's prime minister Mahathir Mohamad showed signs of reconciling himself and his nation to the realities of the new market order. The long-depressed Kuala Lumpur Stock Exchange jumped 10 percent in July 2001 when the government and the exchange announced reforms in corporate governance standards designed in large part to strengthen the rights of minority shareholders. "Dr. Mahathir has taken over the reformist mantle," crowed the director of research for a foreign brokerage firm. "A more enlightened electorate [is] demanding more transparency, accountability and good governance." Another broker reported, "The landscape has changed dramatically in recent months. There is definitely more interest from foreign investors."[20]

Malaysia was not alone; many other Asian nations, struggling to recover from the 1997–98 crisis, moved to make similar changes. "There has been a marked convergence towards 'global best practice' in the formal rules of virtually all the big [Asian] economies," said Jamie Allen, secretary-general of the Asian Corporate Governance Association.[21] By 2002 eight countries in the region had official codes of "best practices," with two more countries actively developing them. Only one nation had such a code before the 1997–98 crisis. Likewise, eleven countries mandated the employment of independent directors on corporate boards in 2002, compared to only three countries five years earlier.

Stock markets clearly rewarded those companies that adopted improved standards of corporate governance. A study conducted by a Hong Kong brokerage firm found that shares of companies ranked in the top quarter by corporate governance standards outperformed the benchmark stock indexes of their home countries by 147 percent in the five years ending December 31, 2001.[22] These results simply could not be ignored by firms seeking to raise capital in the difficult post-1997–98 environment.

It is not only governments and corporations that have been buffeted by the new culture of equities. Within the last ten years, tens of millions of individuals around the world have acquired stakes in the stock market, exposing them to much more volatility and risk than they had previously been accustomed to. In the United States, roughly half of all households own stock, either directly or indirectly through mutual funds and retirement plans. In the early 1980s the figure was less than 20 percent. Much of the increase came from the transition by corporate pension systems from defined-benefit to defined-contribution plans. In Britain, which has lagged behind the United States in the move toward defined-contribution retirement plans, over one-third of households now have interests in equities, a number that continues to grow.

But the really dramatic increases have come outside of the traditional Anglo-American markets. By January 2003 there were nearly 70 million individual stock investment accounts in China, although the number of active traders was probably only a fraction of that amount. Ten years earlier, virtually no Chinese citizens had individual brokerage accounts. According to the Frankfurt Share Institute, 19.3 percent of German households owned shares at the end of 2000, double the level of 1997; the boom in shareholding was first touched off by the giant privatization of Deutsche Telekom in 1996.[23] Between the late 1980s and late 1990s, privatizations in France increased the number of French shareholders from one million to seven million.[24] Throughout Europe, stock markets were dominated by state-owned firms that had been completely or partially privatized. According to the European Union, in 2001, 83 percent of the value of the French stock market represented firms that had formerly been owned by the government. The comparable figure for Spain was 54 percent and for Italy 41 percent.

In 2001 Sweden began channeling a portion of social security contributions into equity mutual funds. Other European nations have created tax-advantaged retirement vehicles similar to the 401 (k) plans in the United States. Intriguingly, an opinion survey in 2002 showed that over half of all the graduates of elite French universities were now interested in pursuing careers as entrepreneurs, up from only about one in ten a decade earlier.[25]

The newfound willingness of Europeans to embrace equities promised to revolutionize the way businesses financed themselves. The *New York Times* observed in 2001 that "after decades of paying little heed to entrepreneurs and new companies, European investors and financial institutions [have] embraced American style capitalism in the last three years as zealously as converts to a new religion." In the late 1990s the principal European stock exchanges began to create so-called New Markets similar to the Nasdaq market in the United States. The objective was to stem the flow of entrepreneurial talent to the United States by making it possible for small, start-up companies with good concepts to get equity funding. Many individuals who had never thought of buying stocks before rushed to participate in the New Markets.

In Germany, market-oriented television shows suddenly became popular, with statements by guests and hosts often moving stock prices. Several new business magazines, with names like *Bizz* and *Teleborse*, found profitable niches. Surprisingly, a few American start-up companies even sought to go public first in Germany rather than the United States, because German investors were willing to pay even higher prices than the sky-high valuations available on Nasdaq. At the German Neuer Markt's peak, an analyst for Commerzbank estimated that the average P/E ratio for stocks in the market's index was 50 percent higher than the average Nasdaq P/E.[26]

Even in Italy, with no history of widespread public participation in equity markets, the new exchanges and initial public stock offerings of speculative companies were met with enthusiasm. Entrepreneurs now had access to a source of funding entirely independent of the banks. In 1999 the founder of a new Italian telecom company marveled at how much things had changed. As a public offering of shares for his company, e.Biscom, was launched, he commented, "Four years ago it would have been impossible to take the company public in Italy. Even two years ago, we had very different plans."[27] E.Biscom's share offering, listed on Milan's Nuovo Mercato, was oversubscribed 26 to 1.

The booming new equity markets were supplanting the traditional universal banks as sources of financing for small and medium-sized firms. In fact, many European banks had already been forced by the changing market environment to withdraw from the paternalistic role they had formerly played in nurturing new businesses. Under pressure themselves from shareholders seeking improved returns, big commercial banks were beginning to see lending to smaller firms as only marginally profitable. International banking reforms encouraged banks to distinguish more rigorously among commercial loan risks; no longer could banks allocate the same amount of capital to back loans to more risky smaller firms that they did for loans to less risky, more established large companies. The more capital that had to be allocated to small-company loans, the less desirable that business became.

Many small-to-medium-sized European firms remain family-controlled, and are wary about going public to secure financing. They have been reluctant to issue financial data for competitive reasons, and often do not want to take on the troublesome chore of dealing with minority stockholders. But they may have no choice. Selling stock to the public, in the new equity markets, may be their only viable alternative.

Unfortunately, like the American Nasdaq, the New Markets in Europe crashed badly after peaking in 2000. Frankfurt's Neuer Markt, by far the largest of the new exchanges, fell a devastating 95 percent from its high. Rainer Reiss, the head of the Neuer Markt, admitted, "There have been lessons learned. This [experience] is an important part of developing a new equity culture."[28] To improve its image, the exchange tightened its rules. Top executives of listed companies were required to disclose their personal transactions in company stock. More rigorous reporting standards were established, and listed firms were required to use either international accounting standards or American-style generally accepted accounting principles.

These measures proved insufficient; the Deutsche Borse (Frankfurt Stock Exchange) announced that it would shut down the Neuer Markt in 2003 and reshuffle Neuer Markt stocks into different categories for trading on the Borse. One European stock analyst explained, "The Neuer Markt was tarred with too many high-profile failures. In the end, listing on the exchange was damaging for a company's reputation."[29]

How would the investing public, and potential corporate issuers, react to the rout? The founder of a high-tech company worried, "We didn't have a real risk culture here." Because of that, he said, "It will take much longer to build [the stock market] back up again."[30] An American investment banker in Frankfurt said, "The jury is still out. When Initial Public Offerings resume in the US, we will see whether issuers return to the Neuer Markt."[31] Another investment banker commented that Germany's standing as the technological hub of Europe would be seriously damaged without a functioning equity market for young firms. Noting the profound changes in the traditional universal banking system, he warned, "There is no way German banks will lend to small companies as they did in the past. This market has to recover."[32]

Whatever the fate of the Neuer Markt, the equity markets in Germany (and most European countries) are in important ways much stronger than they were only a few years ago. Standards of corporate government, and transparency, are vastly improved. (It is important to recall, for example, that as recently as 1994 insider trading by corporate executives was not considered to be a crime in Germany.) Noting the new environment, a partner in a German securities firm told the *Financial Times*, "There has been such considerable progress that it would be very difficult to identify any glaring shortcomings today."[33]

Reforms notwithstanding, the boom and bust of the European New Markets, closely paralleling the bursting of the so-called bubble in the American Nasdaq market, once again raises a question that had dogged organized capital markets since their inception: Were those markets inevitably subject to irrational speculative excesses that could profoundly damage national economies? The boom had actually been touched off in the mid-1990s; the first marker was the frenzied investor enthusiasm for the initial public stock offering (IPO) of Netscape in August 1995. Priced at $28 per share, the stock actually opened for trading at $71. The *New York Times* reported, "It was the best opening day for a stock in Wall Street history for an issue of its size." Many more offerings of small technology stocks followed, rocketing to stunning premiums over their original offering prices.

In some instances, the resulting valuations seemed ludicrous. Amazon.com, upon going public in 1997, quickly attained a market capitalization greatly exceeding that of established (and consistently profitable) booksellers like Barnes & Noble and Borders. Priceline.com, an unprofitable company that booked airline reservations on the Internet, was, on the day of its IPO, valued at more than American, Delta, and United Airlines combined. In perhaps the most outlandish example of all, the telecommunications equipment maker 3Com sold through an IPO 5 percent of the shares of Palm Computing that it owned. Based on the closing price of Palm on the first day of trading, all the shares of Palm were worth a total of $54.3 billion, while, perversely, 3Com, which still owned 95 percent of those shares, was trading at a price that made it worth only $28 billion.

It was (is) very difficult to defend these valuations, lending credence to the notion that the stock market (at least in its pricing of immature technology companies) was behaving irrationally. Such market action jibes neatly with behavioralist theory and Kindleberger's model of speculative bubbles. First, the economy is subject to an exogenous shock from a dynamic new development—in this case radical new technologies. Stocks in companies associated with the new technologies rise sharply, attracting attention from an expanding pool of investors, many of whom are relatively new to the game and hence inexperienced. Easy money (low interest rates) fuels the boom. A "feedback" effect develops as rising prices incite more investors to buy, in turn causing prices to rise even further. (George Soros calls this process "reflexivity," where the market, in effect, acts on itself.) Eventually, prices rise to exorbitant levels far above realistic valuations, until finally the supply of buyers is exhausted and the bubble bursts.

In 1999 Alan Greenspan advanced a "behavioralist" explanation for the ebullience of the technology stock market. At a Senate hearing he testified: "It is, for want of a better term, the 'lottery principle.' What lottery managers have known for centuries is that you could get someone to pay for a one-in-a-million shot more than the value of that chance. In other words, people pay more for a claim on a very big payoff, and that's where the profits from lotteries have always come from. So there is a lottery premium built into the prices of Internet stocks."[34]

The currently accepted interpretation of the Nasdaq "bubble" is that it was but another historical example of crowd psychology gone haywire, where investors, besotted with greed, temporarily abandoned all sanity. But closer examination reveals that, as in other so-called bubbles of the past, the truth is not quite so simple. Much like the "administered" Japanese boom of the late 1980s, where extensive corporate cross-holdings withheld most shares from the public market, the supply of small Nasdaq technology stocks available for trading was constricted, creating an artificial shortage. As in the case of the offering of Palm Computing stock discussed above, where only 5 percent of Palm shares were actually made available to the public, the typical IPO for new Internet companies involved only a fraction of the shares outstanding. For example, Amazon.com issued only 3 million shares (of 23 million total) to the public in its IPO, providing a thin float that was subject to erratic swings in demand, in effect creating an artificial shortage of stock. The same could be said for virtually every Internet IPO in the late 1990s.

The IPO prices for these shares were usually set deliberately low. According to University of Florida economist Jay Ritter, the average underpricing of IPOs (defined as the difference between the issue price and the closing price on the first day of trading) grew from 7 percent in the 1980s, to 15 percent from 1990 to 1998, to 65 percent in 1999–2000.[35] The founders and venture capitalists who had backed the firm were, in effect, selling part of their stock at a level well below what it could otherwise command, but for a good reason. A huge first-day jump in the price of a new issue as the stock rose to market-clearing levels provided invaluable publicity for small companies seeking to gain attention and market share. Company promoters still retained large holdings that they had not sold, and the value of those remaining shares was obviously greatly enhanced. In this way, many of the huge early moves of small Internet companies (which accounted for much of the so-called Nasdaq bubble) were artificial contrivances.

Another important source of hype for the Nasdaq "bubble" came from the Wall Street research community. Equity analysts for major investment banking firms had become increasingly conflicted, with their traditional role of providing investment advice to clients tainted by the need to generate lucrative stock underwriting business for their firms. By the mid-1990s most major Wall Street firms recognized that high-profile research analysts could be extremely valuable in winning underwriting business from the multitude of start-up technology firms seeking to issue new stock. This placed great pressure on analysts to churn out optimistic research reports on companies that had the potential to generate underwriting business; after all, what company seeking to issue stock would choose to do so through an investment bank that had published a negative outlook on the company's prospects? A strongly "bullish" research opinion, written by a well-known equity analyst, could help the company going public to sell more stock, at a higher price, than would otherwise be possible. It could also, obviously, position the investment bank employing the bullish analyst to receive the large underwriting fees that such a new stock offering would generate.

Gary Vineberg, a former top-rated equity analyst, described the process to the *New York Times*. "I've worked at several Wall Street firms," Vineberg said, ". . . and none actively encouraged their analysts to do objective, critical research and protect their non-investment banking clients' interests . . . The overriding concerns were with investment banking deals and marketing . . . Little else seemed to matter. The final product, overall, was highly marketed mediocrity."[36]

Another analyst pointed out how much the environment equity analysts worked in had changed, given the intense competition to win investment banking business. "In the 60's and 70's," he noted, "there was a process, and analysts could not put out wild, unsupported statements and price targets like those we saw taking place [in the 1990s] without being challenged." A telecommunications analyst concurred, saying, "When the bull market took off, because of a competition for banking dollars, you saw a real dilution of ethics. The pressure was—the valuations are up, keep them up."[37] As long as the boom lasted, the underwriting fees would continue to roll in.

Several studies of equity analysts' reports during the late 1990s found that "buy" recommendations outnumbered "sell" calls by lopsided margins; some analysts made no "self" recommendations at all. How much did this hype inflate the so-called Nasdaq bubble? Unfortunately, it is impossible to reach any sort of a definitive conclusion. But it would be very naïve to argue that the drumbeat of optimistic research reports, inspired at least in part by investment banking considerations, did not artificially pump up the enthusiasm for technology stocks.

Also accentuating the Nasdaq "bubble" was the fact that short-selling was often not feasible in many small technology stocks. A short-seller thinks that a given stock will decline, and acts on his conviction by borrowing shares and then selling them, with the intention of later buying the shares back at a lower price. But the small floats of the new technology stocks, and the fact that those shares were often held by retail investors who did not make their shares available for borrowing by short-sellers, meant that bearish investors who thought the stocks were overpriced could not act on their judgment, because they often could not borrow any shares to sell short. This created an imbalance of supply and demand; investors who were optimistic could freely buy the shares of small technology companies, but investors who were pessimistic often were prevented from selling those shares short.

Two scholars from New York University examined this problem in detail in a paper published by the National Bureau of Economic Research in December 2001. They concluded that the "bubble" in Internet stocks was due in part to the inability of bearish investors to sell shares short, and to the fact that most of the shares of the new technology companies were initially held off the market by company insiders and venture capitalists who had signed so-called lockup agreements that prevented them from selling for stipulated periods of time. Starting in late 1999, the researchers noted, growing numbers of these insiders became free to sell their shares. The effect was to increase the floating supply of shares, putting pressure on the stock prices. The increased supply also made more stock available for short-sellers to borrow. The artificial imbalance of supply and demand that had allowed the "bubble" to inflate disappeared, and the "bubble" collapsed under its own weight.[38]

A powerful example of how market imbalances can be created by restrictions on short-selling could be seen in Japan in early 2002. Government authorities claimed that heavy short-selling on the Tokyo Stock Exchange was "destabilizing" the market, at a time when the Japanese banking system and economy were in crisis. It was alleged that as much as 28 percent of all trading volume in early 2002 involved short sales. On February 26, without warning, restrictions on short sales were imposed, and brokerage firms were given only ten days to modify their computer systems to comply.[39]

The result was that many brokers stopped accepting orders to sell short, and market participants that already had established short positions were forced to reverse them by repurchasing the shares. An explosive rally followed, with Tokyo exchange prices jumping more than 25 percent in one month. Critics denounced the government's action as just another in a long series of attempts to manipulate stock prices higher, this time just before the end of the fiscal year on March 31, when banks would have to value their large stockholdings for accounting purposes. With the banking system in dire peril, higher stock prices could provide much-needed relief. Whatever the justification, it is clear that restraints on short-selling can decisively change the balance of supply and demand in equity markets, resulting (at least temporarily) in sharply higher stock prices.

In Chapter 12 it was shown that most of the "anomalies"—such as irrational speculative bubbles—that seem to contradict the efficient market theory and support "behavioralist" interpretations have been found by researchers in studies of small stocks. This is only logical, in that the market for small, immature companies is less likely to be efficient than the market for large, well-established firms. Even though many of the new technology companies at the turn of the twenty-first century had large market capitalizations, the actual supply of floating stock was usually very small. To the extent that an irrational speculative bubble did occur, it is not surprising that it would manifest itself in these "small" stocks. The broader stock market, as reflected by the major world market indexes, did not exhibit such pronounced "bubble" behavior.

The usefulness of behavioralist theory—and the related notion that even mature stock markets are susceptible to irrational speculative bubbles—is really quite doubtful. Ironically, one of the most telling judgments on this subject was rendered by a leading behavioralist, Santa Clara University professor Hersh Shefrin. In his book *Beyond Greed and Fear*, Shefrin offers advice directly to stock market participants. Recognizing that allegedly irrational behavior by investors is hard to predict and therefore difficult to exploit, and that many of the mispricings resulting from irrational behavior are relatively minor, he admits that investors "would be better off . . . acting as if markets are efficient."

Volatility is inevitable in modern stock markets where valuations are based on attempts to project corporate earnings and dividends far into the future. That volatility will obviously be even greater if the projections involve immature companies employing radical, fast-changing new technologies (such as the Internet). Relatively small changes in consensus investor opinion about future growth and interest rates can theoretically cause huge swings in stock prices, as in the 1987 crash. Whether defined as speculative bubbles or not, wide swings in stock prices are not likely to go away.

But beyond lending credence to behavioralist explanations for stock market movements, the apparent excess in the technology stock market concealed a profound change in the willingness of investors to take risks. Joseph Perella, the head of Morgan Stanley's investment banking division, observed, "There has been a fundamental shift in American capitalism. Previously, venture capitalism was a private game. Now, the public is willing to fund the growth of companies that are almost start-ups. Basically, the public is saying, 'I want to own every one of these companies. If I'm wrong on nineteen and the twentieth one is Yahoo!, it doesn't matter. I'll do OK.' "[40]

Greenspan made a similar observation about the technology stock boom. "There is at root here something far more fundamental—the stock market seeking out profitable ventures and directing capital to hopeful projects before the profits materialize. That's good for our system. And, in fact, with all of its hype and craziness, is something that, at the end of the day, probably is more plus than minus."[41]

In *Toward Rational Exuberance: The Evolution of the Modern Stock Market*, this author demonstrated how standards of valuation for American stocks evolved progressively over the twentieth century, from the more conservative to the more liberal. Beginning in the 1920s, investors started to look to future earnings growth rather than simply current dividends as the source of value in equity investments. By the late 1950s, when dividend rates fell permanently below interest rates in the United States and Britain, dynamic valuation methodologies based on earnings growth had triumphed over static approaches relying solely on current dividends.

As the century progressed, investors became more and more willing to take on the risks, and stock prices rose accordingly. An increasingly stable economy with vastly improved regulation and transparency seemed to make the stock market safer. The Federal Reserve Board demonstrated, by its actions after the 1987 crash and the 1998 emerging market crisis, that it would take all necessary steps to prevent a meltdown of the American (and by implication, the global) stock market. And finally, the fact that so much of the money now invested in equities was retirement money meant that the time horizon of investors had lengthened, making them more willing to ride out short-term volatility in the expectation of eventual long-term gains. In effect, the risk tolerance of investors increased, meaning that the *risk premium* (the extra return stocks must generate, compared to bonds, to compensate investors for the greater risk of equity investing) declined.

A lower risk premium results in higher stock prices, as investors are willing to pay more for a given stream of future earnings and/or dividends. An example of how powerful this effect can be is demonstrated by the risk-premium analysis presented by the authors Kevin Hassett and James Glassman in their book *Dow 36,000*. It was generally estimated that the risk premium of the American stock market at its peak in 2000 was roughly 3 percent (meaning that equity investors expect future returns from stocks to exceed bond returns by 3 percent annually in order to compensate them for the extra risk inherent in stocks). This was down from 6–7 percent at the beginning of the twentieth century. If the risk premium were to fall further—say from 3 percent to zero—Hassett and Glassman estimated that the Dow Jones Industrial Average would rise to 36,000.

The willingness of investors to effectively become venture capitalists, providing financing for speculative start-up technology companies, can best be seen as another step in the progression toward greater risk tolerance (and higher valuations) that has occurred over the past century. This has profound implications for all modern economies. In a little-noticed 1984 book entitled *The Share Economy*, the economist Martin Weitzman described how the economy could be transformed if employees were paid part of their compensation in stock (or options on stock) rather than in cash wages. The interests of the firm and its workers would be harmonized, providing a powerful incentive for both management and employees to work together to achieve common purposes. And in a macroeconomic sense, the dislocations (unemployment) of recessions would be minimized, since if employee compensation fluctuated with the fortunes of the firm, the pressure to lay off workers in a downturn would be much less severe.

Weitzman's theory seems to have been validated by the performance of the new companies created during the late-1990s boom. Even when the stock market dropped sharply after 1999 and the economy fell into a mild recession, employment in the largest one hundred American boom-era companies actually rose more than 25 percent. By mid-2002 only eight of these firms had failed, and the combined sales of the remainder had increased by nearly $60 billion over the preceding three years.[42]

While the process of reevaluating equity market risk first started in the United States, most stock markets in developed countries, despite a very difficult environment, seem to have caught up with American price levels. *Barron's* took note of this in 2001 in an article entitled "No Bargain Bazaar." The article presented calculations showing that the French and German stock markets had attained P/E levels roughly equaling those of the United States. Overall, the global P/E ratio of 22 to 1 was very close to the American market P/E of 23 to 1 (as measured by the Standard & Poor's 500).

Would the worldwide bear market that followed the turn of the twenty-first century reverse this trend by causing investors to withdraw from the stock market? (The FTSE World Index declined 43 percent from the peak in early 2000 through the end of 2002.) The early evidence indicates a slackening of interest in some countries, but nothing like a wholesale rejection of the new equity culture. For example, the percentage of the German population that owned stock, either directly or indirectly, which had doubled from 9.1 percent in 1997 to 19.3 percent in 2000, slipped back slightly to 17.9 percent in 2002. The Chinese market decline that began in 2001 cooled investor interest in stocks, but precise figures are impossible to obtain. In the United States the number of households with a stake in the stock market actually rose from 49.2 million in 1999 to 52.7 million in 2002, despite the market decline.[43] Only in Japan, ravaged by a decade-long bear market, did large numbers of investors seem to be abandoning the market. (In 2002 a public opinion poll showed that 83 percent of Japanese had "no interest" in investing in stocks.)

Valuations in emerging markets, of course, still lag behind those of developed countries. This is to be expected, as risks in those markets are significantly greater. Lack of transparency, weak legal systems, endemic corruption, and a lack of respect for the rights of minority investors remain serious concerns. In actuality, the performance of emerging markets since the boom year 1993 has been quite poor. According to Ibbotson Associates, emerging equity markets, in aggregate, posted losses in five of the succeeding eight years.[44]

Significantly, foreign equity investors have not been deterred by these lackluster results. The acceptance of the new culture of equities is evident in IMF data released in 2001, which showed that capital inflows to emerging economies was overwhelmingly dominated by equity investment. In 2000, $150.5 billion of the $154.1 billion total private capital inflow into developing countries consisted of equity investment.[45] The turnaround that has occurred since the early 1980s, when debt, not equity, predominated, is remarkable.

It is clear that the equity culture is here to stay. Despite sharp drops in virtually all market indexes, the globalization of this equity culture is continuing. On the same day that the Deutsche Borse announced that it would close down its Neuer Markt, the European Union revealed plans to sweep aside member-state regulations and create an open market for stocks (and other securities). Investors would be able to trade shares freely across national borders with few restrictions. In an example given by the *Financial Times*, the new "EU-wide financial market" will allow "Greek investors [to] buy Finnish shares from several marketplaces at a minimal cost."[46]

It is also clear, however, that the immense size of the modern global stock market, with its vast number of participants, creates new dangers. The market itself can substantially influence the economy rather than simply acting as an indicator of economic trends. When stocks rise, tens of millions of shareholders feel "richer" and are inclined to spend more money, increasing the demand for goods and services and potentially creating inflation. Conversely, falling equity prices can cause shareholder-consumers to cut back spending, reducing demand and potentially throwing an economy into recession. (This is the wealth effect.) Government officials (like Alan Greenspan) are forced to take stock market movements into account when formulating economic policy.

As more companies become dependent on equity (rather than bank) financing, they also become subject to the vicissitudes of the stock markets. Even without the existence of large speculative "bubbles" or catastrophic panics, the ease with which stock can be sold to large numbers of public investors will vary dramatically over time, and the process will almost certainly be much more complicated than raising money through traditional banking relationships. In "boom" times marginal companies may find it easy to secure financing, while during "busts" even good companies may be shut out of the market, leading to a substantial misallocation of resources.

As Japanese and European critics of Anglo-American stock market capitalism have been wont to point out, excessive concentration on current stock values can distort long-term decision making, because companies are pressured to produce short-term profit gains at all costs. The *Financial Times* cited the example of the British retailer Marks & Spencer, which tried to achieve the rapid profit growth necessary to satisfy stock market investors. According to the *FT*, Marks & Spencer, which had an impeccable reputation built up over many years, "squeezed suppliers, gave less value for the money, and spent less on stores."[47] In 1998 it achieved the highest profit margin on sales in its history. Unfortunately, it had so compromised its position that sales (and profits) subsequently plummeted.

Corporations routinely "managed" earnings to meet stock market expectations, shifting revenues and expenses across accounts or between accounting periods, striving to present an attractive picture to analysts and investors. Many companies went on acquisition binges, motivated by accounting rules that assigned relatively little value to assets acquired through corporate takeovers, enabling the acquiring company to inflate future profits by releasing hidden value from the acquired entities. Corporate share repurchases became commonplace in the 1980s and 1990s, in large part because they instantly increased earnings per share by reducing the number of shares outstanding. But none of these devices really improved economic performance.

As stock market capitalism became preeminent, executive compensation systems designed to align management and shareholder interests proliferated. By 1996 more than half the compensation received by chief executives of Standard & Poor's 500 companies was tied to the stock market, usually through stock options that provided strong incentives to push share prices higher.[48] Critics argued that option awards often distorted incentives, encouraging management to hype the short-term stock price recklessly at the expense of other considerations.

One investment manager in Dallas derisively labeled the prevalent "pay-for-performance" compensation systems as "pay-for-pretense," declaring that the "unbridled greed" of many corporate executives was "poisoning the system that has been the source of our national wealth." He went on to allege, "The impending takeover of corporate America by self-serving elitist managers may prove to be far more damaging to capitalism than anything that Karl Marx may have conceived."[49] This critique echoed Adam Smith, who had warned more than two centuries earlier of the dangers of separating the management of corporations from ownership.

A very different view of high executive compensation—and one that seems to support the "stakeholder" concept of corporate management—is offered by John Plender in *Going Off the Rails*, published early in 2003. Plender believes that most of the value added in new technology companies comes from human, not shareholder, capital. Hence it is only fair that these highly skilled employees receive high compensation. For example, Plender notes that the value of stock options granted to Microsoft employees in 2000, if fully accounted for, would have absorbed 77 percent of the firm's pretax profit; the figure for the entire information technology industry would have been 73 percent. While many critics condemn these seemingly bloated numbers, Plender argues that the high compensation levels accurately reflect the contributions of these people. Human capital, at least in technology companies, is more important than shareholder capital, and thus deserves to earn a greater return.

Most critics of the Anglo-American model have not embraced this argument, instead focusing on recent high-profile examples of malfeasance by American managers. Gerhard Cromme, chairman of the ThyssenKrupp engineering group and head of Germany's corporate governance commission, said, "We [in Germany] must no longer feel inferior towards the practices in the U.S. What has happened in the U.S. has exposed serious weak points of deep concern to us all."[50] A French investment banker noted, "Small savers were encouraged to abandon fixed-income investment and take the plunge into equities during the stock market boom of the 1990's." But those investors had been "badly shaken" by revelations of corporate mismanagement and fraud, as well as sharp declines in stock prices. As a result, the banker admitted, many of the new investors were "clearly reluctant to return to the equity market."[51]

Advocates of Anglo-American stock market capitalism argue that the market itself will eliminate abusive behavior on the part of corporate managements. They point to the fact that stock prices of companies engaged in questionable accounting practices have plummeted, often costing misbehaving executives both their money and their jobs. Other observers attribute the rash of corporate scandals to the unique circumstances of the late-1990s boom itself. Alan Greenspan seemed to subscribe to this view when he testified before the Senate Banking Committee in July 2002. A "once in a generation speculative boom," Greenspan opined, had created "outsized opportunities for avarice." The bear market that followed was not nearly as forgiving.

Revelations of abuses have often followed boom periods in the stock market; unsavory practices that can be hidden when stock prices are rising often cannot be concealed when a market "bust" occurs. But this pattern of cyclical scandals does not diminish the fundamental changes that the new equity culture has wrought. Within the last decade alone, tens of millions of people worldwide have acquired interests in stocks. In the United States and Britain, it is taken for granted that retirement incomes will be greatly affected by stock market performance. With the introduction of tax-deferred retirement savings accounts in European countries such as Germany, millions of Europeans will soon also have significant stakes in the equity markets. China and other Asian countries are actively encouraging their populations to invest in stocks. For many tens of millions of people, the stock market has become, in less than a single generation, a very important factor in their economic well-being.

Around the world, nations are being forced to modify their policies and to restructure their economies to accommodate the equity culture. Traditional practices inimical to stock market capitalism, ranging from lifetime employment in Japan to crony capitalism in Indonesia to management by consensus in Germany, will continue to come under pressure. Leaders such as Mahathir of Malaysia and Jospin of France may struggle to modify or contain the process, but they cannot reverse it. Their economies, and the entire world, will be fundamentally transformed in the years ahead.

Notes

INTRODUCTION

1. *Wall Street Journal*, May 8, 2000.

1: A FINANCIAL REVOLUTION

1. Arthur E. Monroe, ed., *Early Economic Thought: Selections from Economic Literature Prior to Adam Smith* (London: Cambridge University Press, 1934), p. 15.
2. John Chancellor, *Devil Take the Hindmost* (New York: Penguin, 2000), p. 6.
3. *Cunningham's Essays on Western Civilization* (New York, 1913), p. 164.
4. Tenney Frank, *Economic History of Rome* (London, 1927), p. 282.
5. Chancellor, *Devil Take the Hindmost*, p. 7.
6. Fernand Braudel, *The Wheels of Commerce*, trans. Sian Reynolds (New York: Harper & Row, 1982), p. 101.
7. Richard Ehrenberg, *Capital and Finance in the Age of the Renaissance: A Study of the Fuggers and their Connections*, trans. H. M. Lucas (New York: A. M. Kelley, 1963), p. 309.
8. Earl Hamilton, *American Treasure and the Price Revolution in Spain, 1501–1650* (Cambridge, Mass.: Harvard University Press, 1934).
9. Larry Neal, *The Rise of Financial Capitalism: International Financial Markets in the Age of Reason* (New York: Cambridge University Press, 1990), p. 3.
10. Chancellor, *Devil Take the Hindmost*, p. 9.
11. Braudel, *Wheels of Commerce*, p. 97.
12. Timur Kuran, "The Islamic Commercial Crisis: Institutional Roots of the Delay in the Middle East's Economic Modernization" (unpublished paper, University of Southern California), quoted in *New York Times*, November 8, 2001.

13. Neal, *Rise of Financial Capitalism*, p. 87.
14. Braudel, *Wheels of Commerce*, p. 100.
15. Neal, *Rise of Financial Capitalism*, p. 45.
16. David Ormrod, *The Dutch in London* (London: HMSO, 1973), p. 17.
17. S. R. Cope, "The Stock Exchange Revisited: A New Look at the Market in Securities in London in the 18th Century," *Economica* 45 (February 1978): 5.
18. P.G.M. Dickson, *The Financial Revolution in England: A Study in the Development of Public Credit, 1688–1756* (London: Macmillan, 1967), p. 487.
19. Chancellor, *Devil Take the Hindmost*, p. 51.
20. Ibid., p. 52.
21. Ibid., p. 53.
22. Dickson, *Financial Revolution in England*, p. 494.

2: BUBBLES

1. Adam Anderson, *An Historical and Chronological Deduction of the Origin of Commerce, From the Earliest Accounts* (London: A. Millar, 1764), Vol. 3, pp. 91–92.
2. John Carswell, *The South Sea Bubble* (Dover, N.H.: Sutton, 1993), p. 66.
3. Janet Gleeson, *Millionaire* (New York: Simon & Schuster, 2001), p. 142.
4. Ibid., p. 143.
5. Ibid., pp. 144, 146.
6. Ibid., p. 147.
7. Ibid., p. 148.
8. Carswell, *South Sea Bubble*, p. 98.
9. Gleeson, *Millionaire*, p. 161.
10. Ibid., p. 163.
11. Carswell, *South Sea Bubble*, p. 46.
12. Ibid., p. 35.
13. Gleeson, *Millionaire*, p. 188.
14. Ibid., p. 189.
15. Ibid., p. 109.
16. Carswell, *South Sea Bubble*, p. 159.
17. Chancellor, *Devil Take the Hindmost*, p. 71.
18. Dickson, *Financial Revolution in England*, p. 95.
19. Ibid., pp. 457–67.
20. Neal, *Rise of Financial Capitalism*, p. 92.
21. Gleeson, *Millionaire*, p. 208.
22. Carswell, *South Sea Bubble*, p. 148.
23. Gleeson, *Millionaire*, p. 226.
24. Carswell, *South Sea Bubble*, p. 159.
25. Dickson, *Financial Revolution in England*; and Peter M. Garber, *Famous First Bubbles* (Cambridge, Mass.: MIT Press, 2001).

26. Carswell, *South Sea Bubble*, p. 232.

27. Thomas Mortimer, *Every Man His Own Broker: Or a Guide to Exchange Alley*, 3d ed. (London, 1761), pp. 47–49.

28. Dickson, *Financial Revolution in England*, pp. 312, 321.

29. Charles P. Kindleberger, *A Financial History of Western Europe* (London: Allen & Unwin, 1984), p. 98.

3: THE NEW WORLD

1. David Kynaston, *City of London* (London: Chatto & Windus, 1994), Vol. 1, p. 91.

2. Ibid., p. 41.

3. Dickson, *Financial Revolution in England*, p. 520.

4. Frank Griffith Dawson, *The First Latin American Debt Crisis: The City of London and the 1822–25 Loan Bubble* (New Haven: Yale University Press, 1990), p. 41.

5. Ibid.

6. Ibid., p. 61.

7. John Francis, *The History of the Bank of England, Its Times and Traditions* (London: Willoughby, 1948), p. 27.

8. Dawson, *First Latin American Debt Crisis*, p. 89.

9. Ibid., p. 67.

10. E. Victor Morgan and W. A. Thomas, *The Stock Exchange—Its History and Functions* (London: Elek Books, 1962), p. 126.

11. Dawson, *First Latin American Debt Crisis*, p. 106.

12. *The Times* (of London), January 24, 1825.

13. Dawson, *First Latin American Debt Crisis*, p. 98.

14. Jane Ridley, *The Young Disraeli* (London: Sinclair-Stevenson, 1995), p. 31.

15. Ibid., p. 33.

16. Ibid., p. 34.

17. Dawson, *First Latin American Debt Crisis*, p. 107.

18. Ibid., p. 214.

19. Ibid., p. 121.

20. Ibid., p. 140.

21. *The Times* (of London), September 26, 1826.

22. Dawson, *First Latin American Debt Crisis*, p. 140.

23. Ibid.

24. Ibid., p. 141.

25. Charles Freedman, *Joint Stock Enterprise in France, 1807–1867* (Chapel Hill: University of North Carolina Press, 1979), p. 6.

26. Charles K. Hobson, *The Export of Capital* (New York: Garland, 1983), pp. 110–11.

27. Dawson, *First Latin American Debt Crisis*, p. 210.

4: THE RAILROADS AND THE MIDDLE CLASS

1. Leland Hamilton Jenks, *The Migration of British Capital to 1875* (New York: Knopf, 1927), p. 132.
2. Chancellor, *Devil Take the Hindmost*, p. 128.
3. Ibid., p. 138.
4. Jenks, *Migration of British Capital*, p. 146.
5. Kindleberger, *Financial History of Western Europe*, p. 210.
6. Ibid., p. 212.
7. A. Gerschenkron, "The Modernization of Entrepreneurship," in *Continuity in History and Other Essays* (Cambridge, Mass.: Harvard University Press, 1968), p. 137.
8. James C. Baker, *The German Stock Market, Its Operations, Problems and Prospects* (New York: Praeger, 1970), p. 5.
9. Ibid., p. 6.
10. Freedman, *Joint Stock Enterprise in France*, p. 18.
11. Ibid., p. 22.
12. Ibid., p. 24.
13. Ibid., p. 109.
14. D. Morier Evans, *Commercial Crisis, 1847–48* (London: Letts, Son & Steer, 1848), p. 73.
15. Chancellor, *Devil Take the Hindmost*, p. 143.
16. Jenks, *Migration of British Capital*, p. 155.
17. Brian Bailey, *George Hudson: The Rise and Fall of the Railway King* (Stroud, U.K.: Alan Sutton, 1995), p. 88.
18. Chancellor, *Devil Take the Hindmost*, p. 146.
19. Ibid., p. 149.
20. Ibid., p. 120.
21. Ibid., p. 144.
22. Jenks, *Migration of British Capital*, p. 28.
23. Ibid., pp. 246–48.
24. Kynaston, *City of London*, Vol. 1, p. 242.
25. Ibid., p. 260.
26. *Economist*, September 22, 1866.
27. Kynaston, *City of London*, Vol. 1, p. 242.
28. *The Times* (of London), November 13, 1868.
29. *New York Times*, November 19, 1868.
30. *New York Herald*, April 12, 1870.
31. George Crouch, *Erie under Gould and Fisk* (New York, 1870), p. 43.
32. Maury Klein, *The Life and Legend of Jay Gould* (Baltimore: Johns Hopkins University Press, 1986), p. 117.
33. *New York Herald*, March 1, 1872.

34. Ibid., March 17, 1872.
35. John Steele Gordon, *The Scarlet Woman of Wall Street: Jay Gould, Jim Fisk, Cornelius Vanderbilt and the Birth of Wall Street* (New York: Weidenfeld and Nicholson, 1988), p. 358.

5: A GLOBAL STOCK MARKET

1. Salomon F. Van Oss, *Stock Exchange Values: A Decade of Finance, 1885–1895* (London: E. Wilson, 1895), p. lix.
2. London *Daily News*, October 27, 1886.
3. Sidney Pollard, *European Economic Integration: 1815–1970* (London: Thames and Hudson, 1974), p. 71.
4. Philip Ziegler, *The Sixth Great Power: A History of One of the Greatest of All Banking Families, the House of Barings, 1762–1929* (New York: Knopf, 1988), p. 216.
5. Kynaston, *City of London*, Vol. 2, pp. 344, 424.
6. Ziegler, *Sixth Great Power*, p. 239.
7. Kynaston, *City of London*, Vol. 2, p. 426.
8. Ibid., p. 247.
9. Ibid., p. 252.
10. Ibid., p. 343.
11. J. Kocha, "The Rise of Modern Industrial Enterprise in Germany," in A. D. Chandler, Jr., and D. Daems, eds., *Managerial Hierarchies* (Cambridge, Mass.: Harvard University Press, 1980), p. 90.
12. D. Lavington, *The English Capital Market* (London: Methuen, 1921), p. 210.
13. Thomas F. M. Adams, *A Financial History of Modern Japan* (Tokyo: Research, 1964), p. 2.
14. Albert J. Alletzhauser, *The House of Nomura* (London: Bloomsbury, 1990), p. 47.
15. Ibid., p. 48.
16. Ibid., p. 53.
17. Peter Bernstein, *Capital Ideas* (New York: Free Press, 1992), p. 19.
18. Ibid., p. 19.
19. Ibid., p. 22.
20. Ibid., p. 18.
21. Ibid., p. 20.
22. Strouse, Jean, *Morgan: American Financier* (New York: Random House: 1999), p. 659.
23. Robert Sobel, *Panic on Wall Street: A History of America's Financial Disasters.* (New York: Macmillan, 1968), p. 34.
24. Ranald C. Michie, *The London Stock Exchange: A History* (Oxford, U.K.: Oxford University Press, 1999), p. 4.

25. Youssef Cassis, *City Bankers, 1890–1914*, trans. Margaret Rocques (Cambridge, U.K.: Cambridge University Press, 1994), pp. 68, 72.

26. Michie, *London Stock Exchange*, p. 71.

6: A NEW ERA

1. Hartley Withers, *The War and Lombard Street* (London: Smith, Elder, 1915), p. 1.

2. Kynaston, *City of London*, Vol. 3, p. 5.

3. Ibid., p. 28.

4. Ibid.

5. Ibid., p. 29.

6. Ibid., p. 31.

7. Barret P. Whale, *Joint Stock Banking in Germany; A Study of the German Credit Banks Before and After the War* (London: Macmillan, 1930), p. 198.

8. Michie, *London Stock Exchange*, p. 176.

9. Ibid.

10. Gardiner C. Means, *Quarterly Journal of Economics*, August 1930.

11. Ibid.

12. Baker, *German Stock Market*, p. 10.

13. Michie, *London Stock Exchange*, p. 182.

14. Richard Schabacker, *Stock Market Theory and Practice* (New York: Forbes, 1930), p. 407.

15. Kenneth S. Van Strum, *Investing in Purchasing Power* (New York: Barron's, 1925), p. vii.

16. John Brooks, *Once in Golconda: A True Drama of Wall Street* (New York: Harper & Row, 1969), p. 81.

17. Charles R. Morris, *Money, Greed and Risk: Why Financial Crises and Crashes Happen* (New York: Times Business, 1999), p. 71.

18. *New York Times*, September 21, 1929.

19. Ibid., June 12, 1965.

20. Harold Bierman, Jr., *The Causes of the 1929 Stock Market Crash: A Speculative Orgy or a New Era?* (Westport, Conn.: Greenwood Press, 1998), p. 21.

21. Ibid., p. 25.

22. Marshall E. Blume, Jeremy J. Siegel, and Dan Rottenberg, *Revolution on Wall Street: The Rise and Decline of the New York Stock Exchange* (New York: Norton, 1993), p. 95.

23. Robert Sobel, *The Last Bull Market: Wall Street in the 1960's* (New York: Norton, 1980), p. 130.

24. Paul Sarnoff, *Jesse Livermore: Speculator/King* (Palisades Park, N.J.: Investor's Press, 1967), p. 7.

25. Bierman, *Causes of the 1929 Stock Market Crash*, p. 30.

26. Robert Sobel, *The Great Bull Market: Wall Street in the 1920's* (New York: Norton, 1968), p. 113.

7: CRASH

1. John Kenneth Galbraith, *The Great Crash* (Boston: Houghton Mifflin, 1998), p. 98.
2. Ibid., p. 105.
3. Frederick Lewis Allen, *Only Yesterday* (New York: Harper Bros., 1931), p. 330.
4. Galbraith, *The Great Crash*, p. 107.
5. *Saturday Evening Post*, December 28, 1929.
6. James Grant, *Bernard M. Baruch: The Adventures of a Wall Street Legend* (New York: Wiley, 1997), p. 240.
7. Michie, *London Stock Exchange*, p. 263.
8. Alymer Vallance, *The Centre of the World* (London: Hodder & Stoughton, 1935), p. 234.
9. Robert Sobel, *The Big Board: A History of the New York Stock Market* (New York: Free Press, 1965), p. 284.
10. Harold James, *The End of Globalism: Lessons from the Great Depression* (Cambridge, Mass.: Harvard University Press, 2001), p. 6.
11. Karl Marx (ed. Friedrich Engels), *Capital: A Critical Analysis of Capitalist Production*. Vol. 3, pp. 668–69. Trans. Samuel Moore and Edward Aveling (New York: Appleton, 1889).
12. James, *End of Globalism*, p. 22.
13. Robert Shaplen, *Kreuger: Genius and Swindler* (New York: Knopf, 1959), p. vi.
14. Lionel Robbins, *The Great Depression* (London: Macmillan, 1934), p. 63.
15. Sobel, *Panic on Wall Street*, p. 384.
16. Sarnoff, *Jesse Livermore*, p. 89.
17. Sobel, *Great Bull Market*, p. 57.
18. Galbraith, *The Great Crash*, p. 10.
19. Brooks, *Once in Golconda*, p. 82.
20. Bierman, *Causes of the 1929 Stock Market Crash*.
21. David Felix, *Keynes: A Critical Life* (Westport, Conn.: Greenwood Press, 1999), p. 522.
22. Ibid., p. 523.
23. Michie, *London Stock Exchange*, p. 254.
24. Arthur Schlesinger, Jr., *The Coming of the New Deal* (New York: Macmillan, 1959), p. 468.
25. Sobel, *The Big Board*, p. 293.
26. Ibid., p. 294.
27. Ibid., p. 298.

28. Willard Atkins, George Edwards, and Harold Moulton, *The Regulation of Securities Markets* (Washington, D.C., 1946), pp. 70–71.
29. Michie, *London Stock Exchange*, p. 264.
30. Roger Lowenstein, *Buffet: The Making of an American Capitalist* (New York: Random House, 1995), p. 37.
31. James, *End of Globalization*, p. 193.
32. Robert Sobel, *N.Y.S.E.: A History of the New York Stock Exchange, 1935–1975* (New York: Weybright & Talley, 1975), p. 127.

8: BRETTON WOODS

1. Felix, *Keynes: A Critical Life*, p. 274.
2. Robert Skidelsky, *Keynes* (Oxford, U.K.: Oxford University Press, 1996), p. 102.
3. Ibid., p. 33.
4. Moggridge, Donald E. *Maynard Keynes: An Economist's Biography* (London: Routledge, 1992), p. 673.
5. Ragnar Nurkse, *International Currency Experience* (Geneva: League of Nations, 1944).
6. John Littlewood, *The Stock Market: Fifty Years of Capitalism at Work* (London: Financial Times/Pitman, 1998), p. 17.
7. Michie, *London Stock Exchange*, p. 330.
8. Littlewood, *The Stock Market*, p. 30.
9. Ibid., p. 84.
10. Ibid., p. 10.
11. Sobel, *Last Bull Market*, p. 30.
12. Sobel, *N.Y.S.E.*, p. 171.
13. Alletzhauser, *House of Nomura*, p. 114.
14. Milton Friedman, *Essays in Political Economics* (Chicago: University of Chicago Press, 1953), p. 52.
15. Bernstein, *Capital Ideas*, p. 44.
16. Ibid., p. 47.
17. Ibid., p. 50.
18. Moggridge, *Maynard Keynes*, p. 585.
19. Littlewood, *The Stock Market*, p. 86.
20. Ibid., p. 102.
21. *Institutional Investor*, April 1967.
22. Maurice Obstfeld, *Covered Interest Rate Differentials* (Washington, D.C.: National Bureau of Economic Research, 1993).
23. Richard Marston, "Interest Differentials under Bretton Woods and the Post-Bretton Woods Float: The Effects of Capital Controls and Exchange Risk," in *A Retrospective on the Bretton Woods System*, Michael Bordo and Barry Eichengreen, eds. (Chicago: University of Chicago Press, 1993), pp. 515–46.
24. *Wall Street Journal*, May 28, 1975.

9: CHAOS

1. *Financial Times*, August 28, 2001.
2. Bernstein, *Capital Ideas*, p. 127.
3. Blume, Siegel, and Rottenberg, *Revolution on Wall Street*, p. 89.
4. Bernstein, *Capital Ideas*, p. 78.
5. Ibid., p. 77.
6. *Institutional Investor*, October 1970.
7. Eugene Fama and William G. Schwert, "Asset Returns and Inflation," *Journal of Financial Economics* 5, no. 2 (1977).
8. Alletzhauser, *House of Nomura*, p. 144.
9. Ibid., p. 223.
10. Ibid., p. 154.
11. Ibid.
12. Ibid., p. 156.
13. Ibid., p. 160.
14. Ibid., p. 161.
15. Robert Zielinski and Nigel Holloway, *Unequal Equities: Power and Risk in Japan's Stock Market* (Tokyo: Kadansha International, 1991), p. 161.
16. Jeremy Edwards and Klaus Fischer, *Banks, Finance and Investment in Germany* (Cambridge, U.K.: Cambridge University Press, 1994), p. 231.
17. Gabriel Hawawini and Pierre A. Michel, *European Equity Markets: Risk, Return and Efficiency* (New York: Garland, 1984), p. 89.
18. G. Hallett, "West Germany," in *Government and Economies in the Post-War World*, A. Graham and A. Seldon, eds. (London: Routledge, 1990), p. 83.

10: RETURN OF THE BULL

1. Fama and Schwert, "Asset Returns and Inflation."
2. *Barron's*, May 10, 1980.
3. *Institutional Investor*, June 1980.
4. Ibid., June 1980.
5. Ibid., January 1979.
6. Blume, Siegel, and Rottenberg, *Revolution on Wall Street*, p. 92.
7. Sanjoy Basu, "The Investment Performance of Common Stocks in Relation to Their Price/Earnings Ratios," *Journal of Finance* 32, no. 3 (1977).
8. Robert Shiller, "Do Stock Prices Move Too Much to Be Justified by Subsequent Changes in Dividends?" *American Economic Review*, June 1981.
9. Jonathan Isaacs, *Japanese Equities Markets* (London: Euromoney Books, 1990), p. 187.
10. Christopher Wood, *The Bubble Economy: Japan's Extraordinary Speculative Boom of the '80's and the Dramatic Bust of the '90's* (New York: Atlantic Monthly Press, 1992), p. 1.

11. Zielinski and Holloway, *Unequal Equities*, p. 51.

12. Ibid., p. 43.

13. Ibid., p. 127.

14. Ibid., p. 161.

15. Ibid., p. 65.

16. Ibid., p. 52.

17. Ibid., p. 63.

18. Morris, *Money, Greed and Risk*, p. 112.

19. *Business Week*, November 11, 1985.

20. Zielinski and Holloway, *Unequal Equities*, p. 58.

21. Ibid., p. 6.

22. Isaacs, *Japanese Equities Markets*, p. 43.

23. *The New Tide of the Japanese Securities Markets: Tracing the Events of the Past Ten Years and Looking to the Future* (Tokyo: Nikko Research Center, 1988), p. 196.

24. Wood, *Bubble Economy*, pp. 23–24.

11: VOLATILITY

1. *Wall Street Journal*, October 20, 1987.

2. Ibid., November 20, 1987.

3. Robert Kamphius, Jr., Roger C. Kormendi, and J. W. Henry Watson, *Black Monday and the Future of Financial Markets* (Chicago: Dow Jones–Irwin, 1989), p. 40.

4. Ibid.

5. *Wall Street Journal*, November 20, 1987.

6. Kamphius, Kormendi, and Watson, *Black Monday*, p. 57.

7. *Wall Street Journal*, October 22, 1987.

8. Ibid.

9. Kamphius, Kormendi, and Watson, *Black Monday and the Future of Financial Markets*, p. 72.

10. *Wall Street Journal*, October 23, 1987.

11. Ibid.

12. Ibid.

13. Fischer Black, "Noise," *Journal of Finance* 41 (1986).

14. Hersh Shefrim, *Beyond Greed and Fear* (Boston: Harvard Business School Press, 2000), chs. 2, 8, and 9.

15. Werner De Bondt and Richard Thaler, "Does the Stock Market Overreact?" *Journal of Finance* 40 (1985).

16. Victor Bernard and Jacob Thomas, "Earnings Surprises and the Stock Market," *Journal of Accounting Research* 27 (1989).

17. Lawrence Summers, "Does the Stock Market Rationally Reflect Fundamental Values?" *Journal of Finance* 41 (1986).

18. Eugene Fama and Kenneth French, "The Cross-Section of Expected Stock Market Returns," *Journal of Finance* 47 (1992).
19. Eugene Fama, "Attack of the Anomalies," *Journal of Financial Economics* 49, no. 3 (1998).
20. *Wall Street Journal*, January 7, 1988.

12: EMERGING MARKETS

1. Antoine W. van Agtmael, *Emerging Securities Markets* (London: Euromoney Publications, January 1984).
2. Keith K. H. Park and Antoine W. van Agtmael, *The World's Emerging Stock Markets* (Chicago: Irwin Professional Publishing, 1993), p. x.
3. Ibid., p. 48.
4. Ibid., p. 80.
5. "The Visible Hand," *Economist*, June 1, 1991.
6. Steven R. Champion, *The Great Taiwan Bubble* (Berkeley: Pacific View Press, 1998), p. 6.
7. Ibid., p. 10.
8. *China Post*, February 2, 1990.
9. Champion, *The Great Taiwan Bubble*, p. 77.
10. Ibid., p. 23.
11. Ibid., p. 86.
12. Ibid., p. 26.
13. *China Post*, March 10, 1990.
14. Ibid., July 17, 1990.
15. Champion, *The Great Taiwan Bubble*, p. 60.
16. Ibid., p. 64.
17. Morris, *Money, Greed and Risk*, p. 214.
18. Ibid., p. 211.
19. *Wall Street Journal*, September 18, 2001.
20. Ibid.
21. Leonard Gough, *Asia Meltdown: The End of a Miracle?* (Oxford, U.K.: Capstone, 1998), p. 39.
22. Ibid., p. 123.
23. *Asian Wall Street Journal*, April 6, 1998.
24. *New York Times*, January 9, 2002.
25. *Wall Street Journal*, September 18, 2001.

13: CONTAGION

1. *Wall Street Journal*, September 1, 1998.
2. Ibid., September 22, 1998.
3. Ibid.

4. Ibid.

5. Ibid., September 1, 1998.

6. *Far East Economic Review*, March 27, 1997.

7. Gough, *Asia Meltdown*, p. 33.

8. *Far Eastern Economic Review*, March 27, 1997.

9. Robert Slater, *Soros: The Life, Times and Trading Secrets of the World's Greatest Investor* (Chicago: Irwin Professional Publishing, 1996), p. 11.

10. *Guardian*, December 19, 1992.

11. George Soros, *Underwriting Democracy* (New York: Free Press, 1991), p. 3.

12. George Soros, *The Alchemy of Finance* (New York: Wiley, 1994), pp. 362–63.

13. Slater, *Soros*, p. 99.

14. Ibid., p. 71.

15. *Far Eastern Economic Review*, June 12, 1997.

16. Ibid., June 12, 1997.

17. *Institutional Investor*, June 1997.

18. *Asian Wall Street Journal*, August 11, 1997.

19. Ibid., July 14, 1997.

20. Ibid.

21. *Institutional Investor*, May 1998.

22. *Asian Wall Street Journal*, July 26, 1997.

23. Ibid., September 8, 1997.

24. Gough, *Asia Meltdown*, p. 41.

25. Ibid.

26. *Institutional Investor*, January 1998.

27. Ibid.

28. Gough, *Asia Meltdown*, p. 44.

29. Ibid., p. 45.

30. *Asian Wall Street Journal*, September 15, 1997.

31. Gough, *Asia Meltdown*, p. 57.

32. Ibid., p. 49.

33. *Asian Wall Street Journal*, September 8, 1997.

34. Ibid.

35. Ibid., October 10, 1997.

36. Ibid., October 27, 1997.

37. *Asian Wall Street Journal*, November 24, 1997.

38. Gough, *Asia Meltdown*, p. 68.

39. *Institutional Investor*, February 1998.

40. *Wall Street Journal*, July 14, 1998.

41. Ibid.

42. Ibid., June 1, 1998.

43. Ibid., August 20, 1998.

44. Ibid.

45. Ibid., July 15, 1998.

46. Ibid., August 14, 1998.

47. *Sunday Times* (London), March 16, 1993.

48. *Wall Street Journal*, August 14, 1998.

49. Ibid., August 17, 1998.

50. Ibid., February 12, 2002.

51. John Cassidy, *Dot.con: The Greatest Story Ever Sold* (New York: HarperCollins, 2002) p. 38.

52. *Time*, September 14, 1998.

53. *Wall Street Journal*, November 17, 1998.

54. Ibid., September 30, 1998.

55. *Los Angeles Times*, October 16, 1998.

14: STOCK MARKET CAPITALISM

1. Ronald Dore, *Stock Market Capitalism: Welfare Capitalism* (Oxford, U.K.: Oxford University Press, 2000), p. ix.

2. *Financial Times*, March 13, 2002.

3. Ibid.

4. Ibid., December 10, 2001.

5. Ibid.

6. Ibid., December 20, 2001.

7. *Barron's*, January 28, 2002.

8. *Financial Times*, March 5, 2002.

9. Ibid., November 24, 2000.

10. Ibid.

11. Ibid.

12. Ibid., September 18, 2001.

13. *New York Times*, December 28, 2000.

14. Ibid.

15. *Wall Street Journal*, December 28, 2000.

16. *Financial Times*, February 13, 2001.

17. Ibid.

18. Ibid., February 1, 2001.

19. Ibid., July 9, 2001.

20. Ibid., August 22, 2001.

21. Ibid., May 6, 2002.

22. Ibid.

23. Ibid., May 18, 2001.

24. Ibid., November 2, 2001.

25. *New York Times*, March 13, 2002.

26. Ibid., January 28, 2001.

27. Ibid.

28. *Financial Times*, February 4, 2002.

29. *Financial Times*, September 27, 2002.
30. *Wall Street Journal*, September 18, 2002.
31. Ibid., February 4, 2002.
32. *Financial Times*, February 4, 2002.
33. Ibid., September 27, 2002.
34. *Washington Post*, January 29, 1999.
35. *Wall Street Journal*, September 30, 2002.
36. *New York Times*, May 5, 2002.
37. Ibid.
38. Eli Ofek and Matthew Richardson, *Dotcom Mania: The Rise and Fall of Internet Stock Prices* (NBER Working Paper 8630, December 2001).
39. *Wall Street Journal*, March 11, 2002.
40. Cassidy, *Dot.con*, p. 213.
41. *Washington Post*, January 29, 1999.
42. *New York Times*, October 27, 2002.
43. Ibid., September 28, 2002.
44. *Wall Street Journal*, February 12, 2002.
45. *Financial Times*, February 25, 2001.
46. Ibid., September 28, 2002.
47. Ibid., June 29, 2002.
48. John Abowd and David Kaplan, "Executive Compensation: Six Questions that Need Answering," *Journal of Economic Perspective*, Fall 1999.
49. *New York Times*, July 7, 2002.
50. *Financial Times*, June 21, 2002.
51. Ibid., July 3, 2002.

Index

72095967R00208

Made in the USA
Middletown, DE
02 May 2018